Praise for *Island q*

"This story goes reality TV a few step[s] tale about the pitfalls of rigidity and the benefits of adaptability and cooperation . . . Druett, who has written other works of nautical history and a maritime mystery series, wisely lets the details make the point, resisting the temptation to oversell. Her writing style is clear and detached, her touch just right . . . The power of the crews' divergent stories . . . propels the narrative like a trade wind."

—*Los Angeles Times*

"An amazing saga . . . Rarely are the two opposing sides of human nature captured in such stark and illuminating relief."

—*Seattle Post-Intelligencer*

"One of the finest survival stories I've read . . . [Druett's] tale is backed up by a solid knowledge of sailing ships and of the flora, fauna, and weather of Auckland Island, an inhospitable terrain that has defied attempts at human settlement and is now a wildlife preserve." —*The Seattle Times*

"A riveting study of the extremes of human nature and the effects of good (and bad) leadership . . . If the southern part of Auckland Island is all *Robinson Crusoe*, the northern part is more *Lord of the Flies* . . . Druett is an able and thorough guide to the minutiae of castaway life . . . [She] shows that real leadership is rare and powerful."

—*The New York Times Book Review*

"Captivating . . . Druett has a talent for storytelling . . . Those yearning for a classic man vs. nature, triumph-over-terrible-odds story, get ready to set sail." —*Paste* magazine

"Fascinating . . . A surprisingly gripping tale that will leave readers amazed. Grade: A." —*Rocky Mountain News*

"The kind of courage and resourcefulness that would do Crusoe proud . . . Druett's well-researched account earns its place in any good collection of survival literature." —*Entertainment Weekly*

"Using diaries, ship logs, and newspaper accounts, Druett re-creates the different experiences of the survivors of two wrecked vessels . . . Viewers of television's *Survivor* and readers of survival novels will enjoy *Island*." —*School Library Journal*

"Swashbuckling maritime history reanimated by a noted naval enthusiast . . . Druett excels at re-creating the men's struggles and desperation (tempered by boundless hope) . . . Depicted with consistent brio, stormy seas become epic events." —*Kirkus Reviews*

"This is a fine addition to the genre of survival tales like *Endurance* or *In the Heart of the Sea*." —*Publishers Weekly*

"The amount of detail the author has amassed is truly impressive, resulting in an invaluable account of survival." —*Booklist*

"[Druett] writes with a confidence and clarity that makes this account an exciting read and an important addition to our history." —*The Northern Advocate* (New Zealand)

"*Island of the Lost* is one of the greatest yarns I've ever read, surpassing even Shackleton and *Robinson Crusoe*." —*South Coast Register* (Australia)

"Survival stories from earlier ages remain favorite fare, as is underscored by this amazing saga by an award-winning New Zealand maritime historian." —*The Berkshire* (MA) *Eagle*

"It is felicitous that Joan Druett should have found this story. She is one of our most readable historians. Her knowledge of maritime events is encyclopedic. And she can write: vividly, lucidly, accurately . . . Each of the plot's two threads is absorbing in itself. Combined and contrasted, their motif . . . makes this book more powerful still." —*New Zealand Herald*

✠ ISLAND of THE LOST ✠

Also by Joan Druett

ISLAND of THE LOST

An Extraordinary Story of Survival at the Edge of the World

⤜ JOAN DRUETT ⤛

ALGONQUIN BOOKS OF CHAPEL HILL

2019

Published by
Algonquin Books of Chapel Hill
Post Office Box 2225
Chapel Hill, North Carolina 27515-2225

a division of
Workman Publishing
225 Varick Street
New York, New York 10014

First paperback edition, Algonquin Books of Chapel Hill, August 2019. Originally
published in hardcover by Algonquin Books of Chapel Hill in June 2007.
Printed in the United States of America.
Published simultaneously in Canada by Thomas Allen & Son Limited.
Design by Tracy Baldwin.

Illustration on page v © by Ron Druett.

The Library of Congress has catalogued the hardcover edition as follows:
    Druett, Joan.
        Island of the lost : shipwrecked at the edge of the world / by Joan Druett.—1st ed.
            p. cm.
        Includes bibliographical references.
        ISBN-13: 978-1-56512-408-0 (hardcover)
            1. Shipwrecks—New Zealand—Auckland Islands.   2. Grafton (Schooner).
    3. Invercauld (Ship)   4. Survival after airplane accidents, shipwrecks, etc.—New
    Zealand—Auckland Islands.   5. Auckland Islands (N.Z.)—Description and
    travel.   I. Title.
    G525.D78 2007
    919.3'99—dc22   2006031636

ISBN 978-1-61620-970-4 (PB)

10 9 8 7 6 5 4 3

For Roberta McIntyre,
whose early encouragement
could not have been
more well timed.

It has seldom fallen to our lot as journalists to record a more remarkable instance of escape from the perils of shipwreck, and subsequent providential deliverance from the privations of a desolate island, after two years' sojourn, than that we have now to furnish.

— Southland News, July 29, 1865

The man who has experienced shipwreck shudders even at a calm sea.

—Ovid

CONTENTS

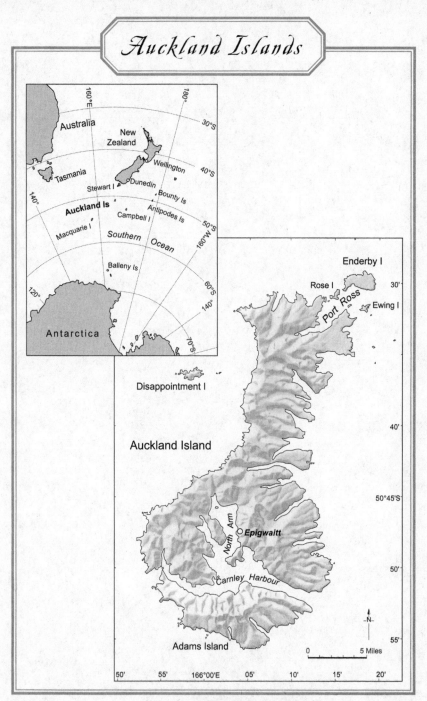

Auckland Islands

Australia

New Zealand

Tasmania

Stewart I   Dunedin

Wellington

Bounty Is

Auckland Is

Antipodes Is

Campbell I

Macquarie I

Southern   Ocean

Balleny Is

Antarctica

Enderby I

Rose I

Port Ross

Ewing I

Disappointment I

Auckland Island

North Arm   ○ *Epigwaitt*

Carnley Harbour

Adams Island

0   5 Miles

Map courtesy of Chris Edkins, Department of Conservation, New Zealand.

ISLAND of THE LOST

ONE

A Sturdy Vessel

It was October 1863, early springtime in Sydney, Australia. The sun was bright, but a chilly wind whisked up the broad surface of the harbor, dashing reflections to pieces. Distant waves rushed against islands and rocky beaches, tossing up sprays of seabirds that cried out a raucous challenge as they circled the tall masts of ships. Wood-burning steam ferries chugged across the harbor from the terminus on Circular Quay, their whistles competing with the nearer rattle of the many horse-drawn trams in the city.

Close by, brigs, ketches, and schooners were tied up to quays, discharging sugarcane, coffee, tropical fruits, and coal, and loading ore and locally made machinery. Because of all this activity, the two men who searched the docks were forced to step around piles of sacks and stacks of barrels, and dodge stevedores who were bent low under heavy loads as they hurried in and out of the gaping doors of pitch-roofed warehouses. The cold wind whistled in the passages and alleys, bringing a smell of soot, dust, and eucalyptus trees, and the two men had their collars turned up, and their cold hands thrust deeply into their pockets. Still, however, they doggedly trudged from wharf to wharf, their eyes moving assessingly from one moored vessel to another.

Though as weatherbeaten as seamen, it was obvious that these two had come in from town. Both were well-groomed, handsome men, wearing city clothes; their good hats were set squarely on their heads, and their boots were decently shined. While they were about the same age, in their early thirties, the dark spade beard of the taller one was peppered with gray, in contrast to the slighter man's luxuriant moustache and whiskers, which were glossy brown beneath a strongly hooked nose. When they talked, it was evident that this latter fellow was French, because of his marked accent, while the taller man's voice held a burr that betrayed his northern England origins. However, they spoke seldom, because they had conferred already, and knew exactly what they wanted.

Everywhere there were notices nailed to walls, doors, bowsprits, and masts, announcing departures, advertising for men, or putting craft up for sale. It was these last that the men inspected, but so far without success, because it was so hard to find a vessel that met their specifications. They were hunting for a schooner that was small enough to be handled by four seamen, but strongly built as well. She had to be cheap, because they had not much funding for the ambitious venture they planned, but it was essential that she be sound. They intended to sail one thousand, five hundred miles sou'sou'east of Australia, as far as the Antarctic convergence, where immense billows rise up before the hurtling winds of latitude fifty, lifting taller than the highest mast before crashing down on ice-sheathed decks. Then they would turn their course to sail six hundred miles northeast and find an anchorage at tempest-swept Campbell

Island. Naturally, then, they were most particular about the ship they had in mind.

All at once, the gray-bearded man spied a likely candidate. He stopped and pointed it out to the other, and then their steps quickened as they approached the vessel. Together, they eagerly read the notice tacked to the post where she was moored. Her name, they found, was *Grafton*. They stood back and studied her, assessing her lines and rigging, and watching the way her short, broad hull rocked heavily in the glossy harbor water. A two-masted craft, she was a topsail schooner, having one square sail set across the upper part of the foremast, and sails that ran fore and aft in the rest of the rigging. This helped make her easy for a small crew to handle, meeting the first of their specifications. What made her particularly attractive, however, were her sturdy build and her workmanlike, seaworthy air.

Again they studied the notice. According to the text, the *Grafton* had freighted coal from Newcastle, New South Wales, to Sydney, and was capable of carrying about seventy-five tons in her hold. It pleased them that she had been a coal carrier. In the tradition of Captain Cook's *Endeavour*, which had also been a collier, she was designed to carry heavy cargoes through gales and wicked seas. She was a little more expensive than they might have wished, but for the adventure the two men had in mind the schooner *Grafton* looked ideal. They turned and went in search of the agent.

NEITHER OF THE MEN was a stranger to adventure. The Frenchman, François Raynal, had spent the past eleven years prospecting in the goldfields of New South Wales and Victoria, until he had had to give it up because of poor health.

First, he had suffered severe bouts of the two diseases that ravaged the Australian goldfields, dysentery and ophthalmia. Though he'd cured the dysentery with a glassful of brandy mixed with pepper, the ophthalmia had involved nine days of blindness so painful and terrifying that a friend had taken his guns away from him, fearing that he would commit suicide. Then he had suffered a near-fatal accident when a tunnel had collapsed on him. No bones were broken, but there had been so much internal damage that back in February he'd been forced to come to Sydney to seek treatment from one of the 118 medicos who practiced here at the time. Now, eight months later, the doctor had pronounced that he was cured, but, while he was free to go back to seeking his fortune, François Raynal was determined not to try the goldfields again.

The taller man, Thomas Musgrave, was a master mariner with the reputation of being a steady captain and a gifted navigator. Fifteen years ago, at the age of sixteen, he had started sailing the Liverpool-Australia route, rising rapidly through the ranks until he was given command. Sometime in 1857, probably because he had an uncle who had successfully set up a drapery business in the city, he had made the decision to settle in Sydney. After finding a house, he had sent for his wife and their children, and for a while he had captained ships on the Australia–New Zealand run. Then his luck had run out, along with his job. Like Raynal, he was ready for another stab at making a fortune. Together, they were pursuing a wild venture that had been proposed by two men they both thought they knew well.

One of these instigators was Musgrave's uncle, and the other was Uncle Musgrave's partner in the drapery business, a Frenchman by the name of Charles Sarpy, one of Raynal's old acquaintances. According to what these two clothiers had told them, there was a rich mine of argentiferous tin on remote Campbell Island, which had not been located yet but was definitely there for the finding. On and on they had gossiped and persuaded, their information and arguments so intoxicating that it wasn't until much later that Raynal—who had been a prospector for the past decade and an engineer before that, and so definitely should have known better—realized that he should have thought much more deeply before going along with the plan.

Mostly made up of volcanic rock torn and dissected by glaciers, Campbell Island was indeed a possible source of mineral ore, but even if the party found this argentiferous tin, they would have to cope not just with the harsh remoteness of the locality, but with an unremittingly hostile climate, too. Both Raynal and Captain Musgrave must have been aware that the constant, bitter winds that burst out of the mountainous interior of the island were notorious. Not only were the primitive charts full of warnings about the dangers of anchoring at Campbell Island, but there were many old sealers in Sydney who knew the Subantarctic well. However, as Raynal ruefully ruminated in the grim months to come, they had both been seduced by the magic term *argentiferous*, which means "silver-bearing." Because of that one enticing word, they had agreed to go along with a scheme that more sensible men would have turned down without hesitation.

At once, they set to the task of adapting the *Grafton* for the job. The first priority was to prepare her for the terrific seas she would be breasting by adding to the weight in her hull, so that she would sit as securely as possible in the water. As Musgrave found, she had already been ballasted with about fifteen tons of old iron to keep her steady when her hold was empty on her return trips to Newcastle for more coal. This was not quite enough weight for what he had in mind, but putting in more was a problem, because above the old iron was a solid, immovable deck, which formed the floor of the hold. He purchased ten tons of sandstone blocks, but the stevedores were forced to pile them on top of this floor, where they were not as stable as the shipmaster would have liked.

Captain Musgrave couldn't do anything about it, so he turned to the task of provisioning the schooner for a voyage that was expected to last four months at the most, this being just a first, prospecting expedition. Twenty casks were stacked in the hold and filled with fresh water, and then he purchased and loaded about three hundred pounds of ship's bread (large round crackers of water and flour that were baked so hard they defied the teeth), two barrels of salt pork, about twenty gallons of molasses, a barrel of salt beef, two hundred pounds of ordinary flour, a few small cartons of sugar and butter, a bag of dried beans and peas, ten pounds of coffee and tea in tin boxes, and a couple of barrels of potatoes. Spare canvas, rope, and spars were also carried for running repairs if necessary.

It was then that the consortium ran short of funds. When Captain Musgrave went to the clothiers to ask for money to buy anchor chain, his uncle and Sarpy quibbled at the cost. Though they reluctantly produced some cash, it was only enough to provide sixty fathoms of chain — thirty fathoms (one hundred eighty feet) for each of the two anchors, and not very good chain at that. Anchoring the schooner close to a rocky shore would be courting disaster, because anchors can drag when the hull is pushed by wind and tide. However, Musgrave was un-willing to complain, knowing that he could be fired and re-placed, particularly after the *Grafton* passed the port surveyor's inspection with *fifteen* fathoms of chain—just ninety feet!—on her "best bower" anchor.

So, instead of backing out of an arrangement that looked in-creasingly dubious, he, with Raynal, turned to the job of finding and hiring two seamen and a cook. It wasn't difficult, because of the constant stream of disappointed gold miners trickling into town, many of them sailors. First to go on the crew list was a twenty-year-old Englishman, George Harris, an amiable fellow who had plenty of sailing experience. Then they found a taciturn twenty-eight-year-old Norwegian with the Scotch name of Alexander Maclaren, who briefly informed them that he was generally called "Alick," and produced evidence of a very good seafaring record.

Once Alick had signed the ship's articles, Captain Musgrave had enough men to carry out the actual sailing of the schooner, because both he and Raynal would take a watch. However, he still needed a cook, and so a fifth was added to the remarkable mix. The recruit they chose was a Portuguese from the Azores who claimed that his name was Brown. However, it didn't take long at all for Musgrave to find that this was completely un-true, the real name being Henry Forgès. This indicated that the Azorean had run away from his last ship, but that did not worry Musgrave at all. He was used to shipping hands under false names, and he didn't expect to sail to any place where Forgès would be tempted to desert.

More notable was the new cook's appearance, which was ugly in the extreme, as some kind of leprosy had eaten off his nose. Intrigued by this, Raynal inquired about his past, asking many questions, which the Azorean answered readily. He had first been shipped ten years ago, he said, at the age of thirteen; the master of an American whaleship had called at his island in need of a cabin boy, and he had grabbed the chance to see the world. At the time, he had been quite good-looking, but on a later voyage, he had fallen ill with the disfiguring disease. His shipmates had been so revolted by his appearance and so afraid of catching it themselves, he said, that he had begged his captain to put him on shore at the Samoan Islands. Luckily, the natives nursed him to health. In fact, as he went on to describe, they had made quite a pet of him, and had been so upset when he swam out to a passing ship that they had chased after him with axes, clubs, and spears. If the ship had not hastily lowered a boat, he might have been killed, but instead he escaped, while the natives roared in savage frustration. Quite a tale, as Raynal, very entertained, readily allowed.

ONCE FORGÈS HAD SIGNED the ship's paper with a cross, the complement was full—five men, encompassing four nationalities and four languages, all with very different natures. Norwegian Alick, though obviously competent, was reticent to the point of curtness, while the English able seaman, George, was much more forthcoming, and Henry, the Azorean cook, was positively garrulous. Captain Musgrave was already showing signs of habitual melancholy, but it was the naturally sunny François Raynal who was suddenly afflicted with a sense of dread, which led him to take a couple of belated precautions.

First, he went to Sarpy and Uncle Musgrave, and asked them to make a solemn promise to send out a search party if the schooner did not get back within four months of departure. When they objected on the grounds of cost, he told them to report the missing schooner to the government of New South Wales. Undoubtedly, the administration would dispatch one of the men-of-war attached to the station, or at least post a message to all the ships in the area. It was a sensible safeguard, he argued. The five men were about to venture onto one of the most dangerous seas on the globe, and on top of that, the charts were vague and sketchy. As he went on to say, "it was of no use disguising from ourselves the fact that we should be exposed to several hazards, and especially to the risk of shipwreck."

It was his second decision—to take along a double-barreled rifle that had served him well on the Australian goldfields, plus a couple of pounds of gunpowder, a dozen pounds of lead for making bullets, and some percussion caps—that turned out to be the crucial one. At the time, it was only on a whim, because Raynal had originally intended to leave the gun in Sydney. Just before he left his boardinghouse, though, he'd had the sudden thought that he might have a chance to amuse himself shooting ducks.

"Little did I think," he wrote later, "how useful this weapon and these munitions were hereafter to prove." In the long, dark season ahead, that gun was to save all their lives.

⤐ TWO ⤇

Open Sea

C aptain Musgrave ordered the anchors hove on the morning of November 12, 1863, despite the fact that it was wet and gloomy, and the tide was on the flood. A spiteful wind whistled from the sou'sou'east, but soon the *Grafton* was under a full press of sail and heading out to the harbor entrance, breasting the sea doggedly while the pilot barked commands. Then at last she was out of the great bay and under the high rocks of the cliffs, and the tall stone echoed with the shouts of the sailors and the snapping of bellying canvas. Round the *Grafton* came, backing her sails to come to a standstill and let the pilot go. Over the side he clambered, and dropped securely in the boat that had followed them out. With a last shout—"God speed you, gentlemen, and take care!"—he was gone, and the voyage was fairly commenced.

Standing out to the open sea was marked by two omens. First, the *Grafton* was almost immediately hit by an unexpected squall from the icy south. This swiftly moderated, but it was a timely warning of what lay ahead. Then, at midnight on November 14, when the wind had completely died and the black water shone like silk, the sky was filled with a shower of meteors that continued till dawn. As Raynal wrote, it was a splendid sight—but the barometer was falling, and it was a grim augury too.

At dawn next day it was still a dead calm. A light air might last a few minutes, the sails would fill, and the ship might sail about half a mile before the sails flapped, sagged, and then hung limp. At the start of the afternoon watch thunderheads gathered, turning the western horizon into a boiling mass of purple-black billows, which progressed slowly and ominously over the sky. At night, torn clouds raced across the face of the moon.

The hurricane grew gradually, taking the next two days to build up to full force. At dusk on November 18 the sky became pitch-black except for a band of phosphorescence on the horizon that delineated a ragged, heavy sea. "The clouds, which are very low, sweep over us with dizzy swiftness," wrote Raynal, using the present tense to convey the dramatic impact of the scene. "Every moment they are furrowed by vivid lightnings. The rain—icy rain—lashes and smites us. At intervals the thunder mingles its formidable voice in a thousand ominous sounds."

At eleven o'clock that night Raynal took over the tiller from the Norwegian seaman, Alick Maclaren, who had been steering. Dazzled by the constant lightning flashes, he could scarcely distinguish the compass in the binnacle, but somehow he managed to hold her onto her course. The ship was pitching and plunging as everything aloft strained and shuddered—and then, just as a deafening crack of thunder crashed out, Raynal was thrown headlong by a sudden squall.

He landed sprawling on the deck, losing his grip of the tiller. The rudder slapped free, and the schooner fell off her course, coming side-on to the force of the waves. A huge breaker reared up as high as the foremast and then crashed viciously down, smashing part of the bulwarks and tipping the hull far over. Crashing noises echoed from below as the ten tons of loose sandstone ballast slid in one mass. Suddenly the *Grafton* fell onto her side, while all men on board held their breaths in terrified suspense. They waited, waited, for her to drop back onto an even keel, but instead she stayed on her starboard side, thumping as she hit the foaming waves. Her deck was slanted too steeply for men to walk on, and the heavy planking of the hull creaked deafeningly, while the strained masts and rigging whined in protest.

Raynal, bruised and drenched, staggered to his feet, struggled along the sloped deck to the stern, and grabbed the tiller again, while Alick clung to a mast. Musgrave clawed his way up the companionway ladder, while the two sailors who were off duty came tumbling and sliding out of the forecastle. With great difficulty Musgrave, Alick, Harry, and George took in sail, while Raynal fought with the tiller, doggedly driving the schooner hard up to windward. Then Musgrave took over, while the Frenchman, with the others, clambered down to the hold, to find everything heaped on the starboard side, which was currently the bottom of the schooner. If the iron ballast had not been held in place by the solid floor, the *Grafton* would have foundered.

The noise was deafening. Waves crashed just inches from their ears as ten tons of sandstone tumbled and slid with horrid thuds. Raynal and the three sailors struggled to secure recalcitrant blocks, barrels, and bags of wet salt. By the time the schooner had been brought upright on her keel, day was breaking. When they clambered back on deck, they were weak with exhaustion, and Musgrave's blue and white hands were frozen by the cold to the tiller.

THE TEMPEST RAGED ON. They couldn't set their sails again until November 21, when they also lit the fire in the galley stove. The sky was thick with cloud, and whales spouted all around them—an ominous sign of another storm to come—but at least it was calm. When Musgrave took an observation at noon, it was to find that the gale had blown them off their course by more than one hundred fifty miles. They didn't glimpse land until November 30, and then it was through a gathering fog, which soon became so dense that it was impossible to see from one end of the little schooner to the other. Throughout that night they lay to under short sail, waiting for dawn. When the sun finally rose the fog had cleared, but Campbell Island was nowhere to be seen.

Coming about, the schooner resumed her course, approaching their target from the west. As the sun rose high in the pale blue sky, tall rock pillars lifted like sentinels from the sea, twisted and eroded by wind and waves into strange, angry shapes, their crowns surrounded by screaming flocks of frigate birds, and white surf at their feet. Beyond, awe-inspiring cliffs reared as much as one thousand feet, their reddish walls shining black where water streamed, the sea pounding savagely at their base. Narrow terraces were crowded with colonies of mollymawk albatrosses, which soared in masses at times, filling the sky with their outstretched wings. The vegetation in the steeply descending gullies was sparse, thin, and pale brown in color; the few shrubs that had managed to survive the year-round freezing temperatures were hunched, blown flat by the constant bitter winds.

If the westerly wind gusted up, they were on a dangerous lee shore—the *Grafton* could be blown onto the rocks and reduced to a whirl of wreckage. Musgrave worked the ship around a massive cape and then coasted along the southern side of the island, where a series of six tall peaks rose from precipitous, contorted cliffs, and more rock pillars reared out of the sea. At last, at dawn on December 2, they turned northeast and sailed past great limestone bluffs that were striped with bands of lichen and loud with the cries of birds. Wrote François Raynal: "11 A.M. Dropped anchor in five fathoms water, at the head of the bay."

They were in Perseverance Harbour, and an unexpectedly pleasant scene lay before them. Dun-colored slopes clothed with tussock and studded with outcrops of white-streaked stone undulated upward to blend with the brown and purple foothills. In the distance, a single pyramid-shaped peak was lighted up by the bright sun that glistened on its closest flank. The weather was warm—so warm that Raynal wondered if the seals that were supposed to be there had been driven away from the beach to find shade. "The sails had scarcely been furled before Musgrave and I went ashore," he wrote—but they didn't find any seals in the scrub, either.

The two men started prospecting for the fabled argentiferous tin at dawn the next day. It didn't take many moments to realize that it was not going to be nearly as easy as Sarpy had promised—after they got into the bush, "more than once we were compelled to lie flat on the ground and crawl under the lianas," wrote Raynal. However, they managed to get to the pyramidal peak, which they named the Dome. Scrambling to the top, they found a grand view to the west, where there was a big inlet, marked on the chart as Monument Harbour. Descending the western side of the hill, they trekked as far as the top of the cliff that overlooked this harbor, and then stood for a while contemplating a roughly tumbled ocean that stretched almost uninterrupted all the way around the world.

There were no seals to be seen on the beach below, just a couple of sea lions. Throughout the long scramble, there had not been a single trace of tin ore to be glimpsed. All they had gained was a voracious appetite. Musgrave and Raynal lit a fire, boiled a billy, and had breakfast.

THE NEXT DAY when Raynal woke he was feverish, and by nightfall he was delirious. The illness that had driven him to give up prospecting had returned, laying him so low for the next three weeks that Musgrave, fully expecting him to die, dug a hole for his grave. Raynal put his relapse down to the change of climate and the unusual exertion, but the dashing of his ebullient hopes must have played a part. While he was confined to his berth, Musgrave, with Alick, took over the quest for the tin mine, but with not the slightest hint of success. "Did it escape his investigations, or does it not exist?" Raynal ruminated later. "I cannot say," he confessed — but must have quietly admitted to himself that the second option was the more likely one.

Their worst expectations were realized. All they could do now was think of some way to retrieve the expedition. Killing seals for their pelts and oil was the best alternative, but still there was no sign of fur seals, and sea lions were very scarce.

This was something that could be directly attributed to the voracity of the early sealers. Within weeks of the moment the discovery of the island was announced in Sydney in 1810, hundreds of greedy, desperate men had arrived, to kill and skin every single seal they found, right down to the last little pup. The populations of the various seal species had never been dense on Campbell, but throughout the southern sealing rush of the first two decades of the nineteenth century, the rapacious gangs had never hesitated to wipe out even the smallest herds of their quarry. Here, the result had been that within three years the fur seal was close to extinction. Fifty years after the sealers had given up and gone, the *Grafton* seal hunt was as doomed as the search for argentiferous tin.

Recognizing the futility of spending any more time and energy at Campbell Island, Captain Musgrave made up his mind to return to Sydney as soon as Raynal was fit to travel. The anchor was weighed on December 29 and the schooner made sail and scudded down the long inlet toward the open sea and home. Fatefully, however, Musgrave—who commenced his journal the following day—had decided to call at the Auckland Islands to assess the seal population there.

THE AUCKLAND ISLANDS group is made up of two hilly, windswept landmasses and a multitude of islets. The larger of the two main islands, named Auckland, lies to the north of the smaller one, Adams, and is separated from its southern neighbor by a body of water called Carnley Harbour, which is actually a strait. The western coast of the group presents a forbidding rampart of tall precipices, while the eastern shores are broken up into headlands, outcrops, and reefs that extend hundreds of feet into the ocean. The islets lie mostly about the northern shores of Auckland Island, where there is another fine harbor, though one large rock, named Disappointment Island, lies off the cliffs of the western coast.

Because of their remote location, the Auckland Islands escaped the notice of explorers like James Cook, and weren't sighted until August 18, 1806. Their discoverer, Captain Abraham Bristow of the South Seas whaleship *Ocean*, was in the employ of the London oil merchant firm of Enderby and Sons. Because he was on the way back to England, and his ship was full of oil, he did not drop anchor, pausing only to name the group after Lord Auckland, a family friend. Returning the following year, this time in command of the whaleship *Sarah*, he anchored in the harbor in the northern part of Auckland Island, calling it Sarah's Bosom. After taking formal possession in the name of the crown he released pigs for future hunting parties, and then departed to spread the news of this rich new seal fishery.

In Sydney, the tidings led to a lot of excitement. Local merchants hired an American sealing skipper, Rhode Islander Samuel Rodman Chace, put him in command of the 185-ton *King George*—the largest vessel ever built in the colony—and gave him the job of freighting men, tools, and provisions to the islands, called Bristow's Islands by the sealers. Others streamed in his wake, leading to a vicious competition for furs that took place at set times of the year.

There were two recognized sealing seasons. The first began in April and extended over the early southern winter, when newly weaned calves were taken. Their soft, chocolate brown furs, once dried, were intended for the lucrative Chinese market, where they were purchased for trimming ceremonial robes. The second killing took place over the southern summer, starting in December, when older seals, both male and female, were assembling on the rookeries to calve and mate over the next four months.

In the weeks before each of these seasons, gangs of men would be set on shore with casks, cauldrons, clubs, and knives, and left to stockpile skins and oil (taken from the layer of fat beneath the skin, and used both for lamp oil and to lubricate machinery), ready for the sealing captains to collect as the killing time came to a close. With no thought for the future, all seals within reach were killed and skinned, and their pelts salted, packed in barrels, and shipped to London. There they were processed for the clothing trade, which turned the best furs into sleek, full-length coats much in demand by both ladies and gentlemen and made waistcoats and hats from the rest. It was like the lumber industry today, where beautiful timbers like mahogany, rosewood, and ebony are used to make fine cabinetwork, while trees of lesser quality are processed into mass-produced furniture or even pulped for paper.

However, like the tearing down of primeval rain forest to make way for roads, the sealing trade was ultimately doomed, because it squandered natural resources without any thought for the future. No one seemed to take into account the fact that if all the cows and bulls were killed off in the southern summer, there would be no pups the following autumn. Initially, the catch was enormous, with just one ship reporting a take of thirty-eight thousand pelts in the first four-month season alone—at the cost of many more than thirty-eight thousand seals, because a lot of the skins were damaged during the attack, or spoiled by mold and vermin. Within just a dozen years, unsurprisingly, the seal population had been reduced to the extent that it was not worth dropping a gang at the Aucklands anymore.

Then, in 1823, to everyone's surprise, Captain Robert Johnson, commander of the New York schooner *Henry,* reported taking about thirteen thousand fine furs at Enderby Island, in the north of the Auckland Islands group. As the sealers realized that the seal population had recovered, another rush commenced, but this one was even more short-lived than the first. The following year, sealing captains reported taking only two thousand pelts; and in November 1825 the Sydney sealer *Sally* lost two boats and six men in the struggle to get just two hundred skins. In January 1830, during the breeding season four years after that miserable excursion, Captain Benjamin Morrell of the Connecticut discovery schooner *Antarctic* dropped anchor in Carnley Harbour — to find no fur seals at all.

For some time after that, though the whaleships hunting the New Zealand ground occasionally called there to forage for firewood, fresh water, and edible vegetables, the island group was of interest only to discoverers. On March 7, 1840, the gun-brig *Porpoise,* one of the six ships of the U.S. Exploring Expedition, called at Sarah's Bosom on the way to New Zealand, and left three days later, after her officers and crew had roamed about the landscape and planted a signboard announcing the date of their arrival and the identity of their ship. Captain Ringgold of the *Porpoise* later reported to Charles Wilkes, the commander of the expedition, that his men had found a little hut that had been built by a French whaling crew, a grave with a wooden cross, and a small garden of turnips, carrots, and potatoes — to which they had added a few onion plants — but no other sign of human life at all.

Just one day after the *Porpoise* left, Wilkes's rival, the French explorer Dumont D'Urville, arrived to find a Portuguese whaleship riding at anchor in Sarah's Bosom while her boats hunted the sea around the islands for whales. D'Urville and his men read the Americans' signboard with interest, and then explored in the pouring rain. They also fished, but the catch proved to be inedible, as it was full of worms. They painted a signboard of their own, and set it up next to the *Porpoise* one, and then, after pausing to record that the grave belonged to a French whaling captain, M. Lefrançois, who had committed suicide in a fit of depression—ostensibly triggered by his failure to invent a gun-harpoon, but perhaps because of the unrelenting weather— they, too, set sail for New Zealand.

Eight months later, on November 20, 1840, the eminent English explorer James Clark Ross arrived with two naval vessels, HMS *Terror* and HMS *Erebus*, which were later to be lost in Sir John Franklin's ill-fated Arctic expedition. Extraordinarily handsome and lionized by London society, Ross was also distinguished by an abundance of energy. After reading both signboards, he organized the setting up of an observatory. Over the next three weeks, measurements were taken and charts drawn. With blithe disregard of possible effects on the natural environment, the party released pigs, rabbits, and hens, and planted gooseberries, raspberries, strawberries, turnips, cabbages, and currants. In a final flourish, Sarah's Bosom was renamed Port Ross (though Ross's personal preference was Rendezvous Harbour). Then they took the observatory down and sailed away for Campbell Island and the Antarctic.

This last visit was to have ramifications. After getting back to Hobart, Tasmania, Ross suggested to the authorities that the

Auckland Islands would make a capital penal colony, now that New South Wales and Tasmania had outrun their usefulness in that respect. Instead, Charles Enderby, scion of the firm of Enderby and Sons that had owned the ship whose captain had first sighted the group, decided to colonize the islands as a whaling settlement.

In the southern summer of 1849–50, Enderby arrived with one hundred fifty men, women, and children to set up a village called Hardwicke, in Erebus Cove, Port Ross, and try to eke a living from soil that had been touted as rich and fertile, but turned out to be acid, salt, and unthrifty, in a climate that was eternally dismal. Within three years, daunted by the isolation, the weather, and the lack of whales, it was decided to abandon the experiment. The pioneers departed, some going back to England, while others headed for the Australian gold rush.

Once more the Auckland Islands were uninhabited by man, known only as a graveyard for ships sailing the Great Circle route from Australia to Cape Horn. Then the *Grafton* arrived.

THREE

The Islands

Captain Musgrave started his journal on Wednesday, December 30, 1863, by noting, "Commences with fresh breeze and dark cloudy weather. At 6 P.M. made the Auckland Group, bearing N.W. about 25 miles distant. Midnight, same weather; all sails set; water smooth under the lee of the island." Morning dawned with an unsteady breeze, and unsettled, threatening weather. The sky was thick with rushing clouds, and the barometer was falling fast. "Every appearance of N. gale," he noted in the log at noon, and added, "I think that Mr. Raynal is a little better since we left Campbell's Island."

The following day they had a sudden squall from the west; then the wind veered about between northwest and southwest, with a very nasty sea cutting up. "I have never seen a sea so agitated," wrote Raynal after paying a brief visit to the deck; "it looks as if it were boiling, and heaves around us in every direction." Musgrave had the *Grafton* on a southward course, being anxious to keep well away from the surf breaking on the reefs directly beneath the tall cliffs — and wisely so, because in the late afternoon a thick fog descended, mixed with drizzling rain.

For François Raynal, back in the cabin, time dragged miserably. Light seeped dimly to his berth, and the sounds of the wind in the rigging and the rhythmic crash of the sea were almost as nerve-racking as the constant jerk and tumble of the hull. When night came the lamp dashed to and fro on its hook, casting wild shadows. The long hours seemed endless, but as the New Year dawned both sea and wind were moderating, and the weather was surprisingly pleasant.

Noted Musgrave: "At 8 A.M. all sail set, and at 9 A.M. made Auckland Islands again." The coast of the southernmost island was again in sight, still about twenty-five miles away. The schooner scudded toward a magnificent vista of great stone ramparts. The scene was so awe-inspiring and the air so warm that Musgrave called François Raynal, who was "much better today," to come up and look. Because of his weakness the Frenchman had to be half-carried, but once he was settled on the deck, propped up against a hatch, he fervently agreed that the view was worth the trouble. The schooner was just two miles from the massive cliffs, and he could distinctly discern the waves breaking at their feet. Every now and then a wave washed into a cavern, and was swallowed up "with a roar like a report of artillery." He could see the rainbows tossed up by the spray, and a multitude of waterfalls that leapt out in a mist of vaporized water.

As the schooner passed the southeast end of Adams Island, the eastern coast of Auckland Island could be seen. It was rugged, rough, and broken up by a succession of promontories, and several lines of reef. Before they had sailed many miles north, however, they found a magnificent bay, lying between two great headlands set about two miles apart. It was the entrance to Port Carnley.

"At 3 P.M. entered a harbour," Musgrave recorded. He had to beat against the westerly wind to get inside, but otherwise everything seemed tranquil. The English seaman, George, was at the tiller, steering. Harry, the Azorean with the colorful past, was in the galley peeling some of the last of the schooner's stock of potatoes for dinner, while Alick, the quiet, strong Norwegian, was perched on the bow dropping the lead line at regular intervals to find out the depth of water beneath the schooner. Musgrave, on the quarterdeck with his telescope, carefully scanned the beaches to the north.

Then, as Raynal went on to relate, Musgrave started visibly, lowered his spyglass, swerved around with an elated expression, and exclaimed, "Good news!"

"Good news?" Raynal echoed.

"Aye — here are the seals that we couldn't find at Campbell Island, I think. Look yourself, and tell me — do you see seals on the rocks over there?"

Raynal took over the telescope, while the schooner worked closer to the shore. Within moments, seals — or sea lions — were plain to be seen, some sleeping on the rocks, others at various vantage points on the beach or on the slopes high above the shingle, while the heads of more seals bobbed about in the water. The animals seemed unaware of the *Grafton*, but then the schooner came about, and the noise of the sails shaken by the wind roused their attention. They reared up and stared, and then plunged into the sea. "In a moment a crowd of them surrounded the schooner, which they regarded evidently with astonishment and terror," Raynal recorded. Instead of coming close, they ranged about the vessel in a big circle, barking and squealing as they swam.

When Musgrave put the *Grafton* about again, and steered toward the southern shore, it was to see a multitude of seal life there too. All five men were elated, Musgrave and Raynal in particular. Conferring animatedly, they came to the decision to stop at the island for a few days, just long enough to fill their few empty water casks with oil and salt down a few furs. After that, they would raise anchor and set all sail to make a speedy return to Sydney. Then, as fast as possible, they would reprovision the ship, and return with about thirty men to pitch a camp and stage a proper hunt.

In this high mood of optimism, they rounded an outthrust of land that they called Musgrave Peninsula, and entered the north arm of the harbor. Musgrave's aim was to find a safe anchorage, but the water was still too deep for the two anchors, limited as they were by the length of chain, to hold on to the bottom and keep the *Grafton* safely away from the rocks. Slowly they sailed on, while Alick stood in the channels swinging the sounding line and counting off the fathoms, but still the sea was too deep for the anchors to find a grip on the bottom.

Silence descended as the feeling of ebullience faded and anxiety took its place. Musgrave was frowning. The wind had fallen, and a dead calm threatened, which meant that the schooner was at the mercy of the tide. When the sun descended behind the mountains they were still without an anchorage, and the stars and moon were blotted out by a flood of brooding clouds. All Musgrave could do was keep to the middle of the bay, judging his position by the sound of the surf, and hope for the best. Raynal lay in his berth listening to the echoes of their captain pacing back and forth, back and forth, then finally went to sleep.

The Frenchman was wakened again by the thunder of rain falling in torrents, and the sound of Musgrave shouting out urgent orders, so he deduced that the wind had risen. When day broke, they were still off the peninsula, however, and the breeze had dropped away, though still the rain poured down. At 6 A.M., after ordering the small boat manned, Musgrave sent it off to look for an anchorage. However, Alick and George came back with no good news at all, and the wind was again beginning to rise.

It quickly became apparent that another storm was looming. Impelled by the gusting gale, Musgrave steered up the long harbor, choosing a northern route each time the bay forked. About three in the afternoon, to the great relief of all, the rain stopped, just as the *Grafton* sailed into a magnificent basin rimmed with precipitous cliffs. At long last the sounding line hit bottom, and Musgrave was able to note that they had "brought up on the N.E. side of the harbour, in 6 fathoms of water, close in shore, about 10 or 12 miles from the sea."

Though the anchors were finally down, he was still very worried. The schooner was much closer to the rocks of the northeast shore than was comfortable, "as there is hardly room for her to swing clear of the rocks should the wind come from the S.W. There is a swell on, and she strains very much at her anchors," he worried. But, it was the best he could manage in the circumstances. Cliffs loomed all around, dangerously close to the limit of their anchor chain, rocks snarling with surf at their feet. Thick, leathery kelp surged back and forth in the foam.

By late afternoon the sky was the color of steel, and a gale was gathering. In Raynal's berth it was very dark, and the night was full of noise—bootsteps hurrying back and forth on the deck above, the drumming of rain almost drowning out the creak and groan of the heavy wooden hull. Added to that, there was a deep, regular, ominous booming. As the men were to find out later, a westerly wind sent great breakers crashing against the western cliffs with such enormous force that each concussion created a roar, setting up echoes in the primeval rock that resounded throughout the land. With each gust the schooner shuddered and pitched her head down. Then back she would rear, to be caught up short by her anchors while the wind wailed through her rigging.

Saturday, January 2, 1864, dawned with constant rain and heavy squalls. "There is a considerable swell running, and the ship has been jerking and straining at her chains," wrote Musgrave in his logbook. Every now and then the gale would let up a little, raising their hopes, but then it would blow with renewed violence. And so the dreadful day wore on.

At seven in the evening there was a sudden uncanny silence — "one of those intervals in which the genius of the storm seems to rest a moment only to take breath," as Raynal described. Then a gust of solid wind and rain slammed the ship; she shuddered hard in response — and the starboard chain snapped.

It broke close to the hawse pipe. The *Grafton* lurched out to the extent of the remaining anchor — which dragged, so that the schooner began to creep toward the rocks, propelled by the wind and the relentless shoreward current. On deck, Captain Musgrave watched in terrible distress, unable to do anything to stop the dreadful progression of events: "She is lying almost parallel with the shore, and should the wind come from the S.W. she must most inevitably go into the rocks, and I have now made up my mind for the worst. I see no hope of her keeping clear.

Barom. 28:99, and falling at 10 P.M. The wind is so that, should I slip the cable with a spring, she would not clear the point, or I would slip and run out to sea. At every heave of the swell she is dragging the anchor home, and getting nearer the shore."

For the next two hours the gale increased, until it was screaming with horrible force. Rolling and pitching, the schooner dragged closer to the waiting shoals. All at once, mercifully, the anchor caught in something on the bottom—"bringing up the vessel at last with her stem about half a cable's length from the shore," as Raynal recorded. The *Grafton* wallowed there for perhaps an hour, and then, with an awful lurch, the anchor wrenched free.

Precisely at midnight on January 3, 1864, she struck on the rocks. "A shock more terrible than any of its predecessors made the vessel shiver from stem to stern," wrote Raynal; "a frightful crash fell upon our ears—the disaster so much dreaded had come about!"

The raging sea swept the helpless schooner's decks, and the wind and rain howled through her rigging as her hull smashed onto the reefs.

FOUR

Wrecked

I n a quarter of an hour the ship was full up to the top of the cabin table and the sea was breaking heavily over her," Captain Musgrave recorded. With frantic haste the five men retrieved what provisions, tools, and personal possessions they could from the hold and cabin, handing them up to the highest part of the steeply pitched deck, and then covering them with the mainsail. Then they huddled there themselves and waited for whatever dreadful scene the dawn might reveal, while the rain lashed down and the wind raged with undiminished fury.

When day finally broke, the men crept out from under the dripping canvas to find that the sea was still high, the wild surf whipped into great clouds of foam. Even in death the schooner offered some protection, however, as the side that reared out from the sea took the brunt of the waves, so that the sixty-yard channel between the *Grafton* and the beach was relatively calm.

Providentially, the thirteen-foot ship's boat, which was lashed upside down above the main scuttle of the schooner, was undamaged. With a great struggle the seamen managed to launch her safely and make her fast under the lee of the wreck. While they were piling as much as they could into her, Captain Musgrave found two long, stout ropes. The end of one of these was secured to an iron ring in the side of the wreck, and the other end to the stern of the boat. That done, the men clambered into the boat on top of the goods, and let her surge out to the end of the tether. Alick took the second rope, attached one end to the boat's bow, and then, while Raynal and the others tensely watched, "at the peril of his life he leaped into the waves," carrying the slack of the second line with him.

"This was a moment of terrible anxiety," Raynal continued. However, the Norwegian was a strong, intelligent swimmer. Instead of striking out blindly for the shore, he made for the nearest rock, and clung to it as the sea boiled around him. Then, judging his moment, he dropped back into the sea and swam for yet another rock, and thus, yard by arduous yard, stepping-stone by stepping-stone, he made his way to shore. With relief the men in the ship's boat saw him scramble out of the surf onto the shingle, and watched him clamber up the steep slope and secure the far end of his rope to a tree.

Now the little boat was secured midway in the channel, attached by one rope to the wreck of the schooner and by the other to the shore, like a bead in the middle of a string. Then, as Raynal went on to describe, they were faced with yet another problem, their lifeline being so steeply inclined. However, it was solved in seamanlike fashion—and a seaman can move just about anything, given two belaying points, a pulley, and a rope. "By means of a pulley, to which were fixed two ends of rope, one of which was thrown to Alick, and the other retained in our skiff, we first passed to our comrade the pitched canvas; this he arranged round the trunk of a tree, in the form of a tent, and under it he deposited the various articles which we kept sending up to him."

Then it was time for the men to follow. Raynal was too weak to hold on, so Captain Musgrave tied him onto his back, and, seizing the pulley, he jumped. For both, it was a terrifying experience. The double weight dragged the rope down so that Musgrave was forced to plow his way through the top of the surf, while Raynal desperately clung to him. A few yards from the beach Musgrave cried out that he could hold on no longer, but Alick dashed into the waves and manhandled them both out of the sea.

George and Harry followed, and at last the party of five was safe on shore. "As for the boat," wrote Raynal, "we left it where it was, securely moored to the rope." Glad to creep into the makeshift tent to escape the pouring rain, they overhauled the bags and barrels that had been so arduously winched up to Alick, and summed up their situation.

There was a cask containing about one hundred pounds of hard ship's bread. A staple at sea, it was usually rationed out at the rate of one pound and a half per man per day, so, with care, they had a good three weeks' worth of that. A smaller barrel held about fifty pounds of ordinary flour. There were two tin boxes, one holding two pounds of tea, and the other three pounds of coffee. A damp hempen bag held a dozen pounds of sugar. In addition, they had a few pieces of salt meat, with mustard and pepper for seasoning. A box holding six pounds of tobacco belonged to Musgrave and Raynal, but they immediately shared it out with the men.

Those were all the provisions they had been able to salvage. Back on board the wreck, secured in the place on the afterdeck where they had waited out the night, were several bags of the salt that had been intended for curing furs, Musgrave's chest, which held navigation instruments, charts, and spare clothes, Raynal's chest with his gun and sextant, and a third chest filled with "useful domestic articles, such as plates, knives, and forks," as Raynal recounted. As well as this, they had saved a big iron pot that had been intended for rendering the fat of the seals they had been so confident of killing. In addition, there were the last remains of the cask of potatoes, plus a couple of pumpkins. Right now, however, those articles were out of reach.

On shore, the only cooking utensil was a small iron teakettle, but at that time hot tea was a very welcome prospect. However, though there was fresh water in abundance, they had no means of kindling a fire: as Raynal wrote, "Not one of us had steel or tinder-box" to strike a spark. Then Harry, the cook, who was going through his wet pockets, suddenly let out a cry of triumph, and produced a box of fusees—large-headed wooden matches used by seamen to light their pipes in the wind. Naturally, they were damp, but George rushed off to find a handful of dry twigs, and the five men crouched close, holding their breaths as Harry gently scraped the head of a match on the friction strip.

Instead of fizzing into life, the match crumbled. Three more met the same fate, and they all sat back a moment, thoroughly discouraged, wondering if they should wait until the matches dried out. Then Harry tried a fifth—and it caught. Scrap by scrap, the men reverently fed the flames, and at last had a fire going—"oh, how our hearts beat!" Raynal exclaimed. The teakettle was filled, and fifteen minutes later the men were heartily enjoying a breakfast of hot tea and hard bread.

It put new life into them. "Our repast finished, my companions sallied forth, each in a different direction, in search of a cave or grotto, whither we might transport our provisions, and which would afford us a shelter from the bad weather," Raynal recorded. First, however, they collected a stockpile of dead wood that was reasonably dry, and left it by the Frenchman's side — "being good for nothing else, on account of my weakness," as he wryly remarked, "I could at least occupy myself, during their absence, in keeping alive the fire."

This was an important responsibility, but it was still very hard to be left alone with relatively little to do while the others battled their way through the dense bush into undiscovered territory. When the sounds of their voices had faded, there were other noises — the hiss and thud of the sea, the cries of restless birds, the pattering of rain, and the rustle and crack of windblown branches — but behind it all lay an oppressive silence, a preternatural awareness of complete and dreadful isolation. Without the reassuring sounds of other men, the knowledge that the nearest inhabited land was two hundred eighty-five long miles away rushed in on Raynal with demoralizing force, and most uncharacteristically he succumbed to utter despair.

"Alone, and abandoned to myself, you may guess of what melancholy reflections I was soon the victim," he confessed. He brooded over his fate, and the doomed hunt for a fortune that had placed him in this terrible situation. "I began to think of my family," he remembered. Not only were his parents half a world away, but it was seventeen years since he had seen them last, on a day in December 1846 when he had parted from them in Paris. All at once, his past life seemed laid out before him like a path that led with awful inevitability to this appalling situation.

FRANÇOIS RAYNAL'S WANDERING quest for riches had begun in December 1844, at the age of just fourteen, after his parents had lost their property in Moissac, a small town in southwest France. Perhaps because he was the eldest of three children, he had decided, quite irrationally, that the responsibility for mending the family fortunes was his. He had left college to go to sea, which was a very bad choice, because a fourteen-year-old was far too young to get any kind of promotion, and no one below the rank of first officer could expect to make money from a seafaring career.

After a couple of voyages this truth had dawned on him, and so, after paying a visit to his parents, who had meantime moved to Paris, François Raynal headed for the island of Mauritius in the Indian Ocean, where he became the overseer of a large sugar factory. There, not only did he learn the hard way, after a couple of mutinies, how to administer large gangs of indentured Indian labor, but he also taught himself how to mend recalcitrant machinery. Then in 1852 a ship had arrived at Port Louis with news of the discovery of gold in Australia, and his dreams of riches were triggered again. Entranced by wild tales of "immense fortunes made in a few days; of ingots of gold, weighing fifty and a hundred pounds," Raynal gave up his job and bought passage on "an ill-found little brig" bound for Melbourne.

Arriving at Port Philip in April 1853, he found Melbourne in a frenzy, with thousands of men desperate to get inland to the diggings. However, Raynal had the sense to realize that if he was to establish himself successfully, he should learn to speak English first. So he joined the crew of a steam packet that plied between Port Philip and Sydney, New South Wales, which should have been a good decision, as seamen were so scarce at the time that he should have been able to command a good wage. However, misfortune seemed to be his constant lot, as he brooded now from his crouched position by the campfire on Auckland Island.

Within weeks the packet ship had been wrecked, and a miserable night of clinging to wreckage convinced him yet again that a life at sea was not for him. Rescued and put on shore in Melbourne, he headed for the diggings — to find that lack of English was the least of his problems. Digging and panning for gold was hard labor, worse than what the most hardened convicts endured. Raynal obstinately persevered. Like a half million other hopefuls, he wandered from one gold strike to another, dressed in the prospectors' uniform of checked woolen shirt, breeches, knee-length boots, and a sunhat woven from stiff dried leaves — the ubiquitous "cabbage-tree hat" of the Australian goldfields. All his belongings were carried in a pack on his back; he worked out how to pitch a tent, and build a hut, and construct a stretcher if he did not want to sleep on the ground; when wet firewood wouldn't catch, he learned how to make a pair of bellows so he could get his mutton cooked. Sheep were abundant on the goldfields, and kangaroos could be turned into stew, but otherwise he had been forced to rely on an indigestible damper made out of water and flour.

He learned to become a good shot — not just to kill game for dinner but for self-defense too. Because this was the so-called golden age of Australian bush ranging, Raynal, like most of the men on the goldfields, carried a revolver and a double-barreled shotgun. That was the same gun that was out of reach — back in his chest on the wrecked schooner, he thought now, and with that reminder of their situation, he was gripped by a terrible sick panic: "How and when should I escape from this island, hidden in the midst of the seas, and lying beyond the limits of the inhabited world? Perhaps, never! A violent despair overmastered me," he wrote later. "I felt my heart swell; I was almost suffocated; tears which I could not restrain filled my eyes, and I wept like a child."

He was saved by his faith. François Raynal was a very pious man, having experienced a revelation his first night at sea, on December 23, 1844, at the age of just fourteen years and five months. As the land on the horizon disappeared, and "the limitless sea surrounded me; the celestial vault was for the first time displayed before my eyes in all its vastness; I was plunged everywhere into the Infinite." Young François was overwhelmed with awe and wonder—"my soul was penetrated with a grave and solemn enthusiasm, the thought of the Supreme Being—of the Author and Lord of the universe—was present to my spirit." Since then, his religion had been a constant support, and in this moment of crisis, just as many times in the past, prayer restored his courage. By the time he heard the crackling of branches as his fellow castaways trudged back to the fire, Raynal was composed and tranquil.

Captain Musgrave, Alick, George, and Harry had endured their own miseries. One by one they straggled back, to confess that they had been unable to find a shelter. The tent was surrounded by a dense tangle of low, grotesquely twisted trees with thick, contorted branches, a ghostly forest, with no undergrowth save thick, spongy moss and springing ferns, and there was not a cave to be seen in the nearby cliffs.

François Raynal had his own news, having made the strange discovery that the peat soil itself burned, and the heart of their fire was now smoldering in a cavity. That information com-municated, a miserable silence descended on the group of ex-hausted men.

Completely discouraged, they slumped to the ground and stared unseeingly at the flickering flames, slapping irritably at the biting, stinging flies that had arrived to add to their tor-ment. All at once, George Harris broke the despondent quiet by lamenting his fate—though all seamen dreaded death by drowning, it would have been better to drown in the storm, the Englishman vowed, than to slowly starve to death in this dismal place.

It was as if he had sparked a general lamentation. When Raynal reminded them all that he had made Sarpy promise to send out a search party if they did not get back to Sydney within four months, Captain Musgrave bitterly declared that not only were they in the wrong place—Auckland Island, not Campbell—but their small stock of provisions would run out long before the four-month interval was up. "Ah, my wife!—my poor children!" he cried; and to the embarrassed distress of the rest, he buried his head in his hands and wept.

"George and Harry were silent," Raynal wrote. "In truth, we were all dumb before this great agony of our unfortunate companion." None of them dared to offer physical comfort, and so the uncomfortable silence dragged on, punctuated by Musgrave's sobs.

Sympathetically studying his captain, Raynal thought he knew exactly how his companion felt. However, he spoke up buoyantly, reminding the others that the wreck was a source of planks, rope, and canvas, which could be used to build a hut where they could live while they waited out the months before rescue. Musgrave calmed down, and they all agreed that to busy themselves constructively was the only sensible way out of their difficulties.

Accordingly, after an uncomfortable night on the wet, spongy ground beneath the shelter of the soggy tent, Musgrave and the three sailors set off for the wreck at break of day, again leaving Raynal to tend the fire.

FIVE

Shelter

The weather remained foul, Musgrave recording that it was blowing a hurricane and raining in torrents. However, without describing the struggle to get the boat back to the wreck, he went on to note in matter-of-fact tones that they managed to detach the sails from the yards and booms, take down the spars, dismantle the topmasts, and gather up a good supply of boards for "building a house, as in all probability we shall have to remain here all next winter; and if we want to preserve life, we must have shelter." In the meantime, the planks could serve as a floor for their tent, so that they could keep clear of the soggy ground. They were fortunate enough to also find a couple of pickaxes, two spades, an awl, a gimlet, an old adze, and a hammer in the flooded hold.

Piece by piece, they got all this lumber and hardware to shore, and after a short pause to eat some salt beef that Raynal had boiled, together with a cup of tea and a biscuit, they set out into the forest to find a better place to pitch their tent. They chose a site near a creek with good running water for drinking, cooking, and washing, and surrounded by trees that would be useful for firewood. A space was cleared and leveled, the tent was taken down and reerected there, and a fire was kindled at its entrance in an effort to keep away the persistent biting flies that had followed them to this new place. After piling the planks and leafy branches on the ground inside, Musgrave and the three sailors lay down and instantly fell into a heavy sleep.

Raynal, who had been relatively idle all the long, miserable day, was not nearly so fortunate. Instead, he lay in deep discomfort, listening to a thousand strange noises. The rush and suck of the surf was identifiable enough, along with the quick ripple of the brook, the rustle of wind in the leaves, and the patter of the rain, but there were also weird cries, squeals, roars, and hoarse coughs, accompanied by crashing sounds in the trees. Then, just as he realized that the tent was surrounded by a commotion of sea lions, all hell broke loose—"an extraordinary turmoil" of bellowing, smashing branches, and great thuds that shook the earth.

Musgrave and the three sailors sprang dazedly to their feet. Arming themselves with a pickax and cudgels of firewood, they dashed out of the tent. Then, just as precipitously, they stopped short, because just yards away two sea lion bulls were ferociously battling.

Both were formidable beasts, about eight feet long and more than six feet broad at the shoulders, their massive bodies covered with short dark hair. Their jaws gaped to reveal huge tusks, and their great moustaches and shaggy iron-gray manes bristled with rage. The sight of the men didn't distract them in the slightest. "Every moment they flung themselves upon one another, and bit and gnawed, tearing away great shreds of flesh, or inflicting gashes where the blood flowed in abundant streams," Raynal wrote with awe. Finally George and Harry, afraid that the beasts would blunder over the tent and demolish it, threw flaming torches at them, and the two bulls roared off, to recommence their battle a few hundred yards away.

THE SECOND DAY after the wreck, Tuesday, January 5, 1864, was a memorable one. Not only was it fine but the sailors held the first of the many hunting parties to come. While Raynal was again left at the camp to make sure the fire did not burn out, Musgrave and the others took up six-foot cudgels and set off into the forest.

Raynal watched them disappear; after about a half hour he heard shouts and exclamations, and realized that the chase had been successful. Later still, the men reappeared, each loaded down with a quarter of a sea lion carcass, the animal being far too big for one man to carry alone. They were scratched, insect-bitten, weary, and bloodstained, but no one had been hurt, and they had enough meat to get them through the next few days. Considering that none of them had been sealing before, and they had only followed the instructions that some old sealer had given them in Sydney—that the efficient way to kill a seal was to club it over the root of the nose, between the eyes, where the bones of the skull were thinnest—they had done very well. It was a triumph.

Revitalized, Captain Musgrave, George, and Alick returned to the wreck to retrieve the three chests and the big iron pot, along with the rest of the provisions, including the potatoes and pumpkins—considered particularly important, because these might provide the seed for a vegetable garden. At the same time, Raynal and Harry, the Azorean cook, took advantage of the dry weather to improve the damp, uncomfortable accommodations.

After taking everything out, they unpitched the tent and lit a big fire where it had stood, to dry and harden the earth, and also scorch and sanitize it, in yet another attempt to rid themselves of the scourge of insects.

There were two kinds of these terrible flying creatures, each carrying its own special torment. The sand flies, *Austrosimulium vexans,* were horrid enough, clinging to every inch of exposed skin and biting viciously, but more revolting were the huge bluebottle blowflies that obstinately burrowed into clothing and blankets, leaving clumps of writhing maggots in their path. These were *Calliphora quadrimaculata,* a sturdily built fly with metallic coloring, that can grow as long as an inch and pollutes everything it touches, because the female has to feed on decomposing organic matter—such as sea lion dung—for the proteins necessary to mature her eggs.

Once the smoke from the fire had sent these insects whirling off in confused clouds, Raynal and Harry directed their attentions to the carcass the hunting party had brought in. Raynal—mistakenly, as the reproductive organs had evidently been discarded with the rest of the entrails when the three hunters had butchered it—estimated it to be from a young female seal, as it weighed about one hundred pounds. Harry hung a quarter from the branch of a tree, and after lighting a fire underneath, Raynal kept it revolving so that it was well roasted by the time the others returned from the wreck.

The salvagers were tired but elated, because they had managed to retrieve the ship's compass, some more sails, and a number of empty bottles, in addition to the pot and chests. The sight of the black meat carved off the roast sobered them somewhat, however, and the first taste was not reassuring, either, being revoltingly coarse and oily. If the meat from a one-year-old was so disgusting to eat, what would it be like when they were forced to kill whatever old sea lions they could find? As Raynal meditated, it was an ominous prospect.

This dubious banquet eaten, they overhauled the chests. Raynal's gun was covered with rust, so he applied himself to cleaning and oiling it while the others took out instruments and clothes, and set them out to dry. Happily, the gunpowder had not gotten wet, being sealed in a tin. Miraculously, too, not only was the chronometer safe in its padded box but it hadn't stopped, so they now knew the exact time of day. "The other instruments," Raynal wrote, "were our sextant, a metal barometer, and a Fahrenheit thermometer." Everything else—books, charts, the small stock of spare clothing—was sodden with seawater. They got it all dried out and stowed in the reerected tent before dark, luckily, because that night the rain came back to make life as miserable as it had been before the sun had come out.

That second night in the tent was very rough, Raynal writing that "on our hard, wet planks, we tasted but a fitful slumber, disturbed by constant nightmares." In the morning the men rose "with stiffened limbs, feverish, and more fatigued than before we went to sleep." It made them all the more determined to build a weatherproof cabin as soon as humanly possible, and so straight after breakfast they went out in search of a suitable site.

This was by no means easy, the coastal forest being "very dense, in fact almost impenetrable," as Raynal described. Because of the constant howling winds, the tree trunks were "twisted in the most fantastic fashion." Every attempt to grow upright was doomed—no sooner had a tree trunk straightened, than "comes the buffeting wind again, and beaten down anew, it bows, and writhes, and humiliates itself, to shoot aloft once more for a foot or so, until soon it falls back vanquished, and is bent towards the ground. Sometimes these trees," he poetically meditated, "being wholly unsuccessful in their attempts to rise, crawl, as it were, along the earth, disappearing every now and then under hillocks of verdant turf, while the portions visible are coated with mosses of every description."

Because he was feeling a little stronger, Raynal went with the others to the mouth of the little brook that rippled near the tent and emptied into the sea nearly opposite the wreck of the *Grafton*. The beach there was reasonably level, so the men cleared a place to draw up the precious small boat and keep it safe from high tides and storms. They then decided to build their cabin on a hillock nearby, about forty feet above sea level, and conveniently close to the tent, the brook, the beach, and the wreck.

It also had the advantage that they would not have to go far to replenish the larder during the busy weeks of constructing the hut, because the sea lions were so numerous in the surrounding bush—"they go roaring about the woods like wild cattle," wrote Musgrave six days later. "Indeed, we expect they will come and storm the tent some night. We live chiefly on seal meat, as we have to be very frugal with our own little stock; we kill them at the door of the tent as we require them."

With more experience in preparing and eating seal meat, they had learned to pick and choose their game. The animal they had killed and eaten first must certainly have been a bull, because they had found the meat so rank and oily. "We cannot use the old bulls," wrote Musgrave. The females and the calves, they found, could be very good eating. "We got one young one which had never been in the water," Musgrave went on; "this was delicious—exactly like lamb."

They had salted down two carcasses for future use, though it didn't seem likely that they would be short of game for quite a while—"we have no occasion to go far after them, as they come close to the tent; indeed we were very much annoyed with them in the night." On one occasion he had been forced to take up the gun and put a bullet through the tail of one invader. "We have not been troubled with them since," Musgrave added grimly.

This was also, though, a mocking reminder of the riches he could have made if only the *Grafton* had not been lost. "If we had been fortunate enough to have kept the vessel afloat, I have no doubt but in two months or less we should have loaded her," he wrote, going on to despair yet again about the hardness of his fate: "After getting to where I might have made up for what has been lost, I lose the means of doing so. The vessel leaves her bones here, and God only knows whether we are all to leave our bones here also. And what is to become of my poor unprovided-for family? It drives me mad to think of it. I can write no more."

The best remedy for despondency was to keep busy, François Raynal recording that Musgrave, George, and Alick were busy felling trees, cutting them into eight-foot lengths, and piling them on the hillside ready for further use. "As for myself, being too feeble for any hard work, I mended the torn clothing of my companions," he wrote. He also cooked and tended the fire, all the time waving away the insects, which continued to plague them horribly. However, "For every ill there is a good," he quoted, going on to describe the abundant, charming bird-life that was attracted to the campsite by the flies. "Never having been alarmed by man, they hovered round about us, and perched themselves on the branches, within easy reach of our hands."

The first to pay a call was a species of little blue robin (probably the Auckland Island pipit, *Anthus novaeseelandiae*), which was so very partial to flies that the men used to catch the insects on the wing for the fun of hand-feeding them to these little birds, which were so tame they would perch on their arms and legs to pick the flies off their clothes.

"We had also for neighbours, in the wood, some small, green, red-headed parrots," Raynal continued. All five men found these astonishing, as they associated parakeets with the tropics: "Ours, however, seemed very well pleased and fully satisfied with their lot."

Known by its Maori name *kakariki*—"green"—in its native New Zealand because of its spectacular coloring, this parrot, a member of the *Cyanoramphus* species, has an emerald body, blue feathers mixed with green and black in the wings, and a bright red top to its head. The bird seen most frequently was "brownish-green, slightly yellow underneath, insectivorous like the robin, and not less partial to flies." This visitor's character was one of "an inexhaustible gaiety," Raynal commented admiringly. "Whether the weather is bad or good, it matters little to him; he sings with a full heart." When the men were pushing their way through the trees flocks of these bellbirds (*Anthornis melanura*, a New Zealand native that feeds on nectar as well as on insects) would accompany them, so that it was as if they "marched to the music of a concert." To Raynal's amusement, if he whistled a cadenza, any bellbirds nearby would puff up their chests and open their beaks—"Then would occur an explosion of harmony!"

Less often, they were visited by another tuneful honey eater, the tui, *Prosthemadera novaeseelandiae,* which the pioneers in New Zealand called the "parson bird" because of its white neck ruff, which forms a fine contrast to its jet black plumage. "Above and on the breast he has two large, white, floating feathers, which give him a very curious appearance, and add to the gravity of his mien."

Despite the commotion Musgrave, George, and Alick created while clearing the hillock, the birds flocked about the site—for protection, as well as company. "Upon these inoffensive passerines a bird of prey wages the deadliest war," Raynal went on, and added, "We frequently saw these birds perched in couples on the dead trees of the shore—motionless, silent, their head half hidden under their wings, their large fixed eyes exploring space." This was the New Zealand falcon, *Falco novaeseelandiae,* a magnificent bird of prey known for its utter fearlessness and disdain of man. It hunts in an unnerving silence, and then streaks in on its prey at speeds of up to one hundred fifty miles per hour, uttering a short, terrifying scream before falling on a hapless small bird in mid flight. Tuis often defend themselves by counterattacking in a flock. The castaways had a simpler ploy: One of the men would take the gun and shoot the falcon dead.

• • •

"BUT WE HAVE other work on our hands at present," wrote Musgrave; shooting hawks was a waste of time and energy as well as precious ammunition. "We must get a place to live in, for the tent we are now living in is a beastly place. I expect we shall all get our death of cold before we get out of it yet; and the blow-flies blow our blankets and clothes, and make everything in the most disgusting state imaginable."

This sentiment was fervently echoed by the men: "We have all worked very hard," Musgrave recorded toward the end of the first week of their stranding; he himself had been so busy that he had not had time to keep up the ship's log or his journal, and so "Mr. Raynal, who is improving fast, keeps the diary. Indeed," he added, "he is so much better that he talks of going to work tomorrow"—and that despite the weather, which was unremittingly foul, "blowing a perfect hurricane from N. to S. all the time," accompanied by torrential rain. "And yet it was the middle of summer!" Raynal expostulated later.

On Sunday, January 10, more than two weeks after midsummer's day in the south, the sun at last came out—"a light breeze from the west has driven away the clouds, the sky is at length visible," Raynal exulted. "Behold how sweet it is—how smiling! Should we not see in this a happy omen, a promise of happiness and approaching deliverance?" For him, it was only natural that he should regard the advent of fine weather on this day, a Sunday, as a sign that better fortune was about to come, and it seems that Harry, George, and Alick shared his sentiments. "In this moment of peace and benediction, after the terrible trials we had undergone, we all of us felt in the bottom of our hearts the awakening of an irresistible need of devotion," François Raynal went on.

The notion was reinforced when Captain Musgrave found a Bible in his chest. "We begged him to read us some fine passage from the Gospels," Raynal wrote; "and ranged in a circle round him before the tent, we listened with the deepest attention."

Musgrave chose the Gospel according to Matthew. Raynal related that when the captain read out Christ's exhortation to His Disciples to love one another, all the listeners "burst into tears." Musgrave himself did not mention the episode, but, as it turned out, for the five castaways this moment was a deeply significant one.

SIX

Prey

When the sun was shining the building site was a very pleasant place—"There is plenty of timber where we are camped, and also a beautiful creek of clear water," wrote Musgrave. However, it quickly became obvious that it would be impossible to build the American frontier-style log house that they had first envisaged, made of straight tree trunks laid on top of each other and the gaps plugged with moss. The local timber was simply too twisted and contorted for this—"not long enough or big enough to make a proper log-house," as Musgrave went on—"so we shall put them (the pieces of timber) up and down."

Fortunately, they were able to draw on Raynal's experience in the goldfields, where he had built huts out of tree branches, used their bark for roofing material, and constructed adobe chimneys out of pebbles and sunbaked clay. His strength was improving daily, and within a few more days he was able to help physically instead of just handing out advice: "I was at one and the same time architect and mason."

After much consultation, the men marked out and leveled a rectangle at the summit of the hillock, twenty-four feet long by sixteen feet wide. Then they dug a four-foot-deep hole at each corner, driving their shovels deeply through the peat. After laying a large stone in the bottom of each of these holes as a foundation, they used masts from the wreck as corner posts, wedging them in with small stones and packed-down dirt. The heads of these posts, about seven feet from the ground, were notched to take crossbeams, which were made out of topmasts and yards. Two more holes were dug, one in the middle of each of the shorter ends of the rectangle, to take two more poles cut from the mainyard of the schooner. Twice as high as the corner posts, these two center posts rose fourteen feet in the air. Then the bowsprit was slung from one of these to the other, forming the ridgepole for a steeply pitched roof.

The next job was to cut twenty-eight rafters, which would link the ridgepole to the lateral beams at twenty-inch intervals, fourteen rafters for each side of the roof. For material for these, Musgrave, taking Alick with him, climbed the cliffs and hunted for poles that were reasonably straight—quite a task in a country where everything grew crooked. Then, while he and Alick clambered all over the top of the framework, lashing these rafters into place, George and Harry dug holes for a pair of strong posts to be set in the middle of each of the long sides of the hut. In the center of the sheltered side, the one that faced inland, the two posts were placed about a yard apart to make the frame for a doorway, while the two posts opposite, set about six feet apart, were to serve as the upright supports for a fireplace.

"I confess that we were not expeditious, and that our work made slow progress," Raynal admitted; "but consider how many obstacles we had to overcome." The first week of foul weather had held them up, plus the constant problem of finding suitable materials. Then there was the want of good tools, to which was added "the necessity of hunting seals." Musgrave had found an alternative source of game, going across the bay in the boat with Alick as oarsman to shoot a dozen birds they called "widgeons"—actually a species of cormorant, *Phalacrocorax colensoi,* native to the Auckland Islands. However, while the fowl made a welcome change of fare, and had the added advantage of being readily salted and smoked, sea lions were their staple.

Over the twelve days since they had been wrecked, the castaways had learned a great deal about their prey, including the best method of tackling them. As Raynal described, the prescription for approaching a mature sea lion was to fix the animal's gaze, "and, without hesitating, advance straight upon him, until you are near enough to deal a blow on his head with your cudgel exactly between the two eyes." It was crucial to hit the target exactly. If the animal did not fall at once with the thin bones of the frontal part of his skull crushed and his brain destroyed, the next move was to whirl about, run like hell, "and leave the field open for him to regain the sea." Not only could a hurt and angry sea lion maul a man with his tusks and crush him to death with his weight but he was unnervingly agile on land, being perfectly prepared to pursue a fleeing castaway up a cliff if he was not given the chance to plunge back into the surf instead.

Accordingly, the men had learned how to attack and kill quickly and efficiently. Quite apart from the danger of merely wounding a sea lion, the more speedily they filled the larder the better, because the overriding priority was to get the cabin built.

Luckily, as Musgrave commented, the weather kept tolerably fine over the second week of their stranding, at the time they were erecting the framework. The major irritant was the sand flies. With the advent of warm sunshine, hosts of *Austrosimulium vexans* hatched in the sea wrack on the beach, and proved well named, being vexing indeed, because "unfortunately," as Raynal recorded wryly, "they found the way to our hillock." Like mosquitoes, they sucked blood, but were even more maddening, because once they latched onto bare skin they would not let go, no matter how the men slapped, wriggled, or scratched. "They flattened themselves down, closed their wings in around their body, so as to take up the least possible space, and continued to bite us and to suck our blood with greedy violence."

Consequently, the men's hands were red, sore, and itching, and their faces were so swollen they could scarcely see. As Raynal went on to observe, anyone who happened on the scene would have wondered about their sanity — "Every moment one or the other of us, tormented by the intolerable bites and stings and pricks, would leave off his work, throw his tool on the ground, and rub himself strenuously against the nearest post." If it hadn't been so painful, it would have been hilarious — and, indeed, the men often did burst out laughing, even the victim himself.

"SUNDAY, JANUARY 17," wrote Raynal. They had been shipwrecked exactly two weeks, and the weather had deteriorated again. "Wind blowing from the north, sky cloudy and threatening, the barometer sinking." Neither Raynal or Musgrave mentioned taking any kind of rest on that Sabbath, but two days later the day dawned clear and sunny, and Captain Musgrave demonstrated his leadership skills by giving his men a much-needed vacation.

Accordingly, they launched the small boat—"which," wrote Raynal, "we had furnished with mast, sail, and oars, as well as with our cudgels and my gun"—and jumped into it. First, they went down the harbor to Musgrave Peninsula and, as Musgrave recorded, "planted a flagstaff, with a large canvas flag on it, where it may be seen from the sea, and we tied a bottle to it, with a note inside it directing anyone who may see it where to find us." Then they steered up the western arm of the harbor, finding an outlet at the other end that confirmed that Carnley Harbour was a strait, not enclosed. "Here we found there was a narrow passage out to the sea, about three-quarters of a mile long, and the quarter of a cable's length in width," wrote Musgrave, "proving the land to the southward to be not a peninsula, but an island."

This passage between Adams Island to the south, and Auckland Island to the north, was an ancient gorge bounded by massive lava flows that plunged precipitously to the shoals below. Musgrave didn't try to negotiate this, considering it too dangerous for a small boat, "as the tide was rushing rapidly through it and there was a heavy swell running and breaking on both sides. It runs nearly north and south," he added, "the south end opening to the sea—I should suppose not far from the South Cape."

So, instead of venturing further, the men stilled their oars and gazed about, overwhelmed by what Raynal called the "wild and majestic beauty" of the scene—"Let the reader figure to himself a kind of ravine, about five hundred yards wide and three thousand long, pent up between two cliffs as perpendicular as walls, and from eight hundred to twelve hundred feet in height." The sound effects, too, were awesome, as the great stone ramparts were "hollowed with numerous caverns, into whose depths the waves plunged with hoarse wild murmurs, which, repeated in all directions," echoed on and on, seemingly for ever.

Musgrave, much more mundanely, recorded, "At this place we saw hundreds of seals; both the shores and the water were literally swarming with them, both the tiger and black seal; but in general the tiger seals keep one side of the harbour, and the black seals, which are much the largest, the other side."

This definition of two kinds of seal, "black" and "tiger," has puzzled biologists ever since Musgrave's journal was first published. Four seal species visit the Auckland Islands—the sea leopard (*Hydrurga leptonyx*), the southern elephant seal (*Mirounga leonina*), the New Zealand, or Hooker's, sea lion (*Phocarctos hookeri*), and the New Zealand fur seal (*Arctocephalus forsteri*). However, only these last two establish breeding colonies there, so Musgrave had to be referring to fur seals and/or sea lions.

All seals belong to a group called Pinnipedia, which have streamlined bodies and flippers for limbs. Both fur seals and sea lions belong to a subgroup, the eared seals, Otariidae, which have small external ear flaps and can turn their hind flippers forward when they are on land, so that they are surprisingly nimble. However, while they have all this in common, New Zealand fur seals and New Zealand sea lions are easily told apart. Not only are sea lions a lot bigger than fur seals, a full-grown sea lion bull being three times the size of a male fur seal, but fur seals, as the name suggests, have much longer fur, the soft, shimmering inner coat stiffened with a top layer of guard hairs. And, though fur seals have pointed noses and long whiskers, the nose of a sea lion is broad and blunt.

The fur seal is chocolate brown in both sexes. While the big, aggressive sea lion bulls are dark brown, too, their much smaller wives are a very pretty caramel color, quite often striped or spotted. Fur seals could perhaps be called "black," especially when wet, but it is highly unlikely that they would have been present in the numbers that Musgrave described. It was just thirty-four years since the Connecticut explorer Benjamin Morrell had described the complete disappearance of fur seals from the Auckland Islands, and, unless augmented by new arrivals, the population could not possibly have reestablished itself to that extent. Later evidence, too, suggests that sea lions would have greatly outnumbered fur seals in Musgrave's time—as they still do today. In 1873 two skulls found near the castaway hut were both sea lion skulls, and in 1916 a scientific expedition found no fur seals at all at Carnley Harbour.

It is much more likely that the animals Musgrave described were all sea lions. The collection of "black" seals gathered on one of the shores would have been a mob of dark brown adolescent sea lion bulls, while the "tigers" on the opposite side would have been sea lion cows, presided over by a few dominant bulls, the "beachmasters." The young males, called "Sams" (Sub-Adult Males) by scientists, are forced to live apart from the breeding population until they are socially mature, though they make constant hopeful forays on the rookeries—breeding platforms—with the object of defeating an old or weak beachmaster, stealing his cows, and establishing a harem.

Male and female sea lions looked so different from each

other that even professional sealers had trouble realizing that they were the same species, calling the males "sea lions" and the females "sea bears." Two or three times bigger than the cows, the bulls can grow to a length of twelve feet, and weigh a thousand pounds. As the name suggests, sea lion bulls have a mane, which, with the moustache, further distinguishes them from the cows. "The upper lip, thick and fleshy, is fringed on either side with thirty hairs, hard as horn, each about four inches in length, and terminating in a point," wrote Raynal, who was a precise and astute observer. "Some of these hairs are marked with transparent veins, like those of the tortoise shell."

Since Musgrave's day, the sea lions of the Auckland Islands have been studied in much more detail, though his observations are still considered valuable and interesting. While the sea lions are present about the shores throughout the year, it isn't until the breeding season that they start to gather on the rookeries. In October or November, the fully mature bulls haul their massive bodies out onto the rock platforms, and immediately start fighting for the best territory, each battling for a shelf from which he will greet the heavily pregnant cows when they arrive about the beginning of December.

At first it seems a waste of time, because the incoming cows haughtily ignore the questing bulls, their minds being otherwise engaged. The moment each one is clear of the surf she rises up on her fore flippers, and looks about for her friends. As a scientific observer noted in 1972, "A plump, wet female sea lion would emerge from the sea, survey the scene, and then hurriedly gallop towards a group of cows as if she were late for an appointment." Presumably, these other cows are her cousins, her sisters, and her aunts, and include her mother and grandmother, too, because she knows them so very well. Having joined the mob, she settles down, often rubbing herself against one of her friends to dry herself off.

For the next seven days or so they huddle together companionably, going into the sea to fish every now and then, and the rest of the time sleeping so heavily their snores can be heard from many yards away. Sea lions have no sense of hygiene at all, freely vomiting and defecating all over each other, as well as indulging in a lot of sand-throwing, but few fights develop, and those are mostly settled with a threatening yawn. Then, about the third week of December, the pupping begins.

When she goes into labor the female shifts away from the mob and twists about, obviously uncomfortable. As the moment of birth approaches she swings her hindquarters vigorously, working so hard that the pup is virtually hurled out of her body, landing some feet away. Mother and calf then get to know each other by sound, taste, and smell, though the calf has to learn how to suckle the thick, creamy milk, which is five times as rich as dairy cow's milk. There are few more contented sights, one scientist observed, than a well-fed sea lion pup sleeping on his back alongside his mother, his brown fur dry and fluffy, his flippers limply extended, and his little stomach bulging.

When the pup is one week old his mother is ready for mating. If the beachmaster does not make any overtures, having given up by now, she will initiate the courting by snuggling up to him, arching her neck against his, and spreading her hind flippers to display her genitals. The bull responds by snuffling and licking that area, and then mounts her, their coupling being a muscular and protracted process that can last as long as forty minutes before she tires of it and starts to bite his neck and tug at his mane. After that, she is not interested in mating anymore, and will take to the forest with her pup, often trekking several miles inland to avoid further attentions.

BY JANUARY 19, the date of the castaways' excursion, the rutting season was almost over. However, a pitched battle was in progress as the small boat drew up, probably between a beachmaster and a Sam who was trying to usurp his rookery. The contestants paid no attention to the *Grafton* sailors, who paddled to keep the boat still in the water while they gazed in fascination. "We watched them about half an hour, and left them still hard at it," wrote Musgrave; "they fight as ferociously as dogs, and do not make the least noise, and with their large tusks they tear each other almost to pieces."

They had seen several of these fights, because during the month of December and the first ten days or so of January, the bulls skirmish constantly to keep dominance over both territories and wives. Musgrave observed that when annoyed, a bull would raise his mane: "It is from three to four inches long, and can be ruffled up and made to stand erect at will, which is always done when they attack each other on shore, or are surprised." With their enormous teeth bared they looked like lions indeed, with "all the ferocity and formidableness which their name seems to imply." He sighted one from the boat whose "neck and back were lacerated in a most fearful manner; large pieces of hide and flesh were torn off, perhaps a foot long, and four or five inches wide."

Up until this day, the sea lions hadn't usually bothered the men, but this situation rapidly changed when they rowed toward the southern shore where the subadult males were assembled.

Instead of shying away, the young bulls gathered and tried to seize the oars in their teeth. Most were easily beaten off with those same oars, but one large specimen became so enraged that he attacked the boat. Horrified at the sight of the great bull clawing his way up the bows with his jaws gaping wide and his moustache bristling above his huge tusks, the men cringed back. Then Alick seized up the boat hook and slammed it down on the snarling head, and, uttering a furious roar, their attacker disappeared beneath the waves.

This fright didn't deter the men from landing the boat on the opposite beach, where they cooked and ate a midday meal while the beachmaster watched from a respectful distance. After exploring the immediate scenery, they returned to the shore and slaughtered a couple of newborn pups, Raynal writing that they considered their flesh "much superior to that of the young who, having given over suckling, have begun to feed on fish."

They also shot a dozen widgeon and some ducks, so they could look forward to a more varied menu than usual. Then, tired but relaxed, they rowed back to their own beach, by now aptly named Shipwreck Cove. There they plucked the birds, cooked what they needed, and then hung the others in pairs on the highest branches of the trees, "to place them out of the reach of the attacks of the flies," as Raynal wrote. For some reason the loathed bluebottles did not rise very high, "probably on account of the wind."

SEVEN

The Cabin

The day after the outing, Wednesday, January 20, the weather turned foul, but the men didn't allow this to bring their work to a standstill. They had a good store of meat, and so could concentrate on the cabin—and right now, the building of the fireplace and chimney was the project at hand. It was crucial that they get it right. Not only would the fire provide vital heat in the winter to come but it had to be safely contained. If the cabin burned down, it would spell the end for them all, so Raynal planned a long way ahead, and the men worked with care.

Because of the danger of the peat beneath the fireplace alighting, they dug out a deep hearth between the two fireplace posts, and filled the cavity with stones. Then they painstakingly chose flat, large rocks for the sides and rear, laying them carefully on top of each other and bracing them with wooden pegs pushed into the ground on the outer side. The next problem was that there was no clay to make an adobe-style mortar to stick the stones together. What they needed, Raynal decided, was cement.

After thinking about it, he went down to the beach and collected a great quantity of seashells. "These," he stated matter-of-factly, "we calcined during the night." In the process called "calcining," calcium carbonate—the hard substance of the shells, in this case—is converted into calcium oxide (lime). It requires intense heat, and is normally done in a kiln. A roaring fire was made, the shells piled on top of the red-hot embers, and the whole covered over and then left to roast.

It was successful, because when the makeshift oven was opened in the morning, Raynal found that he was now "provided with a supply of lime." Normally, to make cement, this lime would be mixed with clay. As there was no clay available, Raynal turned to a process the ancient Roman engineers would have recognized, by mixing the calcium oxide with sand. It was a slow process, and a painful one—by the time Raynal had made enough mortar to cement the fireplace stones together, the lime had burned right through his fingertips.

"This lime, mixed with the fine gravel we found under the rocks of the beach, made a capital mortar for our mason's work. But when the latter was finished," he ruefully wrote, "though I had used a palette of wood as a substitute for a trowel, I found the tips of my fingers, and nearly all of my right hand, burned to the quick." He was gratified by Musgrave's approval, but the most effusive compliments "could not make me forget the intense pain I suffered. However," he added, "constant application of fresh water, and a few dressings with seal-oil, soon cured my wounds."

Getting the materials together for the chimney pot took still more ingenuity. The hull of the *Grafton* had been sheathed with a thin layer of copper below the waterline, a customary precaution because unprotected wood is vulnerable to teredo, the wood-boring shipworm that can reduce hard timber to something as fragile as lace in a matter of weeks. Luckily, the moon was full, and so Alick and George took advantage of the very low tides to wade into the surf and strip sheets of this copper from the sides of the wreck, using a pry bar Raynal had made out of a flat metal rod—a "tringle," which had been salvaged from the foremast shrouds—by splitting it a little way at one end, and then curving up the split ends to make a claw.

Considering that they were standing waist deep in cold salt water, and were forced to duck under the surface at regular intervals to detach the lower edges of the copper plates, the two men were surprisingly efficient. "Though they could not work above two hours at a time, in three tides George and Alick had stripped off enough copper to enable us to finish our chimney pot," wrote Raynal. At the same time, the two seamen carefully collected all the tiny nails that had held the copper to the hull. This was a fiddly job that dragged out the work but was essential because the tacks were necessary for pinning the copper sheets to the chimney framework.

Four poles had been fastened to the walls of the fireplace, leaning toward each other to form a broad pyramid that was open at the top. Crosspieces were bound to these rods, and the sheets of copper were nailed first to the inside of this truncated pyramid, and then on the outside, to make a double lining. With that, the fireplace was finished, and the men could look forward to roaring fires in the winter ahead. However, it was lucky that winter lay many weeks in the future, because the framework of the cabin was still open to the weather.

• • •

BECAUSE CAPTAIN MUSGRAVE did not have Raynal's engineering skills, he took on the responsibility of keeping the pantry replenished, occasionally taking the taciturn Norwegian, Alick, with him to help. Someone always had to venture out with a cudgel—or the gun, if there was any hope of varying the menu with poultry, widgeon being preferred. He and Alick tried fishing off the beach, but did not have much success, because they were competing with the sea lions in the sea lions' natural fishing ground. They had better luck in the creek that was their source of drinking and washing water, finding a small species that "resembled trout and were delicious eating," according to Musgrave, "but were very small, the largest weighing scarcely a quarter of a pound." This was *Galaxias brevipinnis,* a fish native to New Zealand and known to the Maori as *koaro,* an ancient species with just one dorsal fin and no scales, which is very agile, starting life in the sea, like salmon, and then in early adulthood leaping up rushing streams to reach the rocky pools where they breed.

About this time, too, Musgrave took up a habit of going off on long excursions, taking a cudgel and trekking for long distances on foot, sometimes with Alick, but often alone. This is a common phenomenon when people are stranded in desolate, remote places, exhibited by members of scientific discovery parties as well as shipwrecked seamen. Obsessive behavior is characteristic, too, and in Musgrave it took the form of a preoccupation with charts and barometer readings. He carried surveying tools with him, and made charts as he went, determined to map the harbor and the surrounding territory to the best of his ability; not only was it reassuring to have a picture of the terrain in his mind, but his journal and charts would be of use to future travelers, even if rescue came too late to save him and his companions. He and Raynal had already made a grim pact that if they died before anyone came, they would be buried with their journals, so that the records they kept would be uncovered when their bodies were eventually disinterred.

On Sunday morning, January 24, Musgrave was alone when he set out to climb the mountain to the northeast of the camp, as Alick was sick, and Raynal was still not well enough to trudge long distances. To his surprise, there were many signs of sea lions—"In going up I found seal tracks nearly to the top of the mountain, which I reckon is about four miles from the water; and about three miles up I saw a seal."

After reaching the summit he stood a long time, contemplating precipitous mountains stretching to the north and east, covered with long, coarse, dun-colored grass and the occasional patch of stunted scrub, and with a multitude of waterfalls dashing down granite ravines. It was a daunting landscape, far from the touch of man. He could hear a muffled boom every now and then as a large breaker thudded against the tall cliffs to the west. To the north and east of the island group a tumbled ocean extended as far as his eye could reach, unmarked by a single sail. With his head bent dejectedly, battling a fit of black depression, Musgrave turned and set off back to camp.

He returned down the face of the mountain instead of along the spur he had climbed to get to the top, and was forced to traverse a number of swamps to get to the band of thick forest that backed the cove where they camped. "The 'big bush,' as we call it, is where the largest timber grows; it extends about a mile from the water all round the shores of the harbour, which, taking all the bays, is not less than sixty or seventy miles." He identified the trees as the "iron-bark" that grew in Australia, though the bark was different, being much thinner and harder, "as thin as brown paper."

These trees (actually New Zealand rata, *Metrosideros umbellata*) made excellent firewood and were spectacular at this time of the year, midsummer in the south, as they blazed with scarlet flowers. Getting through the forest was a trial, though, because Musgrave was often forced to drop to hands and knees to crawl under the low, crooked branches and around the gnarled roots that rose above the bare, mossy ground. The emptiness of the space beneath the tortured branches was strangely haunted, a preternatural reminder of how far they were away from the lands where other men lived, and it was a relief to get out of it and back to the camp, where he could hear reassuring human voices.

Two days after that, on Tuesday, January 26, Musgrave went out on another such excursion, though not alone this time — which was lucky, because he very nearly shot himself. When he discharged the gun, one of the barrels hung fire; when he turned the gun butt-down to reload it, it went off, sending the ball whistling past his nose and through the rim of his hat. "I thank God, who has protected me thus far," he prayed; "although in His wisdom He has chastised me severely lately, that He had again spared my life."

On Monday, February 1, he was unlucky enough to be overtaken by a sudden storm while out in the small boat. He managed to get the boat back to the wreck, where he moored her, but she was damaged when a heavy wave smashed her bow against the *Grafton*'s hull, and so getting her fixed was yet another job to be done — once the cabin was completed.

FILLING IN THE SIDES of the structure proved a challenging problem, which they solved in a complicated and time-consuming fashion. First, the poles that Musgrave, George, and Alick had cut when they cleared the top of the hillock were stuck upright in the dirt to the depth of about a foot, all along each side save for the fireplace and the door, bound as tightly together as their twisted shapes allowed. Each one was tied at the top to the crossbeams, one after another, until the spaces between the upright posts were more or less closed in. The insides of the walls and roof were crosshatched with horizontal rows of thin laths, and the outside was covered with canvas, a double layer going onto the roof. The cabin was still by no means impervious to weather—as Musgrave commented, "it lets a great deal of wind through"—but the castaways moved into it the moment the last of the canvas was lashed into place.

The date was Tuesday, February 2, 1864. They had been stranded on this desolate and difficult coast for thirty-one long days and nights, and thankful indeed did they feel to be under a roomy shelter at last. Though the cabin was still not much more weatherproof than the tent they had made out of the mainsail, it was a great deal bigger. "The house is 24 feet by 16 feet; the chimney is 8 feet by 5 feet, built of stone," wrote Musgrave. As usual, however, his satisfaction was blighted by dismal thoughts of the plight of his loved ones in Sydney. "We shall be able to have a roaring fire in it in the winter, if we are so unfortunate as to have to remain here till that time; and God help those at home, whom it almost drives me mad to think of. We have, as yet, had plenty to eat," he went on, adding dolefully, "but whether they have or not, God only knows."

By the last week of February not only did they have a

door—"a very good one, made of inch boards"—but they had
a board floor. Raynal, Alick, and George had gone out into the
forest to fell timber and cut it up into suitable lengths for joists,
and had gotten the collection of lumber to the house just as the
heavens opened. While they set up the joists that afternoon, the
rain rattled on the roof in such torrents that they could hardly
hear themselves speak. Within an hour this became a matter for
worry, as the earth was getting wet and boggy.

Advised by Raynal's experience on the goldfields, where it
was quite common for sudden cloudbursts to destroy miners'
huts, they decided to dig a two-foot-deep ditch around the
house to take off the water from the roof. For two days it was
impossible to do this, as it rained too hard to leave the cabin for
anything not absolutely urgent. Finally, however, it cleared, and
Alick and George were able to commence digging. Then they
found that the trench weakened the foundations of the chimney
and the corner posts, so they braced them with still more poles,
placed at an angle.

The fireplace was a huge success—which was lucky, because
there were times when it was as cold inside the house as it was
outside. The wind whistled through a thousand gaps in the
walls, setting the canvas to rattling and lifting, and the flames
to fluttering and roaring in the chimney. Obviously, something
had to be done about it. After a great deal of discussion the
party came to the conclusion that thatching the outside of the
walls was the best way out of the problem. From then on they
went out every day to gather up clumps of the long, coarse,
strong tussock-grass that grew at the tops of the nearby cliffs.

"The reader may think that this occupation was rather amusing," Raynal wrote wryly, going on to relate that it was very

much the opposite. The gatherers set out at dawn, each with a rope, and clambered to the top of the cliff to attack the tussock, which was "not only extremely hard, but jagged at the edges, and sharp as a knife." As a result, when they trudged home, bowed down in the rain with three or four great bundles on their backs, their hands were dripping blood from dozens of tiny but agonizing cuts.

Then the straw had to be tied into bundles, each one about as thick as a man's arm, according to Raynal, and tied with thread unraveled from old sailcloth. After being trimmed square at the ends, they were bound upright to the sides of the house, starting at the bottom and with each row overlapping, so that the effect was like the thatching on the roof of an English cottage. As they went along, the men laid another network of laths over the outside of the thatch, and sewed the outside laths to the inside ones with twine and a wooden needle—"a wooden needle of the size of a sword blade!" Raynal exclaimed—so that the thatch would not be carried away by the next hard gale.

WHEN IT WAS TOO DARK, wet, or windy to thatch, the men built furniture, starting with something to sleep on. According to Musgrave, they made five stretchers out of poles and canvas, and slung them in the roof six feet above the floor, so that by day they could move freely beneath them. Raynal drew a different picture, describing plank beds like long boxes set on legs, which were filled with primitive mattresses of dried moss. These, according to him, were set about the walls, with his bed and Musgrave's at the corners of the northern end, and those belonging to the three sailors at the other extremity of the hut, one against each of the three walls there. While it is impossible to tell which man's version was right, Musgrave's description seems more likely, as suspending the beds overhead would leave space to move around; otherwise, the house would have been very cramped.

A dining table measuring seven feet by three feet was built out of boards and placed in the center, with a long bench on either side, and a keg for the captain's seat at the end. Musgrave had a smaller table, made out of a chest that had come from the *Grafton*'s cabin, to use as a desk, and this was placed at the northern end of the house. The chronometer box was set on this, and above it hung the barometer and thermometer. A shelf held what books they had—the Bible, Milton's *Paradise Lost*, and a couple of English novels, which lacked a few important pages. It was at this table that Musgrave wrote up his journal every Sunday, using seal blood once the little pot of ink he had saved from the wreck had run out.

"This, the north end of the hut, was occupied by Mr. Raynal and myself, the men's quarters being at the other end," he penned. "A cook's table stood behind the door at the men's end. There were two or three shelves round the place, which, with a pair of bellows and a looking-glass, completed the furniture." On these shelves, according to Raynal, pots, pans, and dishes were stored, along with the lamps that the men had made out of old preserved-meat tins, which had wicks spun out of sailcloth threads, and were fueled with sea lion oil.

For the storage of large items, triangular lofts had been erected in the four corners of the roof. Raynal, who had been appointed the group's medic, was in charge of the medicines they owned, of which there were only two. One was the remnant of their stock of ordinary flour, which could be rolled into balls when dampened with water, and swallowed to combat diarrhea. The other was the last of their mustard, which could be used to raise blisters on the skin as a cure for aches and pains. It seems incredible now that anyone should try to cure a headache, for instance, by making a big blister on the nape of the neck, but perhaps it felt as if it worked because the pain of the blister would be so intense that the original pain would seem insignificant by comparison. For whatever reason, it was a popular remedy of the time. Both the mustard and the flour were kept in a bag that was hung above Raynal's bed.

As a finishing touch, openings had been cut in the upper walls, and panes of glass salvaged from the schooner were wedged into the gaps. "These," Raynal continued on a note of pride, "were our windows." Considering their circumstances, to have something so civilized as glass windows was a triumph.

EIGHT

Democracy

The men might have been warm and comfortable, but in the meantime, there was a crisis in the house. The division of the castaway hut into two halves—one for the captain and officer at the more sheltered northward end, and the other for the three ordinary sailors—reflected the placement of accommodations on board ship. By tradition, the captain and his mate lived in the sternward part of the vessel in a cozy cabin, and the men lived forward in a crowded, uncomfortable forecastle. At sea, both Musgrave and the sailors accepted this as the norm—but, while Captain Musgrave was happy that the arrangement of the house they had labored together to build should be so similar to the usual shipboard plan, the sailors did not necessarily agree with the idea of being ranked shipboard-style anymore.

Since they had been cast ashore, a mood of democracy had prevailed in the party, each man being considered as important as the next. Though this had contributed significantly to their survival, it meant that Alick, George, and Harry had become much more cavalier about rank, a sentiment that hadn't taken long to become obvious. As far back as February 7, Captain Musgrave had grumbled that while they didn't actually demur when he gave them an order, they obeyed "in that manner which says plainly, Why don't you do it yourself?"

In a nutshell, they had come to believe that they were just as good as their betters, something that Musgrave, a master mariner of the old school, regarded as the first stirrings of mutiny. "It is true I no longer hold any command over them," he complained; "but I share everything that has been saved from the wreck in common with them, and I have worked as hard as any of them in trying to make them comfortable, and I think gratitude ought to prompt them to still continue willing and obedient. But you might as well look for the grace of God in a Highlandman's log-book as gratitude in a sailor," he grumbled; "this is a well-known fact."

François Raynal, who was acutely aware of the need for solidarity if they were ever to survive this ordeal, became alarmed when he realized what was happening. Up until then, he had been gratified to note that they lived and worked together "in peace and harmony—I may even say in true and honest brotherhood." Occasionally, impatient words had been exchanged, but it had always been just a momentary spat, easily put down to stress. Now, it looked as if the house which they had been building with such unanimity of purpose could prove to be a divider, and "if habits of bitterness and animosity were once established amongst us," he declared, "the consequences could not but be most disastrous: we stood so much in need of one another!"

There was a case for a little human understanding, though. The men had become accustomed to Musgrave's recurring black moods, and realized that this was why he had developed a habit of wandering off for long distances alone. These terrible bouts of depression could be triggered by foul weather, setbacks in the house building, failure to catch seals, or monthly anniversaries, such as that of the departure from New South Wales, or of the night the *Grafton* had been wrecked. All five got depressed at times, but Musgrave was the only one who was married and had family responsibilities. Accordingly, he was prey to a constant nagging guilt that was not felt by the others — "I shall never forgive myself for coming on this enterprise," he once wrote. He'd had the best of intentions, and it would have worked out well "had the old chains only held the ship to her anchors," but it had turned out for the worst.

As captain, he felt responsible for the whole group, too, and was desperately worried about their prospects of rescue, something that he tried unsuccessfully to assuage with his far-ranging excursions into the hinterland. The fact that he didn't trust his uncle — Sarpy's partner — to look after his family implied that he didn't believe in the promise Raynal had extracted from Sarpy and Uncle Musgrave, either. And, even if the two drapers surprised them all by sending a search party, it would not arrive before October at the earliest — "people would not come down into these stormy and unexplored regions in the winter."

François Raynal, though he trusted Charles Sarpy as little as Thomas Musgrave did, was better off in several respects. While he loved and missed his parents, they weren't dependent on his income, no matter how eager he was to return to France with a fortune in his pocket. He had his confident piety and his technical resourcefulness on his side, too, plus a natural unfailing optimism — a faith in the future that he knew Musgrave did not share.

So Raynal fully understood the reasons for Musgrave's moodiness. However, he also sympathized with the sailors' democratic stance. On the goldfields, an aggressive mood of democracy had prevailed—every miner deemed himself the social equal of any other miner, and carried a gun to back it up. Raynal also knew the exhilaration of living in a country where servants and laborers who'd struck lucky were suddenly the equals of the aristocracy who had once employed them. Accordingly, he held egalitarian views of his own.

After putting his mind to the problem, he thought he'd found a way of repairing the rift between Captain Musgrave and the men—by the exercise of democracy itself. "My idea," he wrote, "was that we should choose among us, not a master or a superior, but a 'head' or 'chief of the family'"—a man who would maintain discipline, adjudicate quarrels, and give out daily tasks.

When he voiced this proposal it was heartily approved by the rest, though the sailors wanted another clause included—that if the chosen man proved unworthy he could be fired, and another election held. This was satisfactory to all, so the agreement, after having been rephrased into resounding legal language, was recorded on a blank page in Musgrave's Bible. Then, after clasping hands over the book, and solemnly swearing to obey and respect the provisions of the contract, the men held the vote at once.

Raynal nominated Musgrave, who was unanimously elected forthwith. "Thenceforth," wrote the Frenchman, "he sat at the head of the table, and was released from all share in the work of cooking." To soothe any feelings that might still be ruffled, Raynal then volunteered to take over the cooking for the first week of this new arrangement—a very good move, because in addition to the many surprising virtues he had demonstrated already, he turned out to be a resourceful chef. "Frequently he gave us four courses at a meal," wrote Musgrave. "One bill of fare, for instance, might be stewed or roasted seal, fried liver, fish and mussels."

Despite Raynal's best efforts, though, he had very limited ingredients to work with, and the unbalanced diet was beginning to affect their health. As Musgrave also wrote, they "felt very severely the lack of bread and vegetables." The science of nutrition lay a long way in the future—it was not until 1912 that Professor Frederick Hopkins demonstrated that "accessory factors of the diet" are necessary for survival—but seamen had known since the sixteenth century that people got sick and died if they were deprived of fresh fruit and vegetables for too many weeks, and that six-month voyages out of sight of land were a virtual death warrant.

The symptoms of sea scurvy were generally well known, even if vitamin C—the deficiency of which is the cause of the disease—had not been identified yet. As early as six weeks after the ship's store of fresh vegetables and fruit had run out, and the sailors were existing solely on salt meat and hard bread, small black spots would appear on their legs and arms, then run together until the limbs were entirely purple-black, while at the same time they were afflicted with severe pains in all their joints, particularly when trying to sleep at night. Because the vitamin is necessary for connective tissue, including bones, to stick together, limbs that had broken and healed years before would suddenly break again, with agonizing results. Gums would become spongy, and teeth fall out. Blood would trickle from the eye sockets and nostrils; the sufferer would begin vomiting bloody matter. A ghastly death as the brain swelled and burst inside the skull was inevitable—unless the patient was given fresh fruit or vegetables to eat. Then the cure was miraculous. It was because of this that early discoverers and the sealers and whalers who followed them planted fruit and vegetable gardens on far-flung desolate shores.

However, scurvy was not just a disease of the sea. If people on land were deprived of fresh fruit and vegetables as a result of poverty or a long, hard winter, they would develop similar symptoms. Because Captain Musgrave was acutely aware of this, the twenty potatoes saved from the wreck had not been eaten, but had been planted, instead—a wise and provident move that, unfortunately, did not work. All that had come up was a four-inch growth of leaves with marble-size clumps of potatoes underneath, the soil and climate being so hostile. These had not been eaten, but saved for more seed in the hope that they would do better in the following season—if they were doomed to stay that long. The seeds from the two pumpkins had been sown, too, but had come to nothing at all, simply rotting in the ground.

Consequently, the men hadn't eaten any fruit or substantial vegetables for some significant time. Just as important, since the supply of hard bread had run out, they had eaten no carbohydrates, either. Both Musgrave and Raynal recorded that Harry, who had been the schooner's cook, wistfully reminisced about the buckets of potato peelings he had thrown overboard in the past, declaring how much he would relish them now. It was a natural craving, because the raw potato would have supplied not just essential vitamins and minerals but also the carbohydrates and fiber that their current nutrition lacked.

Despite Raynal's care to add variety to the menu with "four courses" of seal meat and seafood, their diet was still limited to protein, salt, and fat, the latter mostly in the form of seal oil. All five men were suffering from nausea, dizziness, lassitude, and chronic bowel problems. Carbohydrates, not fat or protein, provide fuel for the brain and central nervous system, and so their reactions had slowed. The heart needs sugars to function properly, so, while they thought they were tired because of the very hard work they had been carrying out, their unbalanced nutrition was a factor too.

Despite the high caloric value of what they were eating, they were losing weight, as some carbohydrate is necessary to turn fat into energy; without at least one ounce of starch or sugar a day, the body breaks down its own muscle. "I am getting as thin as a lantern, and some disordered fluttering and heavy beating of the heart, which causes a faintness, is troubling me," Captain Musgrave complained. He put it down to "melancholy," which was one good reason, but another culprit was their limited bill of fare.

The ever-wise Raynal declared that "the exclusively animal diet" was not just boring, but also "unwholesome for Europeans accustomed from infancy to a mixed diet." In his own childhood, "farinaceous food and vegetables" had been just as important as meat—typical fare in France, where country folk lived on a hearty regime of broth, stews, potatoes, fruit, and bread. Even Henry Forgès, who hailed from the desperately poor Azores, where daily existence was a constant struggle, had been brought up on a healthy mixed diet of cornmeal bread, fruit, cheese, milk, and eggs. Musgrave, though he had been raised in England, a country not known for a healthy diet at the time, had lived in a rural village, with access to grains, fruit, and vegetables. George Harris, the English seaman, had possibly fared much worse, but would have been familiar with bread and boiled puddings, which were the staples of the English poor, along with gallons of tea, an extremely popular beverage with all classes. Even Alick the Norwegian, who would have been more accustomed to a fish-based diet, was used to eating bread and pancakes, with vegetables, fruit, and cake.

The men had nibbled at some of the plants that grew around their campsite, risking poisoning as well as dyspepsia in the urge to find some edible vegetable, but with no success. Then Raynal noticed a plant growing by the marshes — "a plant with circular leaves, folded up like a funnel, and broad as a plate, developing themselves in a tuft or cluster on top of a long and tubular stem." Though he did not know it, this plant had been scientifically identified back in November 1840, by Joseph Hooker, the great British naturalist with the James Clark Ross expedition, who was the first to describe the fascinating landscape in systematic detail. Auckland Island held "much to delight the eye, and an extraordinary amount of new species to occupy the mind," Dr. Hooker had declared, going on to write that it seemed to have a natural barrier of almost impenetrable vegetation — "a low forest skirts all the shores, succeeded by a broad belt of brushwood, above which to the summit of the hills, extend grassy slopes. On a closer inspection of the forest," he went on, "it is found to be composed of a dense thicket of stag-headed trees, so gnarled and stunted by the violence of the gales as to afford an excellent shelter for a luxuriant undergrowth of bright green feathery ferns and several gay flowered herbs."

These herbs included one immense species Dr. Hooker called

Arabia polaris, and which he described as having bright green foliage and large umbels of waxy flowers. Though it had a most disagreeable smell, he noted it was greedily eaten by the pigs, rabbits, and goats that had been left at the islands by previous visitors. Known today as *Stilbocarpa polaris,* it is classified as a megaherb, because it grows to a gigantic size (up to six feet) in all the subantarctic islands to the south of New Zealand. The earliest whalers and sealers knew it as Macquarie Island cabbage, and made it their custom to call at the islands and collect a good store, to be cooked with dried peas, dried beans, or porridge oats, as an antiscorbutic stew.

Raynal was most interested in its thick, white stem — actually a starch-storing rhizome — which grew horizontally along cracks in the rock, and "was held to the soil by numerous tiny roots." It looked edible when sliced, so he manufactured a grater by piercing holes in a piece of sheet iron, shredded up some of it, patted it into cakes, fried it in seal oil, and served it up with "a certain degree of ceremony." The men tasted it, and heartily approved — not because it was delicious, but because it was a relief to find a plant that was even marginally fit for consumption. As Musgrave wrote, "We have found a root, which is very abundant all over the island, and it is very good food; it makes a very good substitute for bread and potatoes. There is also a great deal of sugar in it." Because of its sweetness, the *Grafton* castaways called the plant "sacchary."

The sugary rhizomes of *Stilbocarpa* have saved the lives of many shipwrecked people who gnawed them in desperation, though they need to be cooked to be palatable. A strange side effect was that eating *Stilbocarpa* roots bleached the teeth, so that even men who had been addicted for years to chewing

tobacco ended up with teeth as white as a child's. Most important, however, was that the *Stilbocarpa* "roots" added essential
carbohydrates to the *Grafton* castaways' diet, though it took
some time for their systems to adapt to digesting this strange
stuff.

All of the plant is edible. It seems, though, that Raynal didn't
think of trying ways to cook the flower stalks or leaves, probably because of their unpleasant odor. If he had been inspired
to stew the hairy stalks, he would have found that they have a
flavor similar to celery; the leaves can be boiled and eaten, too,
though the result tastes like wet blotting paper. If Raynal had
boiled or baked the root, he would have found that it tastes
exactly like boiled turnip, but there is no record of his cooking
it in any way other than frying it. However, he did turn the
grated root into beer.

There was logic on his side, because it was traditional for
scurvy-conscious ship captains to brew antiscorbutic beers to
deal out to their crews. Back in 1753, in his famous *A Treatise of
the Scurvy*, the navy surgeon James Lind had drawn attention
to an age-old Scandinavian custom of treating scurvy by dosing
the patients with a beer made with an infusion of young spruce
tips. The great discoverer James Cook had set much store by
this, directing his captains to collect the tips of any trees that
looked like spruce, and then make a beer "by boiling them three
or four hours, or until the bark will strip with ease from the
branches, then take the leaves or branches out." The resulting
decoction was mixed with molasses and wort—the infusion of
malt that creates beer when fermented—and "in a few days the
Beer will be fit to drink." His men didn't like it, but the drinking of spruce-style beers, along with the consumption of a wide

variety of strange and wonderful vegetable matter picked up on desolate coasts, had the desired effect. When the *Endeavour* arrived at Batavia (now Jakarta), Captain Cook was able to exult, "I have not lost one man by sickness the whole voyage."

The castaways did not have either wort or molasses, but the second wasn't necessary, as the *Stilbocarpa* rhizomes have such a high sugar content. As it turned out, the wort wasn't essential, either, Musgrave recording that by grating the root, "then boiling, and afterwards letting it ferment, we were able to make a passable beer," which was more sustaining than water, and a reasonable substitute for tea. Freshly made, it would also have been a source of necessary vitamins. However, it almost led to yet another crisis, because George, Alick, and Harry teased Raynal into trying to distill it into brandy. "They began to laugh and jest at me," he wrote; so, naturally, he couldn't resist the challenge.

After fitting one of the barrels from his gun onto the spout of the teakettle, he wrapped it in a cloth. Then, while the beer simmered in the kettle, he poured cold water onto the cloth, so that the alcohol, which evaporated first, was condensed in the barrel and dripped into a waiting container. It worked—but then Raynal abruptly remembered the temptations of hard liquor. "I foresaw, with alarm, the fatal consequences of the abuse of it, which, sooner or later, would take place," he wrote, and abandoned the project forthwith, lying to the men that the experiment had been a failure.

NINE

Routine

The decision to abandon the attempt to distill alcohol was part and parcel of the monastic regime based on study, hard work, and prayer that was established soon after they moved into their home and Captain Musgrave was elected their leader. The seamen needed something to occupy their minds; and so, as Musgrave described, "I have adopted a measure for keeping them in order and subjection, which I find to work admirably, and it also acts beneficially on my own mind. This is, teaching school in the evenings, and reading prayers and reading and expounding the scriptures on Sunday to the best of my ability."

According to Raynal's version of the story, the school was his idea, not Musgrave's. However, it had probably evolved spontaneously. After they had eaten the first tasty supper Raynal cooked in the new house, Musgrave proposed that they should give their home a name. All the men had ideas for this, and so the five names were written down on folded bits of paper and tossed into a hat. George Harris, being the youngest, had the privilege of drawing the winning ticket, which turned out to be Musgrave's contribution—"Epigwaitt," which, he said, was a

North American Indian word meaning Near the Great Waters. It was adopted with enthusiasm, and the house, as well as the hillock on which it stood, was known by that name from then on.

Because the exercise had used up time so enjoyably, someone commented that they should think up other good ways of passing the long, dreary evenings. This was when the idea of a school was proposed—a school that was remarkably egalitarian, according to Raynal's description, and fully in accordance with the democratic way they had chosen their leader. Though Harry and Alick could neither read nor write, they were keen to learn, and so they volunteered to teach the others Portuguese and Norwegian in return for lessons in reading and writing. Raynal himself offered to tutor French and mathematics. Thus, he recorded, "from that evening we were alternately the masters and pupils of one another. These new relations still further united us; by alternately raising and lowering us one above the other, they really kept us on a level, and created a perfect equality amongst us."

As time passed, they devised games as well as lessons. Musgrave made a solitaire board by perforating a bit of wood and whittling pegs for the holes, while Raynal painted a larger piece of wood with alternating squares of lime and soot to make a chessboard, and carved chessmen out of two thin laths, one white, and the other red. Dominoes were marked and whittled next. Then Raynal made the mistake of cutting fifty-two playing cards out of pages from an old logbook, thickening them with paste made with some of the medicinal flour, and painting in the pips. He thought it would be safe, because the men had nothing to bet with, but Musgrave turned out to be not just a bad card player, but a sore loser as well; so, after exchanging "some unpleasant words" with the captain, the Frenchman threw the cards into the fire.

Raynal reckoned that he destroyed them "tranquilly, without saying a word," but, as Musgrave did not mention the incident, it's hard to tell if it wasn't Raynal himself who had flounced into a rage. Altogether, it was a waste of precious flour. After he had made the cards, Raynal had shared the little bit of paste that was left in the bottom of the pot with Musgrave, and, as he wrote ruefully, "truly, I had never eaten anything in my life which seemed so delicious." For the next few days the memory of the flavor haunted him—"I was punished for my greediness."

Besides parlor games and night school, they had pets to enliven their leisure hours. One day in early March, Harry noticed a pretty bird hopping in and out of a hole in the trunk of a tree. This was one of the small parrots they had already noted and marveled about, the sight of a parrot being so unexpected on a subantarctic island. When this parakeet flew away, Harry cautiously investigated the nest, which proved to hold three fledglings. He set to work at once, according to Raynal, "to construct a little cage for their reception, weaving a number of twigs together in the most skilful fashion." Having captured the little birds, he carried them back to the house, to the amazement of the others, Musgrave confessing that he found it "very strange to find parrots here at all, and it is more surprising that they should have young ones at this season of the year." March in the subantarctic south marks the start of autumn, a dangerous time for eggs to hatch.

"We fed them on the seeds of the sacchary plant, which at first we pounded carefully, and afterwards mixed with a little seal's flesh roasted, and minced into very small pieces," Raynal wrote. One soon died, but the other two thrived, the male of the pair amusing them greatly by learning to talk. As the two *kakariki* grew larger, they destroyed the bars of their cage, but by that time they were tame enough to be allowed to live freely in the hut.

They were also thoroughly spoiled. A fresh branch of sacchary, complete with seeds, was provided for them every day; they slept at the foot of Harry's bed, right up against the warm chimney; and they made a fuss if their dish of water, placed at the foot of the roosting branch, was not perfectly clean. "On emerging from their bath, they dried themselves before the fire, and turned themselves first on one side, then on the other, with the gravest air in the world," wrote Raynal. Having washed themselves, they were allowed to join the men at the table, "and, in excellent English, Boss—for so we named the male bird— demanded his share."

The story had a sad ending, alas. Harry, in a hurry to put down a heavy pot of water, unwittingly set it on top of Boss, crushing him to death, and "his poor little mate died of grief."

ACCORDING TO HIS OWN ACCOUNT, Raynal was the person who established the strict household routine. During that first week of duty as cook, he had risen at six in the morning, and had made sure that his companions did too, a healthy custom he insisted they continue. If his cabinmates complained, he simply pointed out that they needed enough firewood to get them through the next twenty-four hours, and sent them out to chop down trees. "And soon they fell into the good habit of early rising," he complacently wrote.

The fire was kept blazing day and night, and so a lot of wood was needed, the best being "ironwood," which came from the twisted branches and contorted trunks of the forest rata. While it had the distinct virtue of burning well, producing a lot of heat and very little smoke, it was very hard to cut—so hard that their one hatchet was notched and blunted, providing Raynal with yet another challenge. After vainly hunting the beaches for a stone to serve as a whetstone, he remembered the blocks of sandstone that had been loaded in the *Grafton* as extra ballast. At the next low tide he clambered on board the wreck, lowered himself into the hold on a rope, and felt around with his feet until he managed to lift a block, tie it to the rope, and haul it up to the deck.

He also found an iron pin that had rusted free from a spar. After heating this until it was cherry red, he hammered one end flat to make a cold chisel—"then, with this new tool and my hammer, I fashioned my block of sandstone into a knife grinder's grindstone." The hardest part was drilling a hole through the center, but once he had done it, he was able to fit it with a wooden axle, to which he attached a handle. Fixed between a couple of trees growing close together near the house, the grindstone became a very useful and much-appreciated gadget for sharpening not just the hatchet but other tools as well.

Meanwhile, yet another instance of Raynal's resourcefulness had made their lives more civilized. Within weeks of being stranded, they had all become uncomfortably aware of their smelly and unkempt condition. It was bad enough that they were wildly bearded and longhaired, but every time they pushed through the forest their clothes caught and ripped, and so they were all wearing a collection of rags. Still worse, those rags stank of rancid oil and decomposed blood, an unpleasant reminder of the many long marches their wearers had made with dripping quarters of sea lion carried on their shoulders.

Making trousers and blouses out of sailcloth to wear as protective clothing during hunting forays was one solution to the problem, but it didn't fix the clothes that had been fouled already. Soaking them in the brook didn't have much effect, so, while the men sat around slapping at insects and frowning over their sailmaker's needles and the sewing thread they had made from unraveled sailcloth, Raynal put his mind to the manufacture of soap. When he described his ambition, it was received with some hilarity, his shipmates asking if he knew the right magic words to conjure soap out of thin air. However, that only added to the challenge.

Not long after, he had the opportunity to experiment in semiprivacy. On a day that dawned fine and clear, Musgrave, George Harris, and Henry Forgès decided to climb to the top of the mountain so that they could take a look at the hinterland and the sea, just on the off chance that they might spy a sail. Alick Maclaren wasn't well—being the strongest of the party, he had done more than his fair share of the heavy work. As Raynal meditated, "Our brave Norwegian, who is full of zeal and activity, has undoubtedly abused his strength of late in carrying bundles of straw, stones, or pieces of wood to the hillock, and the illness from which he suffers is probably the result of his excessive exertions. May it be nothing worse!"

It *was* nothing worse, but very wisely Alick decided to stay behind and rest, so was entertained by watching Raynal collect a good heap of firewood, a bundle of dried seaweed, and a few crushed seashells, and then set fire to the lot. By the time their companions had returned, fatigued and downcast, and with nothing in the way of ship sightings to report, it was well ablaze, and burned nicely throughout the night. "Next morning," Raynal wrote, "I found a mass of ashes."

The previous afternoon he had used the gimlet to drill holes in the bottom of a cask, and had stood it up on blocks of wood. Now he shoveled the ash into the barrel, and slowly poured water over it. A pot was placed under the holes to collect the filtrate — "a liquid charged with soda, potash, and a certain quantity of lime in solution." This was his lye. When he had enough of it, he added seal oil, and boiled the mixture. It smelled unbelievably foul, but at the end of the process, to the amazement of all, he had soap, real soap! — "which was of inestimable value to us," for both cleanliness and health.

Monday became washing day, when all the garments that had been cast aside after hunting trips were scrubbed, though it was impossible to remove the stains of seal blood, even after the clothes had been soaked in lye. The dining table and the cooking table were both well scoured, and the floor was kept conscientiously clean, all with Raynal's miraculous soap. Saturday evening was the time for them to take a bath in front of the fire, in a cask cut down for the purpose, and filled with warm water by the cook.

A great deal of indoor time was occupied in sewing and mending, because their clothes were in what Raynal called "a very singular" state, patched so heavily that the original cloth was barely visible. As rags were used up and old sailcloth ran out, they became desperate for another source of fabric. The pelts of the many sea lions they killed were the obvious substitute, but the blowflies always destroyed them before they were dry. The men didn't want to use salt, preferring to reserve it for salting down meat; but at last, after much trial and error, they found a method that worked. The skins were stretched on a board with the fur side downward, and the flesh side was scraped until every shred of fat was gone. After that, the men took lye and scrubbed the skins every few hours, making their hands very sore in the process, but successfully keeping fly-strike at bay. When the skins were absolutely dry, they scoured them with sandstone from one of the ballast blocks, rolled each one up very tightly with the fur side inward, and hammered it until the cylinder was supple. "By this method injury to the fur was avoided and the skin remained quite soft," wrote Musgrave. Not only did they use the pelts to make garments, each man cutting and stitching a complete suit for himself, but they were quilted into warm bed coverings too.

This did not take care of footwear, which was a matter of some urgency, as they had all worn out their boots, and the seal-skin moccasins they made to replace them were not much good at all. As Raynal wrote, "The skin, not being prepared, and always in contact with a marshy soil, grew flabby, absorbed water, rotted away, and was quickly rent to pieces by the jagged rocks of the shore." However, the problem was not easily solved. As Musgrave had already recorded, they "had no bark that would tan," the bark of the rata being very thin and hard.

Raynal made do with this bark, however, cutting lots of it up very small, boiling it in a great quantity of fresh water, and then, when it was as dark as well-brewed tea, pouring it into a cask. This was set outside to slowly evaporate to an even stronger consistency. "In another cask I made a solution of lime with mussel-shells that I had previously burned to powder; and I put into the bath a number of skins, some as thick and others as thin as I could find." By soaking them in this strong alkaline solution, he hoped to get rid of the oil in the skins.

When he fished the hides out a couple of weeks later, the oil had changed into a kind of soapy foam. Taking a few of the planks that were still on hand, Raynal stretched the skins, securing them with wooden pegs, and scraped off the hard fat—a process that sealers called "beaming." The fur was shaved off, and then the skins were steeped in the running brook for some hours, "after which we subjected them to heavy pressure between planks loaded with great stones, so as to expel all the lime which might still remain in them." This procedure had to be repeated several times, but finally the hides were ready to be soaked in the tanning solution. This soaking process would take months, so all Raynal and his assistants could do now was wait for nature to take its course, but at least it was under way.

It was hard work like this that saved them from brooding over their miserable fate, and giving way to depression. As Raynal philosophized, the constant projects in hand "left us little leisure to think of our misfortunes."

TEN

Dire Necessity

With the month of March, storms arrived—"a succession of westerly gales," as Musgrave wrote, "which only ceased from time to time to blow again with redoubled fury"—bringing rain and sleet and sometimes snow. "We began to fear the oncoming of winter," he went on.

Awful premonitions of starvation were creeping in on them all, because the behavior of their prey was changing disturbingly. Now the sea lions were much harder to find, let alone catch and kill. Raynal put it down to the fact that seals are migratory animals—an ominous thought in itself—but Musgrave, who thought that it might be because the sea lions were learning that men were to be feared and avoided, urged that the cows and calves in the scrub around Epigwaitt should be left alone as much as possible.

Whenever the weather was favorable the men took out the boat to hunt for their prey about the shores and islets of Carnley Harbour. On March 3, George, Alick, and Musgrave discovered a small island, which Musgrave called Figure-of-Eight Island because of its shape; this became a favored hunting ground. At the time they first landed it poured with rain, but, as Musgrave commented, they had been out of fresh provisions for the past three days, and so they doggedly persevered.

To their great relief, they came across three mobs of sea lion females. There were thirty to forty cows in each flock, all fast asleep despite the conditions, "and there were a great many very young calves amongst them." When the three men rushed in with their clubs, shouting and yelling, the females woke up abruptly, stared about in confusion, and then fled to the water, leaving their cubs behind, "and I suppose in ten seconds we had knocked down ten calves from two to three months old, and one two-year-old seal."

This was the usual procedure, because once separated from their mothers, the pups were easy prey. "During the months of February, March, and April, the cows are on shore the greater part of the time, and lie in the bush in mobs of from twelve to twenty together, at the places where their calves are assembled," remembered Musgrave afterward. "They do not appear to have any particular time for going into the water to feed; and they allow their young to suck whenever they please." Once fed, the pups would leave their mothers to play with each other: "The mothers appear to take scarcely any notice whatever of their young," he wrote. And, just as on this day on Figure-of-Eight Island, they would readily abandon their pups to seek safety in the water.

For quite a while the men had been shocked by this apparent lack of maternal feeling. Then they had a distressing experience with a cow whose cub had been killed near the house. She kept on returning and looking for her lost calf, "incessantly bellowing, and without going into the water—consequently going without food—for eight days," Musgrave described. "After the first few days her voice gradually became weaker, and at last could scarcely be heard." He was certain she was dying, but instead she returned to the sea to feed; "but for more than a month afterwards she paid a daily visit to the spot, bellowing in the most doleful manner."

Also, however, there was the common sight of the cows biting their young so badly that the "poor little animals are very often seen with their skins pierced and lacerated in the most frightful manner," as Musgrave commented another time. This usually happened during swimming lessons. The seal pups were not born with the instinct to swim, and indeed were so frightened of the water that they had to be prodded and persuaded before they would leave the safety of the beach and flop into the surf. Then the mothers had to teach them how to get along in what was supposed to be their natural element.

Musgrave found this amusing—"the mother gets it on to her back, and swims along very gently on the top of the water; but the poor little thing is bleating all the time, and continually falling from its slippery position, when it will splutter about in the water precisely like a little boy who gets beyond his depth and cannot swim." The cow would repeat the performance patiently for a while, but after that she would become irritated, and use force where coercion hadn't worked. To the men it looked callous, but it was for the pup's own good.

Feeling sorry for the cubs did not make killing them any easier. After the cows had retreated to the safety of the water, their young would run into the bush, but then they betrayed their hiding places by bleating pathetically for their mothers. Raynal once found a pup huddled with two others who "peeped over his shoulder" from under a fallen tree, and wrote that their huge, terrified eyes "seemed to implore our pity and ask for mercy. We were much moved, and hesitated long; greatly tempted to spare them, yet forced by necessity to obey reason rather than sentiment." As he went on to say, the poor innocents, slaughtered, "freed us for several days from all anxiety about our daily food."

It was this same harsh philosophy that drove Musgrave, George, and Alick to rush into the mobs and pick out pups to kill on this rainy day in March. "We could have got more," Musgrave continued, but at that juncture George was attacked by a gigantic bull. Taking one horrified look at the great beachmaster charging full speed toward him, the Englishman abandoned dignity, dropped his club, and scooted up a tree. Musgrave and Alick came to the rescue, and though they would have preferred to let the enraged sea lion go, they were forced to kill him—"we would have been quite willing to get out of his way, but he would not give us a chance," wrote Musgrave, adding, "This was the greatest piece of excitement I have had for a long time."

It was a profitable trip altogether, because they also bagged a lot of widgeons. The abundance continued. Just three days later, Musgrave went outside to find a seal pup, "not more than a month or six weeks old, sitting shivering at the end of the house. I took him in," he related, "and some of them wanted to keep him; but this of course we could not do, as he would eat nothing but fish, and not even that yet, so we killed him. I think he had lost his mother, for he was very low in flesh and had nothing at all in his inside. So this is more fresh meat," he added on a practical note. "God is certainly good in sending us plenty to eat."

However, he was acutely conscious that the reprieve was only temporary. With the equinoctial gales the surf and tides were often too high to venture out in the boat, and he was terribly afraid that the wreck of the schooner was breaking up. Then March 12 dawned—an anniversary, which was always an occasion for gloom.

That evening Musgrave seated himself at his desk with his heart beating fast, as he described it, "somewhat similar to what it might do if I was about writing a love letter." It was exactly four months since the *Grafton* had sailed from Sydney, and "I know that many a bitter tear has been shed for me by this time." Would he and his adored one ever meet again? "Heaven only knows." These were thoughts that maddened him—"I feel as if I was gradually consumed by an inward fire. I strive, by occupying my hands as much as possible, to dispel these sad feelings; but it is utterly impossible."

Then he betrayed the first hint that he had suffered from some kind of nervous indisposition in the past—"I have felt this before, but only on one particular occasion, and that is some time ago," he wrote, going on to agonize, "Were it not for the hope that I shall yet again be of service to my family, I think my spirit, if not my health, would break down; although under my present afflictions my continual prayer is that God may soon deliver me out of them." The thought that constantly nagged at him was that while he had the comfort of knowing that there was plenty of meat to be had on Figure-of-Eight Island for yet awhile, God alone knew if his family in Sydney had enough to eat.

Musgrave made another trip to the island on Friday, March 18, leaving George, whose turn it was to be cook and housekeeper, back at Epigwaitt, and taking Raynal, Alick, and Harry with him. Raynal, who had not been there before, explored the islet with interest. Penetrating the bush, he discovered "the traces of a small and ancient encampment," evidently left by whalers who had stopped there for at least a couple of weeks, because there was a deep cavity in the peat where their fire had burned. Not only did this give hope that a whaling vessel might return one day, but Raynal, to his delight, glimpsed a small rusted file that had been discarded by that past party.

Pocketing this treasure, he returned to the others, who were attending to the main business of foraging for sea lions. Following the sounds of cows calling out to their cubs, they came out on a beach at one end of the islet, to find a large mob of females suckling their young, while standing in the middle, "an old male, probably the ruler of those parts, took his ease, eying calmly the youthful gaiety which went on around him," as Raynal fancifully described. "He had the appearance of a venerable patriarch pleased with the games of his little children."

This beachmaster was ancient indeed: "When he opened his enormous mouth to yawn, we could see that his jaws were almost toothless, a few black stumps projecting here and there from his gums." Seconds later, however, the men found to their alarm that though this venerable fellow might be old, he still had a firm grasp of his responsibilities as lord and master of the harem. Scenting the interlopers, he rose up on his flippers, and "vented from the depth of his vast chest a resonant and prolonged growl, which attracted the attention of the females, and spread alarm among all the troop."

As usual, while the females scattered toward the sea, the men plunged in and out of the panicked mob, killing seven cubs in the rush. Then, as Raynal described, "Musgrave, Alick, and I, handing our cudgels to Harry, seized each of us a couple of the victims," while Harry grabbed the last with his free hand. Dragging their kill, the men dashed headlong for the boat, piled the carcasses inside, and pushed off from the shore.

To their horror, something happened that had never happened before. The cows furiously pursued the small boat, "accompanied by their patriarch." Their speed in the water was terrifying. Some came close enough to grip the blades of the oars with their tusks, and the oars had to be frantically jerked free. One female repeatedly attempted to leap into the dinghy, hurling herself out of the sea and deluging them all with spray until Raynal, in panicky desperation, fired two volleys into her. She sank like a stone—as always happened when seals were killed in the water—and the rest gave up the chase, but it was a nightmare experience. Shaken, they rowed back to Epigwaitt, and such was their awe that they nicknamed the old beachmaster Royal Tom.

THE EXPEDITION OTHERWISE had been a success. They now had plenty of meat—much more, in fact, than they could eat before it went off. "We thought, therefore, of curing at least half of it," wrote Raynal. To do this, they used up some of their store of salt. "Of our seven seals, four were cut up, and the pieces laid between layers of salt in an empty cask. Some days afterwards, when they were thoroughly saturated, we suspended them to the rafters of the roof in the interior of our hut." It was a reassuring sight. As Musgrave commented, their fears "were comforted by looking upon our stock of meat hanging up in the house." Unfortunately, they hadn't found a way of storing *Stilbocarpa* rhizomes, but had to venture out to pull them up as needed.

The evidence of past visitors that Raynal had found on Figure-of-Eight Island was heartening too. "There is no doubt but that they were killing seals, as we found a number of bricks, which no doubt had been used for their tryworks," Musgrave wrote. "There had been two tents pitched, and, from the appearance of the ground where they had their fire, I should judge that they had remained about a week." Though it was impossible to tell how much time had elapsed since they had left, "I am delighted to see even this sign of ships coming here."

Musgrave felt so buoyant that he decided it was high time they checked their signal on Musgrave Peninsula, so on the next clear morning they launched the boat and sailed off in that direction. They fished as they went, but every time they dropped a line the sea lions came around to snatch anything they caught before they could draw it into the boat: Sea lions, as the castaways were finding out, are very fast learners.

They pulled through surf and around rocks that seethed with kelp to the end of the peninsula, to learn something even more depressing—that the flagpole they had raised with such labor was leaning at a desperate angle. Worse still, the canvas flag had disappeared, evidently whipped away by a hostile gale, and the bottle with its carefully composed message was rolling around on the ground. No sooner had they absorbed the grim fact that their signal would have conveyed absolutely nothing about their plight or their location to would-be rescuers, than another north-northwest storm blew up. Hunched against the rain and blown spray, they rowed as hard and fast as possible—"and it was as much as we could do with three oars and me sculling to get across the bay," wrote Musgrave. Several times they lost ground, but after a long struggle they got close to the head of the harbor. There, with numb, battered hands, they piled in some rocks for ballast, set their sail, and scudded back to the house, where they arrived at five, just as dusk was falling, "drenched with rain and spray, and fainting with hunger; for we had had nothing to eat since breakfast."

It was another two weeks before they could return to the flagstaff, haul it back upright, and put up a huge signboard, four feet long and two feet, six inches wide, with the letter *N* painted on it as a sign to passing ships that there were castaways to the north. "I also secured a bottle to the board, to notify to anyone where we are, and giving them some instructions for working up the harbour," Musgrave wrote. "But should they not be able to send a boat on shore to get the bottle, the letter 'N' will indicate which way they are to turn; and when are round the point we shall see them, and I shall get on board as soon as possible."

A few days afterward, however, with the renewed realization that even the hardiest whalers were not likely to arrive before October, the dawn of the subantarctic spring, depression returned. "The days are getting short," Musgrave wrote on April 10; "and a long, stormy, dreary winter is before us, without the slightest prospect of getting away; and how those dear ones whom I left manage to battle with the misery in which my ambition and folly has plunged them, I dare not think. Oh!" he exclaimed in an agitated splash of seal-blood ink; "if they were only here with me, how happy would be my condition compared with what it is; for I am provided with a good shelter, and plenty to eat, and I should then think that they shared these blessings at least; but as it is, I know not to what extremities they may be reduced."

Epigwaitt was indeed a cozy shelter, as at long last the cabin was completely thatched. It had been a tediously long drawn out job as well as a tough one, because it depended so much on the weather—thatching could not be done in the pouring rain, or when the wind blew hard. It had not been until Sunday, March 27, eight weeks after commencing the job, that Musgrave was able to gladly report in his journal that they had at last filled in the sides of the house. "It has taken 5000 bundles of thatch, each bundle weighing a pound," he wrote, "so that the total weight of thatch on the sides and ends of the house is about two and a quarter tons." They hadn't thatched the roof, being satisfied with a double layer of canvas instead, but this did not detract from the final result, which he described as "very warm and comfortable."

The timing was excellent, because from that day on the weather became very foul. Storm followed storm, accompanied by thunder, lightning, and sudden deafening avalanches as whole cliffs came down, the wild surf having loosened the rocky underpinnings. There were landslides inland, too, with complete slopes brought down by the torrential rain and the weight of snow, which made them fear for their house and thank God that they had built it on the top of a hill. While the forest around Epigwaitt was being rapidly cleared for firewood, they made sure to keep a screen of trees between the house and the shore, to shelter their trembling, rustling thatch from the worst of the prevailing gales. "The hurricane shook, and bent, and twisted the trees, tearing off their foliage, in spite of its tenacity, and carrying clouds of rent and faded leaves to the waters of the bay, which were covered with them," wrote Raynal. At times the spray was blown so high and hard they could hear it hissing on their canvas roof.

Added to the roar of the tempest, the crash of thunder, and the cracking and splintering of branches, there were unearthly howls in the distance, sounds uncannily like the barking of dogs. For a while, the men wondered if it was some strange effect of the wind, but because of the weather it was impossible to investigate. By April 12, however, their stock of fresh meat was so low that they were forced to go out, despite the awful conditions.

Alick and Harry left the house first, but just as Raynal and Musgrave were getting ready to follow, Harry came rushing back. "Dogs," he gasped. "Two dogs on the shore!"

"What?" they cried.

For a moment the Portuguese cook was too breathless for further speech, but then he described what he had seen. "One was a fine shepherd's dog," wrote Raynal, "white and black, with a long plume-like tail; the other, of smaller size, seemed a cross between a bull-dog and a mastiff."

Alick had been left behind to keep an eye on them, and try to entice them closer, if he could. Grabbing a rope and a piece of salt meat for bait, Raynal and Musgrave hurried after Harry, but by the time they arrived on the beach, the dogs were gone. Alick said that he had tried to creep closer to them, but the instant he'd moved they had run off into the trees.

They were all terribly disappointed and downcast. As well as being good companions, the dogs, once trained, would have made the hunt much easier. "I saw their tracks," Musgrave wrote, "and was satisfied that they had seen dogs; and, from the men's description of them I think they were sheep dogs."

Nearby, the men found the corpse of a seal calf which the dogs had evidently killed. After that, they still heard them baying far off in the trees, but the dogs were never seen again. And, though they often saw the tracks of pigs, they never saw pigs, either. It was as if both pigs and dogs were deliberately avoiding Epigwaitt and its inhabitants—as if, like the sea lions of Figure-of-Eight Island, they recognized the castaways as their enemy.

ELEVEN

The Jaws of Hell

Sunday, May 1, 1864," wrote Captain Musgrave. "We now enter upon another month of imprisonment, which is commencing with bad weather." Over the past three days there had been a tremendous gale with terrific squalls, hail, and rain, but before that it had been clear enough for a party of the men to revisit Figure-of-Eight Island, which now seemed to be the only place where the seals congregated.

This meant dealing with Royal Tom, but in the meantime he had become accustomed to the men, to the extent that there was a kind of unwritten truce between them. If they left him and his harem alone, pursuing other sea lion groups instead, he did not attack, merely staring at the intruders disdainfully while his wives and calves made themselves scarce by retreating to the water or the bush. Alick, Harry, and George had become relaxed and familiar with him too — overly so, in Captain Musgrave's estimation, because he had heard, though indirectly, that the men had been teasing the old fellow.

Having noticed that he did not like to go into the water when his coat was dry, they had plagued him into galumphing haughtily down to the edge of the surf. There he remained, however, scratching himself in a leisurely fashion. They kept on trying to torment him into flopping into the water, but he won the psychological battle, rather to Musgrave's satisfaction. He did not want the seal life on Figure-of-Eight Island to be disturbed, except when absolutely necessary, "but as I was not there myself I suppose the boys wanted to have a little fun to themselves, which would have cost them a reprimand had I heard of it in a direct manner."

The "boys" probably deserved all the fun they could find, considering that the prospects were so grim, but Musgrave was gloomy again himself. Not only was the thought of winter a depressing one, but the six-month mark of their departure from Sydney was looming, along with the anniversary of his birth.

"Tuesday, May 10, 1864," he penned at the start of his next journal entry. "For some days back I have not been very well. Today I have had a very severe headache, but as it has now left me, and as I did not write on Sunday as usual, I shall do a little of it this evening; and, moreover, as this is the anniversary (32nd) of my birth, I have made it a point for some years to pledge my mother on this day in a bottle of good old port." This year, he had to content himself with toasting her in a tumbler of sacchary beer. "It is not very good, but still it is preferable to cold water."

Outside, as he noted next, it was blowing a heavy northwest gale with rain, which helped him to be properly thankful for his blessings. Inside the warm and comfortable cabin he and his men had built, he was sitting by a roaring fire, digesting a meal of fresh roast seal . . . utterly unaware that twenty miles to the northwest of cozy Epigwaitt, the great Scottish square-rigger *Invercauld* was ripping out her keel on an Auckland Island reef, and spilling her crew into the depths of the freezing black night.

THE 888-TON *INVERCAULD* had left Melbourne for South America on May 3, 1864, on the second leg of her maiden voyage, with a crew of twenty-five but no passengers. As she was in ballast, being on the way to Callao to take on a freight of fertilizer, she was very light and slow to respond to the helm. She had iron masts and wire rigging instead of wood and rope—common enough at the time, but a circumstance that was to prove dire.

When she sailed from Melbourne the weather was fine, but the first night out the wind began to gust, with heavy showers of sleet and snow. However, regular routine was followed, one of the earliest jobs being to "cathead" the anchor—secure it on the bows—and stow away the cable. The sailor who recorded this was twenty-three-year-old Robert Holding, who, like François Raynal, had spent years on the Australian goldfields, where he had prospected in the winters and run a steam threshing machine in the summers. Holding was a natural wanderer, but currently his ambition was to get back to his homeland, England.

Most of the crew had come on the ship from Aberdeen, Scotland, and were strangers to him. He knew the names of the captain, George Dalgarno, the first mate, Andrew Smith, and the second mate, an American seaman, James Mahoney, who had been promoted to the post the day after leaving Australia, but very little else about them. On May 10, according to his account, he began to learn a great deal more.

The ship was running southeast before the northwest gale, in thick, rainy, snowy weather. At four in the afternoon, estimating by dead reckoning they were close to the Auckland Islands, Captain Dalgarno ordered a double lookout to be kept, so extra men were sent to stare with slitted eyes into the sleet and fog, straining for the first glimpse of danger. At 7:40 P.M., when the lookout forward shouted out a warning of land ahead, Dalgarno instructed the first mate, Andrew Smith, to bring the ship about on the starboard tack, assuming that the sighting was of the southwestern end of Adams Island. Disastrously, however, he was twenty miles out in his estimate, and the land the lookout had sighted was the northwestern promontory of Auckland Island, Northwest Cape. Without realizing it, Dalgarno had navigated the ship onto one of the most dangerous coasts in the world, one that thirty years later a visitor likened to "the Jaws of Hell."

The ship wore her stern round in the stormy darkness, as men hauled at braces and the helmsman heaved down the wheel to bring her to a southern heading. Dalgarno and Smith fully expected that this would take her clear of Adams Island, but, moments later, the lookouts bawled, "Land O!"—as the first mate wrote, "to our wonder and astonishment, land was again reported right ahead." Tall cliffs bulged out of the sea. As Smith stared in horror and confusion, he heard the captain shout urgent orders to brace up and bring the ship about on an eastern heading.

Round they brought the ship's stern again, while the storm gusted and the torrential rain poured, fretted with sleet and snow. Then they were steering north of east. At the same time they crowded on all the sail they could, "thinking to get a passage between the small island that we sighted first and the larger one. There appeared, however," Smith continued, "so many rocks, reefs and breakers ahead, that we saw it would be very dangerous, but still carried on sail, in hopes of getting through this passage, as we knew there was no other chance of getting clear, owing to the direction from which the wind was blowing. It was then very dark, with heavy rain, a hurricane blowing, and a tremendous sea running and anyone who knows about beating a light ship off a lee shore can easily understand what our thoughts were when we expected every minute to strike."

By this time, too, the seamen were exhausted. They had all been pulling and hauling at iron-hard ropes for at least two hours. There was another warning shriek from the lookouts as breakers were glimpsed, and Captain Dalgarno shouted an order to luff—come up into the wind. Instead, the ship fell off, and lost her headway. Her doom was sealed. Gripped by the twin forces of the northwest storm and her leeway, the *Invercauld* sagged sideways onto one of the steepest, most forbidding coasts in the subantarctic.

Holding turned from his work to stare with growing terror. They were just three hundred yards to the shore, a distance that was decreasing with every surge of the waves. Suddenly reefs, seething with phosphorescence, popped out of the sea, while black, streaming cliffs abruptly materialized from the rain and snow. Then they were in the surf. Panic and confusion reigned. The captain shouted out for the sounding line to be cast, yet the *Invercauld* was so close to the cliffs that the royals—the uppermost masts—were snapping off as they touched overhanging stone. When Robert Holding looked around in desperation, it was to see that the mate had broken down in tears, while the second mate was meaninglessly screaming, "*Luff, luff, luff!*" at the man at the helm. Then he heard the captain bawl out orders to drop the anchor—an anchor that, days earlier, had been secured to the outside of the bows.

Surf boomed, while the storm shrieked in crescendo. The boats were still lashed to struts above the deck, and Dalgarno yelled at Holding to cut them free. However, what the captain later called "the fatal moment" had arrived. With a series of dull crashes the *Invercauld* struck, and there were no more orders to be heard.

The jibboom was whirled away. The ship lifted on the crest of a wave, and slammed down. With a sickening crunch the keel caved in, and the ballast plunged through the bottom. What was left of the ship bounced and lurched sideways, and, as Dalgarno put it, "a frightful shock sent both [*sic*] our masts by the board." Disastrously, the three iron masts and wire rigging followed the ballast to the depths, carrying with them every inch of the canvas and rope that could otherwise have been used for shelter on the beach.

The remainder of the *Invercauld* was breaking up fast. When Holding, clinging to the poop with five others, looked over the stern, the wild water between the rocks and the beach was strewn with floating wreckage and struggling men. Another heavy sea struck the ship. He looked back, and to his horror there were only two of his companions left. Then a third great wave overwhelmed what was left of the poop, and abruptly Holding was alone.

The following sea washed him completely off the wreck, carrying him with it as it surged up onto the beach. He staggered out of the water, calling out in desperation, terrified that he was the only one who had survived. Other voices answered from the icy blackness, and the small group huddled together through the rest of the dreadful night.

WITH THE FIRST GLIMMER of light they gathered up the longest planks they could find, and set them tepee-fashion about a hollow in the rocks. Other voices called out from the murk, and more survivors joined them. They all crammed themselves into the lean-to, seeking a little warmth. When day dawned, a roll call established that nineteen men had survived—ten seamen, plus the captain, the two officers, the cook, the steward, the boatswain, the carpenter, and the two ship's boys.

They were soaked through and bruised and chafed. Most, including the captain and first mate, had kicked off their seaboots so that they wouldn't be dragged down in the seas that swept them off the wreck, and their numb, bare feet were battered and bleeding. While Dalgarno and Smith had kept their heavy overcoats, the others had not. The cook was a peculiar sight, because he had gone to his cabin just before the ship struck, and put on his best suit over the clothes he was wearing. Now, as Holding observed, he was so overburdened with tight, sodden garments he could scarcely move an inch.

Their surroundings could not have been more dismal; all of them wondered if the men who had died were the fortunate ones. The narrow, horseshoe-shaped beach where they were huddled was at the foot of an almost perpendicular precipice that reared more than three hundred feet overhead. Water plunged straight down the sheer granite walls, to be blown into spume before it even reached the tumbled rocks and the sea. Though the men were not doomed to endure the agony of thirst that was so often the fate of shipwrecked sailors, the water that they scooped out of rockpools was brackish and slimy.

The only part of the ship still visible was a part of the stern. Shattered wood was strewn all about the surface of the water and the rocks. Apart from the leathery, snakelike kelp, and the birds that circled screaming far overhead, there seemed to be no other life—no shellfish, no fish, and certainly no seals. Searching the sea wrack for food that might have been washed ashore yielded just two pounds of sodden biscuit, and about the same amount of salt pork.

Luckily, they had matches—two boxes, one belonging to the cook, the other to the steward—and so a fire was speedily lit. According to Holding, however, when the cook tried to dry the rest of his matches, he carelessly burned the lot. The mate, Andrew Smith, then tried to do the same with the other box, and would have lost them, too, if Holding hadn't grabbed them away and saved them. After that, the seaman refused to give them back. It was beginning to become clear to him that if he was ever to survive this ordeal, it would be by his own resourcefulness.

Instead of demonstrating leadership, Captain Dalgarno seemed too paralyzed to order a search for shelter and food. The party stayed on the beach a total of five days and nights, of which the nights were perhaps the worst. The lean-to measured only five by eight feet, and so nineteen men had to pack themselves on top of each other for them all to fit in, which led to fights and agonizing cramp. In the process—though it was not noticed for a while—they also caught vermin such as body lice and head lice from each other. Eerily, they could hear a dog howling in the far distance, and conjectured that the captain's Irish setter had escaped.

Daytimes were a protracted ordeal of looking for food. The few small shellfish they found were quickly gobbled down before others could grab them away. Some tried to eat the thick rubbery kelp. Others pulled up some of the *Stilbocarpa* plants that grew in cracks in the cliff, and when they found that the sugary rhizomes were edible, they gnawed at them gratefully. The *Invercauld* disappeared completely, leaving the grisly corpse of one of their past shipmates suspended from an inaccessible bit of wreckage. They had already found the bodies of the other five men who had drowned, and stripped them of their clothing. It was a huge relief when this sixth corpse finally fell off the spar, and they did not have to look at it anymore. When the decomposing body washed up on the beach, however, they removed that dead man's clothes too. Then, after giving out the garments to those who needed them most, they left the stripped corpse for the tides to carry off to scavengers. Like the other five bodies, it soon disappeared.

It became a priority to get to the top of the cliff. A narrow fissure ran up it at an angle, and four men, including one named Tait, made up their minds to climb it, if they could. The others watched them until they were out of sight, and when they didn't come back concluded that they had succeeded. Three returned next day, saying that they had gotten to the top, and had seen tussock and the tracks of sheep. Tait, they added, had fallen onto the rocks.

"Well," declared Holding, the experienced prospector, "if there are sheep on this island I will have some damper and mutton tonight." Forthwith, he set off up the cliff, finding that the *Stilbocarpa* plants clung strongly enough to cracks in the rock to serve as handholds. As he climbed, he listened for noises of others following, but when he finally squirmed over the top and stood up to survey the terrain, he was alone. The freezing rain poured down on him, soaking his clothes, and he had to slit his eyes to assess his surroundings.

He looked downward first. Below, the water was relatively calm. Though he could easily distinguish the rocks where the *Invercauld* had struck, it was impossible to see the beach or the camp, because they were tucked under the cliff he had climbed. Then he looked about the top of the tussock-clad plateau where he stood. To the south, tall, inaccessible mountains lost their summits in the clouds; far beyond them, though Holding did not know it, lay the snug shelter of Epigwaitt on the other end of the island. When he turned and looked northward, the land looked more promising, because, though forbiddingly clothed in scrub and thick, tall tussock, the hills were not high. From his vantage point he could see as far as the northeastern coast, and glimpse two large bays set below hills that sloped much more gently than the cliff he had just climbed, and which looked as if they afforded shelter and food.

The wiry turf beneath the new boots he had bought in Melbourne was boggy and getting more so with the rain, and he could see the animal tracks the other men had described clearly enough to decide that they had been made by pigs, not sheep. It was too late to go back, so Holding went over to some rocks, and curled up in a crevice to shiver through a night that seemed endless. At that time of year it was fifteen hours long, while all the time the freezing rain lashed down.

At long last dawn broke. Holding clambered back down the cliff to the wreck site, to find that three of the men were missing, having gone off on an exploring expedition of their own. Tait, the man who had fallen, had rejoined the party in the meantime, but was quite delirious. Holding told the others what he had seen, describing the eastern side of the island and its promising bays, and eventually the rest agreed that it was a good idea to try to get there. Tait was incapable of climbing, so they left him behind, with a volunteer to watch over him until he passed away.

It took a long time for Holding to hassle and help them all up the cliff, but in the end they arrived at the top, to find the three men who had left the party dashing toward them with the glad news that they had caught a little pig by chasing it down and then falling onto it. Though they'd eaten the raw liver already, they were carrying the rest of the carcass. The party hastily made a windbreak, and lit a fire. "We gave it very little cooking for fear of losing too much of it," wrote Andrew Smith. Some of the men threw themselves flat on the ground like animals, to lap up the drips of blood.

Drawn by the fire and the smell of cooking, the sailor who had volunteered to stay with Tait rejoined them. He told Andrew Smith that Tait was dead, but confided to Holding that it wasn't so. After they had left he had gotten frightened, he said, and then, having decided that his best chance of survival was to stick with the group, he had followed them up the cliff.

Holding didn't blame him, agreeing that keeping together was indeed the best plan. However, the very next morning the cook and three of the sailors took off on their own, saying they wanted to hunt for more pigs. Captain Dalgarno and the two mates, Smith and Mahoney, said nothing to deter them, seemingly sunk in numb apathy. Holding was left with the entire responsibility of directing the trek across the island to the east coast, a slow business because most did not have boots, and many had become very weak.

Still the rain poured down, while the temperature hovered just above freezing. Miserably, in a lengthening line, they straggled across the soggy landscape, while Holding ranged back and forth trying to encourage them. He had to rely on persuasion: being just a common seaman, he did not have the rank to force the party to follow his orders. As darkness loomed, he couldn't talk the straggle of men into taking another step, even though, as he bitterly remembered later, the beach that offered decent shelter was only about two hundred yards away.

As Holding battled to light a fire in the long, wet grass, the pig-hunters rejoined them, empty-handed and without the cook. He had set himself down in the tussock and refused to go an inch farther, they said. It was too dark to look for him then, so after another long, dreadful night spent huddled in the rain, two men were sent in search. It was only a short time before they returned, though, saying the cook was nowhere to be seen. Holding didn't send them back, as it was so likely that the poor fellow was dead of exposure. Not only had the cook endured a week of appalling cold and wet with little or no food but his limbs were cramped by his tight layers of clothes.

For breakfast some of the party dug up *Stilbocarpa* roots, while others tried to eat grass. Holding harassed them into getting under way again, but they were getting weaker and more obstinate by the hour. Later, in a moment of insight, he meditated, "It is probable that had we been better acquainted with each other things might have been somewhat different." They did not even know all the others' names, so there was no camaraderie to bind them. He also had the advantage, as he admitted another time, of having been very well fed the previous summer in Australia, while the seamen who had come out from Aberdeen on the *Invercauld* had been living on basic ship's provisions for months. After a while he went ahead to cut down brush and make the going easier, but when he looked back most of the men had simply lain down in the grass. The officers were ordering the two ship's boys, Liddle and Lansfield, to fetch them water from a rivulet close by, choosing to drink it out of the boys' boots rather than get it themselves.

After three days of this, Holding lost all patience. Leaving the apathetic group camped in the grass alongside an ancient cairn of rocks, he headed back to the wreck site to see if anything useful had been washed up in the meantime. The boatswain, a sturdy, phlegmatic, older man, went with him. It was amazing how easily they moved without the impediment of the rest—the half mile to the top of the cliff above the wrecksite was no more than a stroll. On the way, they came across the corpse of the cook, but, lacking tools to dig a grave, they simply covered it with grass. Then they carried on.

After clambering to the bottom of the cliff, they found Tait where they had left him; he was dead and decaying too. They put the body under a rock and covered it with brush, and then searched the piled-up wreckage for food, finding a few pieces of unidentifiable putrid meat.

Without even a pause for revulsion, they lit a fire, cooked, and ate it. "It was too rotten to hold on a stick and was difficult to eat," wrote Holding, adding darkly, "The rest can be imagined." About noon the next day four other men joined them, having left the rest of the party at the cairn. Soon afterward, someone glimpsed the corpse of the ship's pig stuck under a large rock.

Holding climbed up to it, grabbed its legs, and hauled—and with a sodden plop the lower half of the carcass came away in his hands, ripped across the loins. "Did we eat it?" he wrote, and answered, "Of course."

In view of the fact that there were no seals or sea lions on this part of the coast, the next ghastly step was obvious. It was the boatswain who first made the suggestion that they should draw lots for which of them should be the first to die, in order to save the rest. Revolted, Holding exclaimed that he would never kill and eat another man—but then realized that the alternative was outright murder, with himself the most likely victim.

That night, he was too scared to go to sleep, and the instant dawn broke, he was up and away. When one of the seamen, Big Dutch Peter, said he would come too, Holding hastily turned down the offer. Knowing that a blow on the head while his back was turned would spell the end for him, he scaled the cliff as fast as he could. Then he ran off across the tussock, in fear for his life.

TWELVE

Privation

Winter is coming on apace, and the cold begins to make itself keenly felt," wrote Raynal. "The seals are getting rarer and rarer, so that the future does not present itself to our eyes under the most radiant aspects; the spectre of Famine rises menacingly on the horizon, and every day draws nearer with gigantic strides. If the weather were but less inclement! We might extend our researches further. But it is only now and then that we can make an excursion on the waters of the bay."

The past few days had certainly been strange, Musgrave recording on May 15 that they had had "the most varied and extraordinary weather" he had ever experienced. The wind had blown all around the compass, and was calm one hour and blustery the next; at one moment there had been bright sunshine, and the next it would be pelting rain, sleet, and snow, "generally accompanied by thick fog." The temperature at noon was recorded as 34° Fahrenheit, close to freezing, and yet there had been no frost.

Early that morning there had been another strange phenomenon—the men had been shocked awake by an earthquake. It arrived with a sound like hundreds of clattering chariots, and was violent enough to hurl the burning firewood out of the fire. "We were frozen with terror," Raynal frankly admitted. Too frightened to sleep, the five men sat up till dawn, reading the Bible for reassurance.

It didn't make it any easier that they were so often forced by the gales and rain to be cooped up indoors, save for essential trips for firewood and water, and that it was impossible to go out to hunt game. "The weather is variable, but generally cold and damp," Raynal recorded on May 20. The temperature had hovered at three degrees below freezing in the shade, and at night was frequently lower. "In the shade! What a mockery!" The sun was a stranger, peeping out from the heavy clouds only once or twice a week—"and what a sun! so pale, so cold!" Like the rest of the *Grafton* castaways, he craved the sight of blue sky, and was afflicted with "a kind of suffocating anxiety; namely, the monotonous and incessant beat of the waves upon the shore, at a few paces only from our hut, joined to the not less continuous murmur of the wind among the neighbouring trees. It incessantly recalls to us our cruel destiny."

Because the men were so dependent on the sea lions for food, they were very anxious about their seasonal behavior, not knowing what to expect next. The five-month-old pups had learned how to swim, and were taking to the water instead of rushing for the forest, and so hunting them had become as difficult as cornering and killing the adults.

Worse, however, lay ahead. "Monday, 23 May," Raynal wrote. "A thick mantle of snow covers the earth." An extraordinary calm had arrived, and as day broke the bay was as smooth as a mirror, and the air utterly crystalline. Then, all of a sudden, the calm surface of Carnley Harbour was ruffled, and everywhere troops of sea lions were swimming energetically back and forth, occasionally leaping out of the water like porpoises.

The men rushed down to the beach, to realize the dreadful truth. Their major source of "daily food, the support of our lives"—as Raynal agonized—was heading for the open water, where during daylight hours the sea lions would spend the whole of the winter. Panic-stricken, they ran to their boat and rowed madly for Figure-of-Eight Island, hoping to fall in with a few stragglers, but it was deserted. Despair threatened to overwhelm them. "Before us was the prospect of many months of misery, many months of distress. How could we support them?" Raynal agonized.

Musgrave correctly conjectured that the seals were in the water because it was warmer than the land, and that they would return to the shore every time the sun peeped out, but a week later he, too, had to admit that matters looked bad. Not only had the seals disappeared from the local vicinity but the beaches for three miles about the house had been cleared of mussels. Yet, because of the awful weather and the shortening of the days with the coming of winter—"We have only eight hours daylight"—the men could not safely forage any farther than that.

Musgrave continued, "We have to look pretty sharp after our bellies now, and I fear very much that we shall go hungry yet before the winter is out." Most of the time, the weather didn't allow them to do anything more than venture out for firewood—a most necessary task, because, as he noted, they burned the equivalent of a cartload each day. This meant that they were confined to eating salt meat and roots, without even the sacchary root beer to wash it down; it was no longer an alternative to plain cold water because, as he confessed, "it gave us all the bowel complaint." To add to their problems, Raynal was sick with a festered finger, and Alick was also laid low, with a sprained ankle.

Then, on June 11, matters looked up. Raynal recorded that though it was very cold, the sun shone at last, and the sea was tolerably calm. As Musgrave noted with relief, Raynal's finger, which had been so badly infected that he had thought he would lose it, was now out of danger, and Alick's sprained ankle was better. It was a rare chance for a hunting expedition. Leaving Harry to look after Epigwaitt, the others sailed off at dawn, taking a cauldron of embers and a piece of sailcloth in case the short day ended before they returned, and they were forced to camp on the beach.

They steered up the western channel, discovering a little inlet that led to a sheltered beach. Upon landing, to their delight and surprise, they found more evidence of earlier parties—a clearing in the trees that had obviously been made by a man with an ax, the rotting remains of two huts, and a pile of discarded bricks. After breakfasting on some birds they shot and naming the bay Camp Cove, they carried on, heading for Adams Island.

There they made another discovery, but this time a foreboding one—timber from a shipwreck, including a rudder made of fir. "Whence came these waifs and strays?" Raynal wondered. They knew they had been washed up just recently, because the sea wrack had not been here at the time of their last visit.

The men lit a big smoky fire on the beach as a signal, and waited—"were there any shipwrecked men in the neighbourhood they could not but see." They did not give up until dusk, when they put the fire out and headed back to Epigwaitt, feeling mystified and downcast. There had been no response to the beacon, yet they would have greatly welcomed the company of other men, no matter how destitute and wretched.

TWENTY MILES TO the north of Epigwaitt, Robert Holding wandered about the clifftop plateau "in search of food and adventure," as he ironically put it, having successfully escaped from the cannibalistic group. He, too, found reassuring signs of earlier visits. In a clump of tall grass he discovered the frames of two tents, perhaps left by past sealing parties, sited close to the first of the two sheltered bays he had spied the first time he arrived at the top of the cliff.

Looking down the slope to the sea, he was even more gratified to glimpse seals. As he was by himself and knew nothing about the seal-killing business, he decided to leave them alone and hunt for shellfish instead. When he got to the beach, he found large limpets on the tidal rocks, and after some experimentation discovered that they were easily plucked if he slid the blade of his knife quickly between the foot of the shellfish and the surface of the stone. Having the matches, he was able to light a fire, and noted delightedly that when they were roasted they tasted rather like eggs, and were fully as nourishing.

Putting a few shells into his pockets to prove that the food source existed, he climbed the hill and set off across the tussock again, heading for the cairn where he had left Captain Dalgarno and the others. Incredibly—though not to Holding's great surprise—they were still lying about the fire gnawing *Stilbocarpa* roots, which was all they had eaten over the twelve days since he had left them to go back to the wreck site. As he quickly learned, they had scarcely moved at all in the meantime.

Admittedly, Holding had the matches, so the fire had to be constantly tended. Most of the party, including the captain and first mate, had bare, lame, frostbitten feet. The date was June 2, so they had been deprived of substantial food for twenty-three days. All of them would have displayed the classic symptoms of starvation — dull, listless eyes, dry, cracked skin, hair loss, muscular weakness, mental lassitude, and loss of bladder control. Their feet and hands would have been constantly numb, and their legs and arms twisted up with agonizing cramps. However, that Captain Dalgarno — who should have exhibited the leadership expected of a man of his rank — was so extremely apathetic boded badly for them all.

When the mate, Andrew Smith, asked Holding what had happened to the boatswain and the other men who had gone to the wreck site, the seaman evaded the question, preferring not to describe his brush with cannibalism. Instead, he claimed that he had urged the others to come back to the cairn but they had declined, even though he had warned them that if they stayed there they were bound to die — which is what, in fact, probably happened, as they were never heard from again.

Then he changed the subject, telling the party about the limpets on the beach. At the sight of the shells they seemed quite enthusiastic about the idea of moving on. Holding didn't want to be back in the situation of hassling a long straggle of weak, reluctant men into trudging a few pathetic yards each day, though, so next morning he chose the five who were most able to walk — Captain Dalgarno; the first mate, Andrew Smith;

the boy, James Lansfield; the carpenter, Alex Henderson; and a seaman named Fritz Hansen—to make up the pioneering party. He told the others he would either come back himself to fetch them, or send someone else after they were established in the new camp.

Then he led the way northeast. For a while it was hard to keep the five going, but Holding was determined to get them down to the shore, and once they sighted the limpet-encrusted rocks on the beach, they moved along more eagerly. Even better, as they were gathering the shellfish, he managed to knock down a large bird, which they plucked and roasted. Then, after what Holding called the most comfortable night they had experienced on the island, he sent Fritz to fetch the six others.

By the time Fritz Hansen returned, twenty-four hours later, Holding had a feast of fish and shellfish ready, having found a way of catching fish by tapping them on the head with a stick. However, Fritz had only four men with him, instead of the six they'd expected. The seaman informed Holding that the other two had refused to move, but, according to the story he told Andrew Smith, he had woken up that morning to find they had died in the night.

So, Smith glumly noted, the number of *Invercauld* survivors had been reduced to ten. However, as the first mate went on to say, it was not surprising: "Up to the time that we got to the rocks—I think about twenty days after the wreck—we had had nothing to live upon except the small piece of pork and the handful of bread which came from the wreck, the small pig which we had killed, and some wild roots." Added to that, it was the depths of a subantarctic winter. Death from exposure was just as likely as dying from starvation, yet they had hardly any shelter at all.

This was a problem that was about to be solved, in a measure. After they had cleaned all the nearby rocks of limpets, the party of five, again led by Holding, climbed the nearest bluff. On the top they noticed little red berries growing on some of the bushes, and, finding they were sweet, they ate hungrily. Then, realizing that the bushes showed signs of having been systematically pruned in years gone by, they pushed through the growth to the edge of a hill, so they could get a better view of their surroundings. Finding a faint track that zigzagged downward, they followed it. Then all at once Andrew Smith, who was the tallest, electrified them all by crying out that he could see a chimney near the water.

Where there was a chimney, there surely must be a house! Holding dashed after Smith, who screamed that he could see a village close to the beach—a village where men might be living! "With what strength we had left," the mate himself wrote, "we ran eagerly through the scrub to get to them." They called out as they ran, desperately hoping to hear answers.

Instead they lurched to a stop, engulfed by a twelve-year-long silence. Around them lay the last ruins of the settlement of Hardwicke.

THE GRANDIOSE SCHEME to found a British colony in the remote subantarctic south had had its foundation in 1846, when Charles Enderby, of the London whaling firm Enderby and Sons (the employer of Abraham Bristow, discoverer of the Auckland Islands), had published a pamphlet called *Proposal for re-establishing the British Southern Whale Fishery, through the medium of a Chartered Company, and in conjunction with the Colonisation of the Auckland Islands as the site of the Company's Whaling Station.*

Sir James Ross, the popular and much-feted explorer, who was one of the very few Englishmen who had actually visited the island group, thoroughly approved, declaring that "in the whole range of the vast Southern Ocean" no better spot could be found for a whaling station. The British administration agreed, one dignitary calling the plan the "well judged project" of "one of the first citizens of London." Accordingly the Enderby firm was granted a royal charter and a thirty-year lease. As it turned out, only three of those years were needed.

On December 4, 1849, the first ship of the expedition, *Samuel Enderby*, arrived, and the flag was raised in a short ceremony on shore. The joy of the occasion was blunted, however, when they found that a Maori party had beaten them here. The new lieutenant governor, Charles Enderby himself, was formally welcomed by Matioro, a Ngati Matunga chieftain, who, with about seventy of his people and their Moriori slaves, had arrived here from the Chatham Islands—a small group to the east of New Zealand—in 1843, six years earlier. They had built a couple of fortified villages and established potato and cabbage gardens, plus some flax plantations, and so, with good reason, they reckoned the territory was theirs.

Enderby was even more disconcerted to find that the ground was peaty and swampy; that the scrub was almost impenetrable; that the bitter winds blew constantly; and that the rain poured down with depressing persistence. Back in London, he had claimed that the climate was healthy, the virgin soil rich, and that cattle, sheep, horses, and crops would thrive, basing his assumptions on the reports of Captains Bristow, Morrell, and Ross. Now it dawned on him that he might have been overoptimistic.

He compensated for a while by seizing the land the Maori tribe had cultivated, though he did allow them a share of the potatoes and cabbage they had grown. On New Year's Day of 1850, he was backed up by the arrival of the *Fancy*, which carried an assistant commissioner, the first of their surgeons, eighteen laborers with their families, eight thousand bricks, and a number of portable wooden houses. However, most of the incoming settlers, including the surgeon and many of the wives, gave their new quarters one horrified glance and promptly took to the bottle. Before it had even started, the settlement, christened Hardwicke, was doomed.

By the end of the first summer the colonists had somehow managed to erect eighteen cottages and a barracks out of the precut material that had arrived on the *Fancy*. Of prime importance was the fourteen-room Government House, into which Enderby gratefully moved on February 25, 1850. Building a jail, however, had proved an even more urgent matter, which was solved for a while by setting up a large oil cask on a nearby islet, Shoe Island, for the accommodation of dissidents, drunks, and thieves. Later, the barrel was replaced by a proper little prison, which was nicknamed Rodd's Castle in honor of one of the surgeons, J. S. Rodd, MRCS, who was imprisoned there for habitual insobriety. He nearly drowned after falling off the wharf while drunk, and his wife, who was equally fond of the bottle, was notorious for embarrassing behavior on public occasions.

The settlers also constructed workshops, a lot of thatched

windbreaks, and a half mile of road, but generally had dismal success. They liberated rabbits, goats, pigs, and sheep, but, though these animals overran much of the surrounding territory, none of them thrived. The whaling, too, was unprofitable, while all the time the problems with law and order continued. When grog was banned, the men distilled their own. The assistant commissioner went around getting people to sign the Temperance Pledge, but it made no difference whatsoever to their drinking habits. Church services had to be canceled because no one attended.

In October 1850, Miss Hallett, the sister of one of the two surgeons, tried to shoot her brother dead and then kill herself. Probably because they were both drunk at the time, the business was bungled, and so the affair was hushed up. Dr. Hallett quit the colony early in 1851, which posed yet another problem, because the colonists, the whalers in particular, were starting to develop scurvy. A replacement, Dr. MacNish, arrived, but he was a habitual drunkard, too, and twelve weeks later he departed the scene. His successor, Dr. Ewington, lasted just five months; when he went he was so keen to quit that he left his wife (another tippler) behind, rather than wait until he had enough money for her fare.

The governor of New Zealand, Sir George Grey, paid an official call in November 1850. After inspecting the settlement in the pouring rain he went away again, expressing grave doubts about the future of the colony. In the meantime, Lieutenant-Governor Enderby was falling prey to violent apoplectic attacks. By July 1851, rumors of the collapse of the settlement were rife in Wellington and Sydney. In December of that same year a party of special commissioners arrived, and in January 1852

Enderby was asked to resign, an order he doggedly refused to obey, vowing instead to shoot anyone who attempted to remove him. After the commissioners threatened to put him in shackles, he caved in, however, and went with them to Wellington. The end of the grand scheme was nigh.

On August 4, 1852, the colonists departed, taking almost everything with them. The sheep and cattle had been slaughtered to provision the ships. The portable houses, including Government House, had been dismantled and repacked; the bricks were loaded on the *Earle of Hardwicke* as ballast, and the workshops, storage sheds, and prison were taken away, too, along with all the furniture and tools. In 1856 the last of the Maori settlers followed, having chartered a whaleship to carry them to New Zealand.

Once more, the Auckland Islands were uninhabited. When the *Invercauld* castaways stumbled on the settlement on June 5, 1864, all that was left of Enderby's experiment in colony building was one last house, in sadly broken-down condition.

THE FIVE DESPERATE SAILORS who were gathered together in the tall weeds surveyed the ruin numbly. Many of the boards had been stripped away from the framework, so that it was open to the wind and the rain. However, a large fireplace and chimney stood in what had been a kitchen, and the roof of that room was covered with shingles in a fair state of preservation, so, while it was by no means ideal, it was a much better shelter than anything they had found up till now. In addition, after glimpsing some planks sticking up above the high, rank grass of what had been a garden, Holding found a lean-to that was more weatherproof than the house.

Leaving the other three to look around, Holding and the second mate, the American John Mahoney, went to the beach to find something to eat. Robert Holding saw a bird like the one he had knocked over three days earlier, and was creeping over to it when he heard Mahoney call out, "Bob, for God's sake, come back, here is a seal!"

Holding ran back, but could see nothing. "Where is it?" he demanded.

"There," said the other, pointing to a rocky outcrop. "There, in the water!"

Sure enough, Holding could see a seal poking up his nose, his whiskers quivering as he breathed. The only weapon the seaman had to hand was a rotten branch he had been about to throw at the bird. Wading up to the seal, he struck him over the nose with this, but to his horror it broke.

He called out to Mahoney, "For God's sake, give me some stones!" Instead of waiting, however, he ducked down and grabbed rocks from the water around his feet, and used them to pound the seal about the head. The American joined him, and together they grabbed the animal's front flippers, and heaved him over the rocks. When the sea lion shook his head, appearing to recover, Holding took out his sheath knife, and tried to plunge it into its chest, but it bounced back from the thick, rubbery skin and slid down his hand, cutting two fingers to the bone. Ignoring the pain, Holding tried again, doing his utmost to cut the sea lion's throat, and finally, after an awful struggle, the animal collapsed and died. Holding bound up his hand in a handkerchief and headed for the ruined settlement, leaving Mahoney to look after the carcass until he returned.

Needless to say—as he himself ironically remarked—he

had no trouble finding volunteers to help with the butchering. Luckily, too, when the other three had been clearing out the house, they had found a triangular piece of galvanized sheet iron about eighteen inches at its broadest part, which gave capital service as a frying pan. For the first time since the day of the wreck they could eat their fill, Andrew Smith remembering "the flesh, we found, was very good."

They then prepared the lean-to as quarters for the night. After clearing off the long grass, they found that the front of it had fallen in, but this was an advantage, as the boards covered the ground, forming a floor. They crawled in together, and although it was very cold, the captain and the first mate being the only ones with coats, the men slept the better for being under cover.

THE NEXT DAY, a good breakfast gave them the strength to rummage about the ruins some more, finding a number of preserved-meat tins, which proved very useful for boiling shellfish and seal meat. They also uncovered an old adze and a hatchet, both thrown away by the settlers as no longer of any use, but which the castaways found invaluable for cutting the firewood that up to now they had been tearing with their bare hands. Holding also found an old half-gallon water can. Its bottom was rusted out, but later on he made it serviceable by putting in a wooden bottom. Some lengths of fencing wire turned up too, along with an old spade, some roof slates, and a few bricks.

"The party that we left soon joined us and took up their abode in the other house," Andrew Smith wrote. This was now much dryer and more habitable, because they had kept the fire in the old kitchen fireplace going. They shared the rest of the sea lion with them, "and as long as it lasted we found ourselves gaining strength." However, it was soon gone, "and when it was finished we had to take to our old style of living on roots and limpets."

Holding had made another interesting discovery—a pebbled walk that led to what had obviously been a plantation of gardens, fenced off from each other with thatched windbreaks. There were potatoes still growing, but they were only the size of marbles, and impossible to boil soft. There were abundant signs of domestic cabbage run wild too. However, instead of hunting the plantation for vegetables and taking down the thatch to improve their accommodations, the men waited for the people who had lived here to come to their rescue, blindly refusing to recognize the self-evident fact that the settlement had been abandoned for a very long time.

Even Holding, the most practical member of the party, indulged in the delusion. A cat made its appearance, half wild but obviously originally domestic. The second mate drove it away when he threw a brick at it, but, though it never came back, the men became even more foolishly optimistic, thinking that its owner might return. In the end, it was Andrew Smith who recognized that it was all in vain, "though it was evident that a great deal of work had been carried on here at one time."

Despite the disappointment, their circumstances were greatly improved. At long last, they had the resources to establish a secure base. Captain Dalgarno had another opportunity to step into a leadership role and organize his men into work parties and hunting groups. However, the psychological paralysis that had afflicted him ever since he had lost the *Invercauld* still held him in its thrall. Judging by what he told journalists later, all he apparently remembered of this interval was that they remained several months at Port Ross, sleeping "under the trunks of trees like wild beasts," and subsisting "on limpets or other shellfish," which was so far from the truth that it seems possible he had totally lost his grip on reality.

Despite his poor example, some of the group became more enterprising. Andrew Smith recorded that when a long spar was found on the beach, it was cut into lengths and then bound into a raft. Poling about the rocks on this, Henderson, the carpenter, and James Mahoney, the second mate, blundered across another seal, different from the first, being mottled rather than an even dark brown. The skin of this seal, like the one earlier, was eagerly cut up by those who didn't have boots, and fashioned into moccasins to cover their battered bare feet—which, as Holding admitted now, "may in a measure account for their not having tried to get about more."

Then they had the bad luck to lose their raft. It had been tied up with a piece of seal skin, but lost its tether, and drifted away. This was a huge loss, because the rocks about the settlement had been scoured of shellfish, and they had been using the raft to hunt more distant beaches. The obvious solution was to shift their camp yet again, but Holding could find no one willing to leave the warm hearth of the ruined house and accompany him on a search for another site. "By this time we were all getting again very weak," Andrew Smith wrote in justification. "We had had no seal for some time, and some of us were so feeble that we could hardly crawl."

So Robert Holding, as independent as ever, went off on his

own. If he had traveled south, braving the mountains and lighting fires as he went, the story might have been different. Considering the strong moral caliber of Musgrave and his men, if they had been alerted to his presence it is certain that they would have done their utmost to make contact and assist—even if they lost their own lives in the attempt. However, they were not forced to take that terrible risk, because Holding headed east along the shore and then climbed north, to get to the northwestern tip of Port Ross.

THIRTEEN

The Hunt

On June 19, encouraged by the continuing fine weather, Musgrave staged another exploratory expedition. Leaving Harry behind to look after Epigwaitt, he, Raynal, Alick, and George clambered to the top of the high mountain he had scaled alone five months before, "taking the same track up that I took on the 24th January."

The climb went so well that they kept on going until they reached a great slab of rock they had named Giant's Tomb for its resemblance to a coffin. Because this was the highest part of the island (about eight hundred or even one thousand feet, according to Musgrave's reckoning), and the atmosphere was particularly clear that day, they were able to see all the way from Adams Island in the south to Enderby in the far north. As usual, Musgrave made sketches and took extensive notes.

"The whole extent of the group from north to south I judge to be 30 or 35 miles, and about fifteen miles east and west at the widest part," he wrote. The high, bold precipices on the distant north-western shore—where, though he did not know it, the *Invercauld* had found her grave—were particularly striking, while on the east coast there appeared to be "a number of dangerous sunken reefs, upon which the sea breaks heavily." The land toward the northeastern extremity looked much lower than their own area in the south, sloping in undulating ridges to the coast, which was deeply indented. "From the appearance of this part of the island, I have no doubt but it is swarming with seals," he wrote, with no idea that he was studying the terrain where Robert Holding was exploring. "The shores are clad with scrub and stunted timber."

Immediately before the little group of men lay a magnificent but daunting prospect. "There are chasms and perpendicular precipices, hundreds of feet deep, down which it is fearful to look." The ocean was as depressingly empty as ever, but looking seaward was nevertheless "a beautiful relief to the eye." It was good, too, to turn back toward home. "We were seven hours out," Musgrave concluded. Because the marshes were frozen over, the traveling had been easy. On the way back they caught a bird like a water hen, and discovered trees with small red berries that were delicious to eat.

Better still, they found a vegetable that was common on Campbell Island, but which they hadn't seen on Auckland Island until now. This was *Pleurophyllum speciosum,* a megaherb like *Stilbocarpa* but even more magnificent, its rosette of ribbed emerald green leaves measuring as much as twenty inches across. After taking this back to the house, the men chopped it up finely and boiled it and found that it was perfectly edible, making a healthful and welcome addition to the soup they made from preserved seal meat. Up to now they had disliked the sea lion broth because it gave them diarrhea, but the *Pleurophyllum,* being costive, had the benefit of neutralizing this unpleasant side effect. The reason they had not found it closer to Epigwaitt was that wild pigs, released by Captain Bristow in 1807 and by various expeditions afterward, had greedily dug them up, almost completely eradicating the plant. Even now, on Auckland Island, *Pleurophyllum speciosum* is abundant only on scattered rock outcrops and coastal cliffs.

Over the next few days, further invigorated by the capture of a seal and a good haul of mussels, Musgrave began to think optimistically of spring and the hoped-for rescue mission. He talked of setting up a lookout station, fearing that a vessel might pass by without anyone realizing they were there, and on July 14, he and Raynal went down the harbor in the boat to look for a likely place. However, luck was not with them. Not only did they fail to find anywhere suitable that was close enough to Epigwaitt to be serviced regularly, but they were caught out when the wind turned against them.

Taking the boat's sail on shore, they made a shelter and lit a fire, but the rain fell in torrents, and the sail was full of holes. As Musgrave noted wryly, "This, it may be easily understood, was not very comfortable in 51° south latitude, in the middle of winter." The temperature at that time averaged 30° Fahrenheit at noon, aggravated by the chill factor of the hard rain and gusty wind. To add to their discomfort, they had nothing to eat, because the cold seal meat and roots they had carried with them had been used up at noon.

The next morning the contrary wind blew still more strongly, and the rain continued to fall heavily all day. They managed to shoot two widgeons—"one we roasted, and the other we stewed by piecemeal in a quart pot, which is used as a bailer for the boat," wrote Musgrave, who was growing anxious about the chronometer at the hut, which needed winding if it was not to run down. In the end, he decided to go back on foot. Raynal refused to be left alone, and so they pulled the boat up as far as they could, though not in a position that Musgrave considered safe, and set off.

"It is needless to detail our troubles in getting through the scrub and grass in a pelting rain," Musgrave wrote. "Suffice it to say that we were six hours in going the distance of five miles, and arrived home an hour after dark. We had not a dry thread on us, and were almost sinking with exhaustion from fatigue and hunger." Suffice it to say, too, that the other three men, who had been afraid that they had been blown out to sea, were very glad to see them.

By great good luck George and Alick had managed to catch a young seal that morning, "which was quite a treat, for it was the first young seal we had got for a long time, and assuredly we did ample justice to it; immediately after which we went to bed, and required no rocking to put us to sleep." Then, in the morning, Musgrave was pleased to find that it had stopped raining, because he and Raynal had to get back to the boat.

Again their luck ran out, because it poured down before they had gotten half a mile. However, they pressed on, being worried about the boat, "for should we lose her we lose our means of getting a living." Fortunately she was exactly where they had left her, half full of water but undamaged. "After bailing her out we made a fire, stripped off our clothes one piece after another, and managed somehow to get them dry some way or another, and had something to eat in the meantime."

Then they waited for the weather to change. At midnight the wind turned fair at last, enabling them to sail home.

MUSGRAVE GAVE UP the idea of keeping a lookout close to the open coast, satisfying himself with a vantage point on the hill about two miles above the hut, where a man could see a long way down the harbor and warn the people at Epigwaitt to launch the boat if a sail should come in—"and surely one will. On the first day of October I intend to go to keep the look-out myself," he vowed. "I shall remain there until we give up all hopes of any one coming."

October was a long way off, however, as it was still only mid-July, with the worst of the winter yet to be endured. In the meantime, Musgrave resumed his habit of long, solitary wanderings, and went back, too, to the detailed study of barometer readings that had become an obsession with him, comparing them with actual weather conditions and finding very little correlation.

When the barometer rose, traditionally a sign of fine weather, he was likely to wake up to find it "dark, gloomy, and misty," with a nasty gale on the way—"another instance of its deceitfulness, and almost uselessness, in this locality." In fact, he added wryly, he had found that the blowflies were his best barometer, swarming when it was about to rain, and perhaps even predicting a gale—because those maddening flies were still around. During the last week of July the temperature dropped as low as 22° Fahrenheit, and yet the bluebottles survived, polluting meat, clothes, and blankets almost as revoltingly as in the height of summer, and the sandflies were biting as furiously as ever.

"I may here describe our precise mode of dragging out our miserable existence at this time," Musgrave wrote. "Breakfast—seal stewed down to soup, fried roots, boiled seal or roast ditto, with water. Dinner—ditto ditto. Supper—ditto ditto. This repeated twenty-one times per week. Mussels or fish have become quite a rarity, and we have been unable to get any for some time." On July 18 they found a sea lion mob and managed to kill three six-month-old pups and a cow in calf (pregnant), but the seals that escaped the cudgels moved off to another camp, and it proved impossible to find them again.

By the last of July, Raynal was recording that they were reduced to eating salted meat, which was almost inedible, being rank and rancid despite their best care. Though the hunting parties stayed out as long as they could, they trudged home head down and empty-handed. After three days in a row the five men became so depressed that instead of holding school they went to bed as soon as prayers had been said, seeking relief from hunger in sleep—"and as we were always weary, we slept."

Then came a natural phenomenon that the desperate men interpreted as an encouraging omen. George, who had gone out of the hut to relieve himself, rushed back inside exclaiming, "Come, come; come and look!" They all dashed out into the freezing darkness, to see what Raynal described as "sheaves of fire of different colours," leaping, snaking, and darting up the arch of the sky, paling the stars with ghostly radiance, a vast fireworks show that happened in utter silence. Awed, the men stood and watched the aurora, overwhelmed by this manifestation "of the grandeur of nature and the power of the Creator," until the cold drove them inside again.

Early the next morning Raynal and Alick went out in the hunt, going in different directions. Raynal brought down a couple of small cormorants with his gun and carried them back to

Epigwaitt, but when they were cooked and ready to eat, Alick had still not returned. It was not until after the others had eaten their midday dinner—being careful to set aside the Norwegian's share first—that they saw him trudging down the cliff. To their joy he was carrying a great burden on his back.

"We ran to meet him," Raynal wrote, going on to exclaim, "O happiness!" Alick was carrying the entire carcass of a young sea lion, weighing more than one hundred pounds. "With such a burden he had returned from the head of the bay, and along the most difficult paths imaginable! Our Norwegian was a brave and stalwart youth; and if he spoke little, he knew how to act." Alick had tracked the seal and its mother by the marks they made in the snow, and had managed to kill them both. Now he insisted on leading the way to where he had left the carcass of the cow, for fear it might disappear in the night, because several times lately they had been roused by the yelping of dogs.

Leaving Harry to butcher the yearling and cook the roast, the others followed the Norwegian. Musgrave was close behind Alick, while Raynal and George trailed by more than a hundred yards. Being anxious to catch up, Raynal took what he imagined was a shortcut through the forest, and found himself overlooking a marsh fed by a stream of water that plunged down a crevasse in the side of a cliff. Then he was brought up short by the sound of a seal's bark.

Next moment, he saw the animal—a young male sea lion. "Cudgel in hand," he wrote, "I started in pursuit."

The seal was moving fast. Suddenly, as Raynal followed close behind, it vanished. The crevasse yawned dead ahead, and Raynal only saved himself by grabbing a handful of ferns, which, luckily, held even after his feet slid out from under him.

As he clambered upright he heard the sea lion splashing through the water at the bottom. He shouted out to George, who had gone around to the bottom of the ravine, to lie in wait for the seal as it came out. He heard the Englishman answer; he heard him take up his position. Then, nothing. Ten minutes went by, but still there were no sounds.

Determined to drive the sea lion out, Raynal looped his cudgel around his neck by its thong, and slid feet first into the dark crevasse, gathering speed as he went, and then landing knee-deep in freezing water. He stood rigid and still. Though he could hear the animal, he couldn't see him clearly, because he was on the other side of a curtain of roots and creepers that hung from the roof. Ducking carefully under this, Raynal found himself in a gloomy cavern. The stream ran down the middle, and on one side the sea lion lurked, looking nervously from Raynal to George, who was silhouetted in the entrance.

When the sea lion finally attacked, he flew with a roar at the Frenchman. Raynal raised his cudgel to shoulder height, holding it in two hands like a bat, knowing he had only one chance. "Now, with open jaws, he springs upon me! I strike; my cudgel whistles through the air, and alights full upon his head." Finishing off the animal with his knife, Raynal rolled the carcass into the stream, where the current carried it to George.

Unfortunately, the only way to get out of the cavern was by the same route. Plunging full length into the ice-crusted water, Raynal crawled down the ravine, and "rose from it dripping like a Triton, shivering in every limb, and my teeth chattering, under the influence of a keen wind which glued my wet clothes to my body."

Hastily cutting the big sea lion carcass into four pieces, the two men hung two of the quarters from a tree and carried the rest of the carcass on their shoulders to Epigwaitt, where Raynal changed into dry clothes. Night had fallen, but Musgrave and Alick had not returned; obviously, they were waiting for them to catch up, and getting more anxious by the moment. Carrying a lantern, the two hunters sallied out again, and this time took the right route. By the time they found Musgrave and the Norwegian, they were chilled to the bone again, so the four of them lit a fire to warm themselves. When it burned out, they made their way back to the house through the icy dark night.

"We opened the door; we crossed the threshold; what an enticing spectacle was presented to our gaze!" wrote Raynal. "What a contrast to the scene we had just quitted! *Without*, night, and intense cold, and a whistling, biting wind; *within*, light and warmth."

The fire was crackling in the hearth, all the lamps were brightly lit, and their places at the table were neatly set, while an enormous savory joint smoked and steamed in the middle. Harry Forgès, that week's cook, had indeed done well. First giving thanks to "the Providence who had so manifestly heard and answered our prayers," the *Grafton* castaways fell to with a will.

TWENTY MILES TO THE NORTH, Robert Holding was braving the bitter cold to trek across a peninsula to the northwest tip of Port Ross. He was aware that the *Invercauld* survivors he had left behind at the ruined settlement of Hardwicke were gathered around the fire he had left in the hearth of the one remaining wreck of a house. They might be a great deal warmer than he was, but he was convinced they were signing their death warrant.

As he ruminated, it was impossible to tell what horrid scene he might find when he eventually returned. They might be dead, or they might be still clinging to life by eating the few *Stilbocarpa* roots that grew in the area, plus whatever stray shellfish those who still had the strength to forage could find on the beach. Right now, though, his main preoccupation was to find a more promising place to camp. Then—but only then—he would go back to fetch whoever might still be alive.

Because the rocks on the beach were so slippery and dangerous, he was forced to go inland and negotiate the thick, scrubby, contorted forest, which was so tangled that much of the time he had to crawl on hands and knees. Once he was startled by the bark of a seal; then the animal lunged up at him from the gloom of the forest floor. Being taken by surprise, all he could do was hastily get out of the way, but it gave him great hopes for the future. Meantime, just as he did every night of the trek, Holding lit a fire, cooked what shellfish and roots he had gathered that day, and then lay down to sleep in the wet moss and rotted leaves.

Finally he broke out onto a bluff overlooking the bay and the sea, and stood with his club in his hand, staring about intently at the same scene that Musgrave had glimpsed in the far distance, from the top of the mountain above Epigwaitt. Directly in front of him was an islet, two-thirds covered with grass and scrub, where he could glimpse seals on the distant rocks. It was out of reach, being on the far side of a passage five hundred yards wide, but closer to hand were rocks covered with limpets and mussels. After lighting a fire and building a brush wigwam, Holding camped here for several days.

Eventually, however, the urge took him to return to Hardwicke, a journey that took a much shorter time than the trek out—just half a day. Getting there, he walked into a grim and depressing scene. Not only had the party done nothing to improve their circumstances but the steward and the two boys, Liddle and Lansfield, had died. According to a story Captain Dalgarno later told a reporter from the *Aberdeen Herald*, after he had been out looking for food one day, he came back to find the men in a tight group around the fire, leaving no room for him. Reluctant to disturb them, he had paced back and forth to keep warm, and after a while one of the seamen, noticing this, had nudged the man next to him to move along and make a place for the captain. The fellow had made no reply, and when the seaman prodded him again, it was to find that he was dead.

"Our condition, as may well be imagined, was most miserable," wrote Andrew Smith; "our clothes were all very much torn, and at that time it was bitterly cold. Some days we had very fine weather, but in general we had heavy gales from S.W. with great falls of rain and snow. This was, I think, about the month of July." The warmth of the fire was all that had kept them alive.

As Holding found, that fire was now burning at the bottom of a deep hole, the peat beneath having given way. The hearth had collapsed, and the fiery cavity was rimmed with the bricks that had fallen into it. Though there was no fear now of it going out, most of the party had been too weak and apathetic to leave it to hunt for food. One of these was the second mate, Mahoney, who had made the two boys bring him water and roots instead of fetching them himself. Then, however, they had died. It was obvious that he had taken the clothes from the corpses, because he was now wearing so many garments that he could scarcely shift his limbs.

The others told Holding that two of the seamen, Harvey and Fritz, had left the camp some days earlier, deciding to emulate his own example and look for fairer fields. No one had heard from them since. Perhaps they were dead. If they had found food and shelter and were still alive, they hadn't bothered to come and tell their shipmates about it.

Realizing yet again that staying here promised nothing but a slow death from starvation, Holding tried to persuade the men who were so obstinately huddled around the fire to come to the northwestern promontory of the harbor, telling them there were plenty of shellfish there. However, as Smith wrote, "all declined to go, with the exception of myself."

On their way out, Holding and Smith met Harvey and Fritz, returning in defeat, having gotten lost. The two seamen readily agreed to join them, and, after promising to send back the good news once they had established a camp, the four set off along the beach.

This time, Holding led the way around the coast instead of crawling through the forest—a fortunate move, because they not only managed to gather a rich harvest of shellfish but also stumbled over a large seal asleep on the rocks. Holding dropped a stone on its head and finished it off with his knife—this time without cutting his fingers, which he had been lucky not to lose from infection.

He skinned the big carcass and then cut it up so it was possible for them to carry it all to his camp. Three of them shouldered the meat, while Fritz was given the liver, skin, and head, and then they set off. After a few moments, Holding, Harvey, and Smith realized that Fritz wasn't following. When they turned around to look for him they found him crouched on the ground, gobbling the raw liver like a dog.

Saying nothing, the other three went on ahead to Holding's camp, where they built two more brush wigwams. They lit a fire and cooked the meat, but Fritz did not catch up with them until nightfall. He was empty-handed, and when they asked what had happened to the skin and head, he mumbled that he had stowed them in a bush.

It was too dark to go back, but the instant day broke, Holding went out in search, and found them very quickly because a flock of albatrosses was tearing them apart. "Say, was I mad?" he wrote. The head, which had a lot of meat on the bones, was ruined, and he was only just in time to save the skin, which they badly needed for moccasins.

Worse was to come. As Andrew Smith wrote, "We were not long without fresh sorrow, however, for one of the two that Holding and I persuaded to come with us died the day after."

It happened in the middle of the next night. Holding was awakened by Fritz's voice, and when he sat up, the seaman was standing nearby with a can in his hand. When Holding asked what he was doing, Fritz said vaguely, "Did I hear you calling out for water?"

Holding said, "No, I don't want any," and lay down again. However, Fritz went to the nearest waterhole and filled the can before going back to the brush wigwam that he and the other seaman, Harvey, shared. When he tried to get inside Harvey shoved him out—so hard that Fritz fell flat on his face, and didn't get up again. In the morning, when Holding discovered him, he was dead, his corpse frozen stiff.

The ground was too hard to dig a grave, so they put the body under a tree and covered it with boughs. "Two or three days after this I sent Harvey to try to get the Captain's party and told him to bring them down to us," remembered Holding. Then, after the seaman had gone, "the Mate and myself found that Harvey had been eating some of Fritz."

Covering up the remains of the corpse, Andrew Smith and Holding waited, but Harvey did not return. "We waited anxiously day after day in hopes of some of them joining us, but none came," wrote Smith. They were back to living on roots and limpets — "It was always roots and limpets, limpets and roots, day after day, but we had to rest contented with what we could get, although our hunger was never satisfied."

After four days of this, Holding decided to go and find out what had happened, leaving Smith to look after the camp. When he got to the ruined house, the fire was burning deeper in the hole than ever, and only Mahoney and Dalgarno were crouched before it. Where was Harvey? Dead, they said. Holding asked what had happened to the carpenter, and Dalgarno told him that when he and Henderson had been away searching for limpets that day, the carpenter had collapsed. Dalgarno had carried him as far as he could, but weakness had forced him to put the sick man down and come back to the camp alone.

Robert Holding immediately set out to look for the poor fellow, which took a while because the carpenter had crawled into a kind of grotto. He was barely alive, quite beyond speech, his only movement a flicker of the eyes. Holding felt sick and sad, but he, like Dalgarno, was forced to leave the pitiful wretch to die alone, as dark was falling, and it was impossible to carry him to the camp.

When he arrived back at the house Mahoney, now lying on a stretcher by the hearth, ordered him to go and get him some roots. Holding flatly refused. In his candid opinion, the two boys had died because the second mate had overworked them, being too idle to fetch his own food and water, and he had no intention of joining their number. At that, Mahoney unfolded his jackknife and, as Holding related, threatened to use it. Picking up a brick, Holding invited Mahoney to try, vowing that he was too old a hand to be cowed by an Irish New York bully, and Mahoney subsided.

The night that followed was silent and unpleasant. At first light, Holding went to check on the carpenter, but his body had been washed away by the tide. Deciding against returning to the ruined house and a fruitless attempt to persuade Dalgarno and Mahoney to accompany him, he headed for the northern promontory, where he conveyed the grim news to Andrew Smith that the party had now been reduced to four. All the seamen save Holding himself had died, leaving just the captain and two officers. The men of rank had survived where the common sailors had not, perhaps because they had been better fed on board ship, or perhaps because they had looked after themselves instead of exerting leadership.

Smith wrote, "Holding said that the captain and second mate would join us soon, but that at present the second mate was unable to walk, as he had a very bad boil on his leg; the captain was to stay with him until he was better." While Holding and Smith waited for Dalgarno and Mahoney, they shifted their camp to a place closer to the beach, where it was just as easy to build light tepees, and where they had a better view of the ocean.

There Holding, who had learned the ways of poachers when his father was gamekeeper for the duke of Manchester, devised new stratagems for catching food. When he had left Hardwicke he had remembered to bring the fencing wire with him, and now, using the cooking fire for heating and stones for hammer and anvil, he made a spear with one length, and fashioned a hook at the end of another. With the hook he gently turned the weeds in rock-pools, and with the spear he caught the fish that darted out of hiding. He also cut sealskin into ribbons and wove these into a bow net, making the hoops out of bent twigs, then bracing them with sticks. After baiting this with entrails, he lowered it into deep water. His success was limited, however, as the fish liked the soaked, soft sealskin as much as they liked the offal, and soon tore the net to shreds.

"After a time the captain joined us," Andrew Smith recorded. Dalgarno came alone. The second mate was not yet recovered, he told them, but would follow him when his leg got better. Days passed while they lived on limpets and roots and the oc- casional fish, and watched endlessly for ships. Then Holding began to wonder about Mahoney. Finally, curiosity became too much for him, and he went back to Hardwicke to see what had happened. He was alone, as the other two opted to stay and look after the camp.

He found Mahoney lying on his back with one leg extended and the other hanging over the side of the stretcher, exactly as he had seen him last, though the fire had gone out, extin- guished by the bricks that had collapsed from the sides of the hole. The second mate had been dead a long time — "His body was too much decomposed to even touch."

Holding took one of the roof slates and scratched a message with the tip of his knife, commemorating not just the dead man's name but the date he had been wrecked as well:

JAMES MAHONEY, WRECKED WITH THE
SHIP INVERCAULD.
MAY 10th '64.

It was August 12, 1864, almost exactly three months from the time when the *Invercauld* had foundered.

✦ FOURTEEN ✦

Equinox

S unday, August 14, 1864," wrote Captain Musgrave. "Since last
Sunday we have had what we call very fine weather—that
is to say, we have had no gales; but otherwise the weather has
been very variable, with frequent showers of rain and snow."

The men had taken advantage of the moderate days to go seal
hunting, and had managed to kill a yearling, plus two cows,
which, when slaughtered, proved to be in calf. They were also
glad to see Royal Tom, who had been absent for what felt like a
very long time. It was a good augury, Musgrave hoped—perhaps all the sea lions would come back, it evidently being close
to calving time.

Otherwise, he felt "unaccountably fidgety and uneasy, as if I
were every moment expecting some extraordinary occurrence,"
perhaps because it was the nine-month anniversary since their
departure from Sydney. "Yesterday I got to where I could see
well down the harbour, and sat on a rock all day, expecting to see
a vessel coming in," he wrote. "This morning I walked all about
the beach, expecting the same thing." He knew he was only
tormenting himself—"I have no right to expect such an event
for at least two months to come"—but he couldn't help it.

Determined, for once, to look on the bright side, Thomas Musgrave then meditated that having no gales was a very pleasant change indeed. The previous Sunday he had recorded a series of violent storms, including a hurricane that had blown so hard the surf had been dashed over the roof of the house. "Had it not been well built and secured it would inevitably have been blown down, and we should have been house-wrecked as well as shipwrecked," he commented with uncharacteristic dry humor.

To his surprise and gratification, too, the wreck of the *Grafton* had survived the tempest almost unchanged, the only part to come adrift being part of her decks. She had held together through the storms of winter, and now even this latest terrific gale had apparently had little effect.

Realizing that she must have been very strongly built gave Musgrave the idea of heaving her over onto her other side to have a look at her bottom, hoping to find that "it might not be impossible to make something of her after all," and maybe even get her into a fit state to sail to New Zealand.

It was an extremely ambitious proposal. Heaving the wreck over would involve wrapping heavy chains about what was left of the main mast, and then finding a pair of strong blocks, one to be attached to the chains, the other to be securely fastened to a belaying point on shore. In a shipyard this belaying point was a sturdy post called a heaving post, built into the timbers of a wharf, but the *Grafton* castaways would be forced to use a well-rooted tree. A cable rove between the multiple sheaves of these two blocks would tail through another, smaller block to some kind of revolving winch. This, when turned, would gradually haul in the cable, bringing the *Grafton* over on her other side—and that would only be the start of the work, if she was indeed found to be worthy of repair.

It was a great deal for Musgrave to expect of his men. However, when he and Raynal talked it over, the Frenchman thought that he could manage to assemble the blocks and chains, and the men, when they were told about this chance of getting the schooner into a fit state to sail to New Zealand, were very keen to give it a go. First, they had to clear away all the rocks from the area where they expected her to fall, which should have meant that they would wait for warmer weather. However, they were so enthusiastic that even when the weather abruptly changed, bringing an eighteen-hour gale with heavy snow, they couldn't wait to get started.

After working for days in waist-deep, near-freezing water, the biggest rocks had been removed from the area where she would fall. The next job was to lighten the *Grafton* as much as possible. The holds and cabin were already empty, but the sandstone ballast had to be removed block by block, while all the time frost stood on the ground, and the temperature hovered three degrees below freezing. That done, they did their utmost to pump out the water in her holds, but this proved impossible, as the water rushed in as fast as they could get it out. It was a very bad sign, but still they persevered with "great spirit and energy," Musgrave noted rather apprehensively, as he was beginning to wonder if he had misled them.

With considerable difficulty they heaved her over onto her other side, only to find that the arduous exercise had been pointless. Musgrave's worst hopes were realized. The hull on the newly exposed side was holed like a sieve, and the planking was wrenched and splintered all the way from the sternpost to the main rigging in the middle of the hull. It was impossible to mend her, so they let the cable out, and back she flopped.

Perhaps, Musgrave admitted, he had been wrong to give the men encouragement, because they were so horribly disappointed. As for himself, it triggered one of his fits of deep depression, worsened by the fact that September had arrived, "making a count of eight weary months since we were cast away. How tardily they had passed, and with what anguish of mind I suffered it would be impossible for me to describe."

With the coming of the spring equinox, the weather became worse than ever, with gales, snow, and heavy rain—so bad, as Musgrave wrote, "that it was not fit to go outside the door if it could be avoided." There were times, however, when they were forced to battle the elements to hunt for food, and then, if they did manage to kill seals—which were always females in calf—they had to carry the meat home on their backs, because it was far too rough to launch the boat.

Then, to the horror of all five, the sea lions vanished yet again. There were none in the forests, none on the beaches, and none swimming in the water. It was as if they had left to meet and breed on another land altogether.

The seal meat they had salted, dried, and smoked was supposed to stand them in good stead now, but, as Musgrave observed with distaste, it was almost impossible to eat. Given a choice of the sacchary roots, which he had come to hate, or the smoked meat, he would take the roots. "We are sick and feeble," wrote Raynal, who hated "the indigestible plant" even more passionately than the rest; "our position becomes more and more critical." Musgrave felt particularly bad on behalf of his men. They had never complained, he wrote, even though they "had to be pulling about in the boat, in the storm and wet, from morning till night, and then scarcely getting enough to subsist on."

In his journal entry for Wednesday, September 21, he recorded a particularly dismal hunt, after they had been desperate enough to launch the boat though the sky foretold a storm. When the gale arrived, attended with hail and rain, they were eight miles from Epigwaitt, and were forced to make preparations to camp on shore.

By midnight, it was so bitterly cold they realized it was suicidal to stay, so they launched the boat again "and arrived at home about two o'clock on Tuesday morning, wet through and almost famished with cold," and with nothing to show for their efforts. At the end of the entry Musgrave noted without comment, "Tenth anniversary of my marriage." For once, he left his deep distress undescribed.

On September 25 the weather was a little more promising: "Today, the wind having somewhat subsided, we have taken advantage of the respite to launch our boat, to see if in the West Channel we cannot fall in with a sea lion or two," Raynal wrote. However, beaches where seals were guaranteed to be found in the past were now completely deserted. Back across Carnley Harbour they pulled—and then Musgrave held up his hand, hissing that he'd heard a seal bark.

Mooring their boat, they crept up the beach, to find the old bull they had nicknamed Royal Tom, with two equally elderly wives. As brave as ever, the ancient seal advanced with a belligerent roar to meet them, but the men were desperate. "It cost a pang to kill these poor animals, and particularly the old lion, whom we had always respected, but necessity pressed us, hunger threatened us, we could not recede," Raynal wrote. The cudgels did their murderous work, and within minutes the three carcasses were loaded into the boat. Once again, in the meantime, starvation had been fended off.

Then it was October. "The long looked for month has arrived at last (God send relief before it passes)," Musgrave noted, and added, again without elaboration, "It is nine months today since the wreck." The time had come for rescue to finally arrive—if Sarpy and Uncle Musgrave kept their word.

AT THE OTHER end of the island, Robert Holding was also hoping desperately for any sign of a rescuing ship. With the advent of spring the weather had become pleasant, but it only served to make him feel more isolated than ever, and so he had adopted the habit of sitting on the cliffs overlooking the ocean, endlessly watching for a sail.

He was alone by circumstance as well as choice, because his return from Hardwicke with the news of Mahoney's death had brought unpleasant and unexpected consequences. Considering that Captain Dalgarno and Andrew Smith must have suspected the worst, their stunned, shocked reaction to the tidings was out of all proportion to their almost matter-of-fact response to earlier tragedies, perhaps because he had been a fellow officer. Perhaps, too, Dalgarno felt conscience-stricken because he had been the one who had abandoned the poor wretch to his lonely fate.

After Holding had conveyed the details, a cloud of black gloom settled over the camp, with Holding and Smith constantly speculating about who would be the next to die—"Who will be the next to be numbered with the dead?" as Smith rhetorically wrote. Their nights were restless and wracked with nightmares, and the days were equally fraught with despair and foreboding, because food was shorter than ever—the limpets, their spawning season over, had vanished from the rocks.

That was when Holding's isolation began, because instead of cooperating in the hunt for other sources of food, the men quarreled. For example, Holding had found another way of catching fish, tying long lengths of seal entrails about his legs and then wading knee-deep into pools with the bait trailing behind him; a questing fish would grab an end, try to twist off a mouthful, and get entangled long enough for Holding to pluck it up. He got good quantities, which he shared with the other two—until the day he asked the mate to help him carry an unusually large haul. Smith refused, so Holding curtly informed him he could catch his own fish from then on.

There had never been much of the camaraderie and solidarity of purpose that could have saved more of the group (and was such a crucial factor in the survival of the *Grafton* castaways), but now the temper of the remnants of the *Invercauld* crew became more surly, uncooperative, and rancorous than ever. Captain Dalgarno and Andrew Smith, being officers, expected deference and servitude from Holding, who was just an ordinary seaman. He, however, considering himself as good as they were (if not better) in this situation, refused to kowtow to their demands. So Dalgarno and Smith set up a separate camp sixty yards away, and for several weeks they ostracized the man they considered their social inferior.

Holding, while admitting that it "was a disgraceful state of affairs in our position," was obdurate in his refusal to recognize their superior rank—"Whether it was their fault or mine the reader must be the judge." Instead, in typically single-minded style, he spent much of his solitude hunting seals and devising ways of killing them. Because of his background as a game-keeper's son (though the quarry was new to him), he was adept at tracking his prey through the dense bush, often by just the way a leaf had been turned to show its wet side, or a blade of grass that had been knocked awry. If he was on the beach, and had the hide of a newly killed sea lion, he would drape it over himself as he crawled among the rocks. However, putting an end to the animal, once he had it cornered, was a problem. He had the old adze they had found at Hardwicke, and put a handle on it, but found it too unevenly weighted to make a good weapon.

Eventually he came to the conclusion that the ideal instrument would have been a baseball bat. Using a cudgel of wood he shaped in that fashion, he developed a method of crippling the seals by smashing out the left eyeball. If the victim still managed to get away, it made him easier prey the next time, because after taking out the remaining eyeball, it was merely a matter of pounding at the poor beast until either Holding got too tired to lift his club again, or the sea lion gave up the struggle.

Grilling a steak over the fire always fetched the captain and the mate, who deigned to share the food despite their continuing hostility. Holding, though he tried to shame Andrew Smith for his lack of enterprise, and was derisive when the other simply ignored the taunts, divided up the catch willingly, because the never-ending plague of bluebottle flies quickly spoiled the meat. Otherwise, he and the two officers lived entirely separate existences.

Holding's next project was to build himself a decent hut for protection from the blustery, changeable equinoctial weather. Choosing a spot where the tussock grew high, he cut it down and set it aside to dry. Then he made a set of sturdy poles, bound them into a framework with strips of sealskin, and thatched the roof and three sides. When finished, it measured six by eight feet. After building a bunk inside and making a door that could be lifted into place, he lived comfortably enough to consider himself well fixed.

It was impossible, though, for him not to dwell on how different the situation could have been for the rest of the *Invercauld* castaways, if Captain Dalgarno and his two mates had listened to his advice back in May. The priority had been to find a good camping spot and then build a sturdy shelter. With a strong hut at their backs, Dalgarno could have organized the men into foraging parties to get food for the benefit of them all. As Holding grimly added in his memoir, "It was now late October." In the intervening five months sixteen men had died of privation and neglect, mostly because his advice had not been followed.

"SUNDAY, OCTOBER 23, 1864," wrote Musgrave. "Week passes on after week. Another one has passed like its predecessors, and thus I suppose it will continue till time shall be no more."

He was very depressed. Every spare moment had been spent looking out for a sail, and he had not been able to sleep for fear that a ship might pass by in the night. October was the month that they had all waited for, being the time they could expect the ship Uncle Musgrave and Charles Sarpy should have sent out in search of them, and yet there had been no sign of rescue.

"My eyes are positively weak and bloodshot with anxious looking," Musgrave wrote. He was terrified of going mad—"I was mad once"—but at the same time felt sure he was not insane, because if he did go mad, it would bring blessed forgetfulness with it. Raynal, who as always found Musgrave's awful despondency alarming, recorded him crying out just as he had a hundred times before, "If it only affected myself! But my wife, my children, of whom I am the sole support, are the victims of my misfortune."

Were Uncle Musgrave and Charles Sarpy asleep, or dead? Had they completely forgotten the five men they had sent off on the Campbell Island mission? Musgrave became desperate enough to suggest that he and Raynal take the dinghy and try to get to New Zealand for help, but Harry, Alick, and George were so horrified at the suggestion that he let the idea drop. Perhaps, he thought, his fears were groundless, and a rescue ship would arrive in a mere matter of days—most surely it would come before the end of the following week. As evidence of his growing pessimism, however, he started another garden, planting a few leftover pumpkin seeds and the marble-size potatoes, but with little hope of producing a harvest.

The sea lion cows had still not assembled on the rockeries, so the men were reduced to killing the bull seals as they came on shore to battle for the best breeding platforms. They had been pulling about the harbor in the boat, searching in desperation for game, when Musgrave glimpsed an old black bull on a small island. This specimen, being ancient, was guaranteed to be tough, but their empty bellies growled so voraciously that they stilled their oars and studied him as a prospect for the larder.

The problem, as Musgrave went on to describe, was that he was "lying amongst the rocks close to the water—so close that it would have been impossible for us to have got him if we had landed to attack him." From experience, the men knew that the closer a sea lion was to the surf, the more easily he could escape, and it was no good killing one that had reached the sea, because the corpse always sank. Besides this, the nearer to the water a sea lion was attacked, "the more tenacious it is of life."

Not only was this big old bull right on the tideline, but he'd seen them. "Suddenly, raising his head and looking over a large stone, he perceived us," described Raynal.

The men stared right back, not daring to move in case he took to the water—"would he return to the sea, and so escape us?" Stealthily, Raynal loaded his gun. It was not usually advisable to shoot sea lions, because the explosion simply persuaded them to flop even more quickly into the waves, even if they were mortally wounded. However, he had no choice.

Musgrave whispered, "Don't hurry—give yourself time to take aim."

Raynal knew that already, thinking, "Should I fire? The distance was so great!"

But, as his mind ran on, if he delayed the seal might escape. He made his decision. "I fired. The seal was hit, but not killed: his jaw was broken, and he was stunned."

The men rowed frantically, and jumped out of the boat the instant the bottom grated on shingle. "We leaped on the beach, pounced upon him, and before he had recovered his senses, terminated his existence with our cudgels," Raynal concluded. One of the tusks that had been knocked out by the gunshot was almost four inches long and six inches around at the base.

They had good hunting that day, taking another bull at the western head of the harbor, and seeing more in the same place. "Not very long ago we thought it would be impossible to eat this kind of seal," Musgrave remarked; "and indeed they are not by any means fit for food, for the strong smell of the meat is enough not only to disgust but to stifle a person. But what are starving men to do?" As he went on to say, "Hunger is certainly a good sauce."

Soon, though, the pantry was empty again. The sea was too rough to launch the boat, so Musgrave, with Raynal, Alick, and George, trekked along the southern coast—but, Raynal wrote, it was "all in vain, for there were no seals." They walked ten miles, but still without success, and then at noon belatedly realized that they had passed the point of no return, and that it would be impossible to get back to Epigwaitt before nightfall. "And what good was to be gained by returning with empty hands?" Raynal demanded of the rest. "Was it reasonable?" They decided it was not, and kept on across the isthmus of Musgrave Peninsula, still hunting fruitlessly for seals.

By dusk all they had found was a basketful of mussels, which they roasted. After eating them Captain Musgrave was almost immediately doubled up in agony—"he endured the cruellest pain," Raynal recorded anxiously. Musgrave remembered later that he had eaten too many, and in too much of a rush, "and this, with walking and fasting so long, very likely made me ill. This is picnicing in reality," he ironically commented. "God protect us from having much of it to do!"

Raynal found Musgrave's sudden prostration terrifying, as his greatest dread was that illness or accident should strike their small group. "I have experienced, on the appearance of the slightest indisposition, a terrible fear," he had written earlier, going on to predict, "I am persuaded that the death of any one of us, in our present circumstances, would more injuriously affect the *morale* of the others, and perhaps be attended with fatal consequences to all of us. So my constant prayer is, that in our already severe afflictions, God would spare us this trial."

While Musgrave was hunched over with the cruel spasms in his gut, darkness fell. The footing was far too treacherous for them to attempt to get back to the house in the dark, so for fifteen hours they huddled close together behind a rock, soaked through, icy cold, one in terrible pain and the others desperately hungry. The dawn did not break until nearly eight, and then revealed a chill, dank fog, which was followed by a dense, fine, icy rain. Summoning their strength, they started to retrace their steps along the shore, with Musgrave and Raynal in the lead, and Alick and George following behind. "We spoke but little; our reflections not being of a nature to inspire one another," wrote Raynal—but then a rattle of pebbles sounded from behind an outcrop of rocks. "We halted, that we might listen the more attentively."

They saw a head pop up—"a young seal preparing to descend to the water." She saw them; she saw their lifted cudgels; she hesitated; she turned toward the trees—and Raynal quickly fired his gun before she could get away.

His aim was unerring; the bullet went right through her head. Miraculously, weariness vanished. Cutting up the carcass, they shouldered the pieces and marched back in triumph to Epigwaitt, where Harry, "on seeing us return, shed tears of happiness; the poor boy had spent a night of agony in thinking of all the misfortunes of which we might have been the victims."

Providentially, this was the first of many seals. Rushing out of the hut one morning in early November, the men were delighted to see a band of about twenty sea lions in the bay opposite. More arrived over the following few days, and according to the men's calculations the pupping season was only five or six weeks away.

"Not only was their return a guarantee to us against famine," Raynal exulted, "but it had also the same comfort as the arrival of swallows in France or England: it announced the approach of summer."

FIFTEEN

Summer

With the start of the southern summer, seabirds came flocking to the cliffs about Port Ross in the far north of Auckland Island, fighting each other for the best nesting terraces. Robert Holding spent many hours studying them, fascinated with their competition for territory, and their clever way of flying high with crabs or shellfish and then dropping them to crack the shells.

Watching them glide in from far across the sea inspired new hopes of rescue, and caused him to look thoughtfully at the small island—actually Rose Island, but named by him Rabbit Island—on the far side of the five-hundred-yard channel. Because it was closer to the open sea, it was a better place to watch for passing ships. He glimpsed seals on the distant rocks, so he knew there would be a food supply if the camp was shifted there. The problem was how to cross the passage.

His solution was to build a coracle by making a wickerwork frame out of wattle branches and covering it with skins. However, it was too difficult to accomplish by himself, so he approached the others with the proposal. To his relief, Dalgarno and Smith listened with unusual interest. "We had always been very careful of the seals' skins, which we stretched and used for a good many purposes, principally for making shoes," Andrew Smith noted. Accordingly, they had quite a number, of which the hides of bulls were considered the best for the boat, being the strongest.

Having sorted out some of these, the trio hunted for suitable wattles, which they found two miles from the place where Smith and Dalgarno were camped—"which distance we walked every night and morning," Smith went on. While Smith and Dalgarno cut and trimmed the branches, Holding experimented with weaving, finishing up with a frame that he described as about eight feet long by perhaps three feet wide and about sixteen inches deep.

"She was sharp at both ends; her bottom and sides were wrought in the same style as a basket," Smith recorded later. "It required five of the skins sewed together with strips of themselves to cover the wicker work. We cut the skins into the shape of the frame, and then stretched them taut to the gunwales."

Though weaving the wicker frame had been reasonably straightforward, lashing the skins to the wood gave them a lot of trouble, because of their lack of tools, but they managed to bore holes with an awl made out of a stub of hardwood. The job would have been much easier if they had thought to steam the skins to make them easier to stretch, but Holding excused the others as well as himself with the admission that none of them had had any kind of experience in this kind of work.

They finished the job on November 5, and launched her with some ceremony. The craft was only big enough for one, so Holding, being the common seaman, was given the job of poling off to try out her sailing qualities. They were awful, as he swiftly found out. Not only did she leak like the basket she truly was, but the seal hides became so heavy and soggy that she was almost unmanageable.

However, Holding returned to shore with three lobsters, which he had scooped off the surface where they had been feeding. He had seen a great many more crawling along the bottom, but the coracle had been too unstable for him to lean over the side and reach down for them. Accordingly, he made a long hook out of fencing wire, and carried it with him the next day when he went out again. It worked so well that he returned with four dozen after just two hours of fishing. Unhappily, however, it was a short-lived treat, because a couple of days later the lobsters vanished. Like the limpets earlier, their spawning season was over.

At the same time, the number of sea lions diminished dramatically, as the bulls retired to their old rookeries to meet the females, who were hauling themselves ashore to pup. Remembering the seal life he had sighted on Rabbit Island, Holding decided to cross over the five-hundred-yard channel "or die in the attempt." After making a couple of oars and telling Dalgarno and Smith not to expect him back for a few days, he set off, taking his club to keep body and soul together while he was away.

The attempt did indeed almost cost Holding his life, because, as he admitted, he was "wrong for once," in miscalculating the tide. Then an oar snapped as the ebb carried the increasingly waterlogged coracle out to sea. Just as he was giving up hope, an eddy caught hold of the sinking boat and whirled him up into the surf. By this time Holding was up to his waist in water, but he managed to bail out the boat and drag her up the beach.

The coracle needed stripping, drying out, and reassembling, but once he had done that and made a new oar, he circumnavigated the little island, landing every now and then to inspect the scenery. It was about a half mile wide and a mile long, with high bluffs on the seaward side that sloped gently to the bay; the tussock was busy with rabbits, and the shores seemed to have a good seal population too.

After camping the night, Holding stalked and clubbed a sea lion pup. "Poor little fellow," he added, "it did look like a shame to kill it." The rabbits had eaten every blade of grass and eradicated the *Stilbocarpa* herbs, but nonetheless, after Holding drifted back on the breast of the incoming tide, he told the others that he thought it would be a better camp than the place where they were currently living.

The problem was getting all three there, as the leaky, unstable coracle couldn't carry more than one man. "It was now proposed that we should go back and knock down the last house we were in which was built of wood, and try to build another and better boat with it," Smith later reminisced. According to Holding's account, Holding himself was the one who made the suggestion.

The three of them trekked back to Hardwicke, which meant that Dalgarno and Smith were finally forced to face the sight of Mahoney's dead body. He was reduced to bones and moldering clothes, but nevertheless they couldn't bring themselves to touch the remains, let alone give him a decent burial. Instead, they worked around the corpse to detach serviceable boards from the derelict walls.

Using stones as hammers, they drove out the rusted nails and wrenched away the planks. Then, after Holding had cut them into lengths with the adze, they took away as many as they could carry. Back at the camp, they used the boards to build a boat that was eight feet long, thirty inches wide, and twenty-four inches deep. This had used up only about half of the available wood, so, as Holding later related, he requested the other two, who up to now had never "hurt themselves with work," to take the boat to Hardwicke, lash the remaining boards into a raft, and tow it back to the camp.

They started off in the morning, and Holding watched them until they were around the point and out of sight. He expected them back before dark, but night fell and morning dawned before they returned—with neither raft nor boat. When he asked what they had done with the planks, they said that the raft had caught in some weeds, and so they had tied it up. However, when he went to look for it, the raft had been carried away by the sea. So, Holding asked, where was the boat? Beached, they told him. Holding said that he hoped it was pulled well up, and they assured him that it was, but when he hurried to the place they indicated, the boat was gone as well.

According to Smith's version, the culprit was a heavy gale, "which brought a great swell onto the beach, and carried off our boat before morning." Whatever the truth of the matter, the result was the same—the three *Invercauld* survivors had to build another vessel. "This renewed attempt was on the whole very successful," wrote Smith. "Indeed the boat was somewhat better than the other one—we had gathered some experience by our former work."

Holding agreed with this, adding that they were lucky that there were suitable boards still available at Hardwicke. Before the boat was finished he strengthened the lower part of the sides with a wale—a double plank—to keep it stable, and this time he made sure that it was fitted with a good strong painter made of plaited strips of skin. "I think this was about November or December," Andrew Smith added.

AT EPIGWAITT THE MEN were delighted to see the weather improve. With the dawning of December, blue sky was a much more familiar sight, though occasionally winter would return briefly and without warning—the temperature would abruptly plunge to zero, and then soar to over 50° Fahrenheit, a strange effect that Raynal theorized was caused by icebergs floating by. Looking back, Musgrave meditated that while the winter had been bitterly cold and often foggy, it had not been as severe as he feared.

He, like Raynal, expressed his vast relief to see the sea lions return. During that first week the men went out and got four, "and saw upwards of fifty within the distance of half a mile. The shores appeared to be literally crowded with them," he wrote.

Depressingly, however, there was still no sign of a ship. What were Sarpy and Uncle Musgrave thinking? Surely they had informed the colonial government that the *Grafton* had failed to return—which they should have done, "at the outside, five months after we sailed." However, it was becoming more obvious as the weeks dragged by that they had neglected even that basic duty, "for the New South Wales Government is not slow to move in such matters." He and Raynal had climbed to the mountain crest they had named the Giant's Tomb—"I suppose we had a clear view all round of not less than fifty miles; but no sail blessed our longing eyes."

They had then trekked up another mountain, farther north,

and studied the northeast coastline, taking renewed note of the treacherous reefs that straggled into the sea for as much as ten miles off shore. "I hope no vessel will go humbugging about these places looking for us," Musgrave wrote anxiously; it would be ironic indeed if a rescue ship arrived, only to be wrecked itself. Finally, he and Raynal gave up and returned to Epigwaitt, but not before "setting fire to the homeward side of the mountains; it was very dry, and burnt well all night, and would have been a good beacon for anyone near the island." However, the days dragged by with still no sign of rescue, and Musgrave's depression deepened.

"At times his exasperation grew so violent that his mind wandered," remembered Raynal; "and he adopted the wildest resolutions." Again he proposed taking a small boat and sailing alone to New Zealand. When Raynal pointed out this not only would deprive the others of the dinghy, which was necessary for their survival, but was tantamount to deliberate suicide, Musgrave exclaimed, "What matters it, since we are destined to die here? Better bring our misery to an end at once. What use of living? Of what profit is life in such circumstances as ours?"

Raynal could have heartened him by pointing out that their circumstances were surprisingly comfortable, considering what they had been through, and that under Musgrave's leadership they had accomplished a great deal. Instead, as serenely optimistic as always, he said that he was certain a ship had been dispatched. It had probably been compelled to put into some port, perhaps in New Zealand, so, "why give way to melancholy? It was but a delay of days, or, at the most, of weeks."

The *Grafton* castaways' remedy for depression was, as always, to immerse themselves in hard work. As Raynal observed, strenuous activity had already proved their salvation. Musgrave busied himself setting up the lookout post, "going to much more trouble than is absolutely necessary, so as to divert my mind as much as possible from melancholy thoughts and forebodings. To judge by the pains I am taking with it," he added wryly, "any one would suppose that we intended to pass the remainder of our days here, which may be the case; but if life and health are spared me, I shall not remain here another twelve months, if I go to sea in a boat and drown like a rat."

Raynal, too, was busily employed. At long last the leather steeping in his tannin solution was ready to be worked, much to the relief of them all. They had been wearing clogs whittled out of wood, which were dangerous on the stony beach but were better than the moccasins they stitched out of green skin, which smelled horrible, absorbed water, and rotted to pieces on their feet.

The soaked hides had gone red, hard, and wrinkled, but after they had been taken out and partially dried, the men stretched them out on the inside walls of the hut, where the heat of the fire finished the drying process. "A few days afterwards they were dry, and the largest creases had disappeared," wrote Raynal; "in fact, they furnished us with excellent leather."

In order to manufacture shoes from that leather, however, he needed cobbler's tools. Two awls of different sizes were made out of sailmaker's needles, one fine, one stout, which were inserted into hafts of ironwood. Then, in a group operation, lots of little wooden pegs were manufactured. Raynal found a plank made of Norwegian fir, and cut it into many little pieces, each about an inch in length, which he handed to Alick, who split them into matchlike wedges about a tenth of an inch in thickness.

Then the other sailors finished off the pegs by shaping one end into a four-sided point.

Cobbler's thread was another challenge. Raynal went to the wreck and scraped some dry tar out of the seams of the hull, which he brought back to the hut, warmed, and mixed with sea lion oil. Taking long threads unraveled from old canvas, he spun them together with hairs from the manes of sea lion bulls, and after dipping them in his pitch he had a strong, rigid yarn that served his purpose. He also carved shoemaker's lasts, having to make several attempts because the wood he was working on split rather easily. Finally, he produced a pair of these cobbler's forms, and "*thought* myself successful, but experience afterwards showed me that I had been mistaken."

Having lasts, Raynal set to work on the shoes. "At the end of a week's hard labour I had produced a pair which perhaps a village cobbler's apprentice might have induced a ploughman to accept for wearing in furrowed fields," he self-deprecatingly remarked. However, he was pleased enough with the result—until he tried to pull the wooden cobbler's lasts out of the shoes. Not only had he hammered a lot of the pegs into the last itself, but the fit of the shoe on the last was so tight, and the opening of the shoes so small, that the combination seemed irretrievably welded together.

Raynal finally got the lasts out, but only by splitting the shoes down the uppers, which weakened them sadly. Obviously, he had to devise a better method. Cutting each shoemaker's last crosswise into a heel piece and a toe piece helped, but the two halves moved about so much that it was hard to manipulate the leather around them. In the end he hit on the idea of joining the two pieces with a wedge that held them firmly together while he worked, but could be pulled out with a string that had been fed through a hole in the wedge, so that the two bits of the last fell apart and were easily removed from the finished shoe.

The final result was a resounding success. Raynal, having made excellent footwear for himself, manufactured a pair for Captain Musgrave, who warmly recorded in his journal that Mr. Raynal "proved himself a skilful shoemaker, although he had had no previous experience." Soon all five had shoes, the seamen learning the cobbler's art from Raynal.

"I will not go so far as to pretend that our *chaussures* could have figured advantageously among the elegant exhibitions of our best Parisian shoemakers," said the Frenchman; "but then *elegance* was not the problem *we* cared about solving. We had manufactured for our feet a solid defence against damp, cold, and a rough soil; our end was fully attained."

SIXTEEN

Raynal's Forge

Christmas dawned a fine and sunny day, but nevertheless it was a miserable reminder of how far away they were from home. "It was the 25th of December—*jour de Noël*—a day of sacred rejoicing for all Christians, of domestic happiness for all families," wrote Raynal, in a rare mood of utter gloom. He found the day one of the most painful yet—"It was impossible for me to undertake any work, or fix my mind upon the reality. My thoughts flew away, beyond the seas, to my native land." Here he was seated under the trees in the sun with the sturdy cottage they had built at his back, but he imagined snow-drifted streets thronged with merrymakers, church bells clanging in the frosty air, the singing of choirs—"how keen was my suffering when I reflected that *I* could take no part in all the mirth, that I was separated from it by an impassable abyss!"

Worse still, he pictured his elderly parents sitting alone by their fireplace. "Their hair was white, their faces were worn and wrinkled; they wore mourning attire," and they were weeping for their son, "whom they believed to be dead." Horrified by the vision, Raynal leapt to his feet and looked around wildly.

"My companions were lying on the ground, silent, their coun-
tenances dark with the dreariest melancholy."

This was not good enough! "With a firm, strong voice"—as
he put it—Raynal upbraided them, reminding himself as well
as all the rest that giving in to despair just because it happened
to be Christmas Day was weak and cowardly, and achieved
nothing useful at all. "If men abandon us, let us save ourselves."
Somehow, by their own devices, they would escape from this
prison! "Courage, then, and to work!" he cried.

The men looked at him blankly, startled by his abrupt pas-
sion. Then, someone ventured to ask, probably sardonically,
what kind of scheme he had in mind this time.

"We're going to New Zealand," he firmly announced.

That, as someone else pointed out, was impossible. New Zealand was two hundred eighty-five miles away. The only boat
they had at their disposal was far too small and frail for such a
rough, long passage.

Raynal agreed. So they had to make another craft, he said—
"a larger and stronger one."

The audience response to this bold ambition was not at all
encouraging—"they did not welcome my proposition so eagerly
as I had expected," he wrote. "Some turned pale, and were silent
before the terrible prospect of venturing on a sea incessantly
vexed by storms; others objected the insurmountable difficulties
which, according to them, must necessarily prevent the execu-
tion of such an enterprise."

Captain Musgrave had already considered knocking up a
small vessel out of the wreck of the *Grafton*. "If nothing comes
after us, we shall commence at the New Year to pull the *Grafton*

to pieces, and try what we can do with her bones," he had written back on October 30, when he was coming to grips with the awful realization that the long-awaited month had passed by without rescue. "It is an undertaking the success of which I am exceedingly doubtful of," he privately admitted, however. "If we had had tools I should have tried what we could have done long before this time; but who expected that we should be left here unlooked for like so many dogs!"

After more thought, he had rejected the idea, for the good reason that they did not have the necessary carpenter's tools, being limited to an ax, an adze, a hammer, and a gimlet—"a mighty assortment to take our ship to pieces, and build another one with, if even there was any carpenter or blacksmith among us, which there is not." So now, though he privately felt as if he would "go to sea on a log in preference to dragging out a miserable existence here," he kept quiet.

Raynal was silent too. Instead of making another effort to persuade his fellow castaways, he made up his mind to start on the project by himself, because he reasoned that a "successful beginning would be the most powerful argument to convince my companions." Being fully aware that the lack of carpenter's tools was the major stumbling block, his first move was to set about building a forge—"that is to say, of a furnace, an anvil, and a pair of bellows"—so he could manufacture the implements they needed.

The last of these three items, which promised to be the most difficult to construct, was the one he tackled first. Early next morning he went to the wreck, pried off "a few sheets of copper, a tolerable large quantity of broad-headed nails, and numerous planks," and got back to shore with his booty just as the tide came in.

Then he set to work. First, he made three wooden panels out of narrow planks that he pegged together and caulked with tow, "which I procured from untwisted ropes." With his knife, he shaped these panels so that they were semicircular on one side and came to a point on the other. The middle plank, the longest, was fitted with a copper tube, which narrowed at the far end, and which he rolled himself, joining the long edges by folding and doubling them over each other, "just as tinmen do." He enclosed the base of this tube with "two little pieces of wood hollow in the middle, which, when brought close together, formed *une sorte de virole*" — a ferrule, or collar. "This I fastened with pegs to the extremity of the panels."

The pointed sides of the two other panels were joined to this middle panel by hinges made of sealskin, so one panel was above the central one, and the other below. "In this way," he went on, "they were movable, could rise or sink, as wanted, on the middle piece, which remained immovable, when the bellows were fixed in their place between two posts erected in the rear of the fire." Holes were bored in the middle of two of the panels, and fitted with leather valves. "Finally, I completed this wonderful instrument by covering the sides with seal skin of a suitable shape, nailed to the edges of each of the three panels."

The men were now the proud owners of a double-action forge bellows capable of furnishing a continuous jet of air, and were suitably admiring. When Raynal asked his comrades whether they had changed their minds about building a boat, a "unanimous shout of assent was the reply," and all three sailors immediately offered to help out with the work.

THE SUCCESS OF THIS project posed yet another problem, however. As Raynal pointed out, back in the early days they had been able to devote most of their time to house building, because they had had the provisions saved from the wreck. Now they were almost entirely dependent on sea lion meat, and if the boat was to be built, two of the men would have to take over the whole of the hunt, which up to now had been the job of them all. The challenge was "bravely accepted by George and Harry, the two youngest," Raynal wrote. "Upon them alone fell the heavy labour of hunting and fishing, as well as of cooking and washing, the repair of our clothing, and the management of our household affairs."

Alick took on the task of supplying the forge with fuel, a responsibility that used up close to twenty-four hours of each day. Not only did he have to cut firewood, but he had to turn it into charcoal. This involved making a pile of wood from seven to nine yards thick and then overlaying it with turf so that it would smolder in the middle. The wetness of the peat was a problem, because it either extinguished the fire by dampening it, or else dried into an airtight shell, which had the same effect by blocking the supply of oxygen to the embers. Consequently, Alick had to lay the turf very thinly, watch it for cracks, and, if any chinks appeared, block them with a pellet of fresh peat. This meant he had to check the fire a score of times in the night—"Yet he laboured to the very end without a single complaint. Such absolute self-denial is above all praise," as Raynal declared.

The Frenchman's description of Musgrave's contribution was somewhat more muted. "As for Musgrave, he assisted me in building the boat, as well as in the labours of the forge," he wrote. Musgrave himself displayed very little enthusiasm, saying, "We shall shortly commence to pull the schooner to pieces, and I have no doubt but we shall feel truly interested in the work of trying to get away. I hope we may succeed," he added on a dubious note. "It is quite true that by energetic perseverance men may perform wonders." The men were all "very sanguine," but he did not feel "quite ready to commence yet."

Instead, according to his own account, he was deeply involved in a different project, that of building a substantial lookout hut—so he and Raynal could live apart from the men. "Raynal and I have not finished our new place, where we intend to live," he wrote. Raynal himself made no mention of this. Back in November, after he and Musgrave searched for a suitable site for a lookout hut on Musgrave Peninsula, he had dismissed the project as unworkable. "One of us being necessarily kept at home to attend to our various domestic cares, three only would be left to go in search of food, and to carry provisions to our sentinel. This would never suffice. And when the bad weather rendered navigation impossible, what then?" The plan was nothing but "a chimera conceived in a moment of illusion," he said, and decided emphatically, with no further ado, "We would abandon it."

So Musgrave's idea that he and Raynal should live in splendid isolation in the lookout hut had never been discussed with Raynal himself. Certainly, the Frenchman would have dismissed the notion out of hand. Not only was it physically impossible for Alick, George, and Harry to build a boat by themselves, as well as hunt for game, look after Epigwaitt, and get provisions to the lookout hut, but he was utterly firm in his conviction that they could only survive if they worked and lived as a close group. Also, he was far too busy at the forge to spare the time to work on another house, let alone argue about it. However, Musgrave clung to this private fantasy for some weeks, which indicates that he had become delusional.

He was extremely depressed, commemorating the New Year by glumly noting that it marked the one-year anniversary of their arrival in the Auckland Islands, "and in all probability another will at least pass before I get away, unless by chance of some sealers coming in the meantime." He had given up the last dim hope that Uncle Musgrave and Sarpy would meet their responsibilities, and was in very poor health. His hair, which had gone quite gray, was falling out, and he was afflicted with a plague of boils.

Though the rookeries were busy with calving cows as January drew on, Musgrave remained miserable—"I have never suffered as I do now; it is no use talking about what I have suffered—God alone knows that extent of that since I have been here," he wrote. At last, however, he took an interest in the boat building. Together he and Raynal made a shed to house the forge, roofed with sheets of copper torn off the hull of the wreck. A brickwork furnace was constructed inside it, and the bellows set up horizontally between two stout posts at the rear of the hearth. A block of iron from the old ballast of the schooner served as an anvil, and Alick accumulated a good stock of charcoal for fuel.

"On the morning of 16 January," wrote Raynal, "our forge was set to work for the first time. The charcoal glowed and crackled," he went on; "and the bellows, manoeuvred by Musgrave, gave forth a sonorous roaring, which to our ears seemed the sweetest music in the world." The first job was to manufacture a pair of strong pincers out of two rust-corroded bolts, so that he would be able to manipulate red-hot pieces of metal without getting burned. Naturally, not having tongs to hold the bolts still, it was a tricky job — "what trouble I underwent before I succeeded in fashioning this simple tool!"

Every time Raynal despaired, however, Musgrave would tell him to take courage. "Try again," he would say, according to Raynal's description. Then, when at last Raynal succeeded, "Bravo!" Musgrave cried; "victory is ours! Look at the master blacksmith, the most accomplished in his trade! To work! Let us beat the iron while it is hot!" As for Raynal himself, he was not ashamed to confess that he wept for joy.

By the end of January he had three pairs of pincers of different sizes, three punches, a mould for nails, a pair of tongs, a cold chisel for cutting iron, a large hammer for beating it, and a stock of carpenter's tools. According to Musgrave, the men, meantime, had been lightening the wreck of the schooner by taking down the lower masts and removing the last of the iron ballast. They then secured seventeen empty casks about her bows, hoping to get her higher on the beach, and make it easier to strip off her planking, as otherwise they had to work at low tide, waist-deep.

However, the remains of the *Grafton* proved to be impossible to shift, mainly because she was so weighty. "She is built of very heavy hard wood," wrote Musgrave. Originally she had been constructed out of "the wreck of a Spanish man-of-war; but I am sorry to say they took care not to put any copper bolts in her: but perhaps there were none in the original wreck. But they have not been sparing with the iron," he added. "She has got any quantity of that about her." The iron was very useful, but copper would have been easier to work, and not nearly so rusty.

The plan was to build a ten-ton cutter—a decked craft, perhaps thirty-five feet long, most probably rigged for a big gaff mainsail, a triangular staysail, and a jib set from a running bowsprit. By the end of the first week in February they had the blocks for this laid down, and curved timbers had been cut from suitable rata trees, ready for the framework of the hull. Now all they needed was the tools, the most important being an auger, a large drill used for boring holes in the heavy wood, into which strong wooden pegs called "tree-nails" would be inserted to join the pieces of the framework together. "Mr. Raynal is Vulcan; he has had some little experience in blacksmithing, which will now be of the greatest service to us," wrote Musgrave. Raynal had produced a lot of tools already, but the job of twisting the biting bit of a big auger promised to be very taxing indeed.

Everyone "works cheerfully and well," Musgrave went on; his best hope was that nothing would happen to dampen their ardor. He had not a notion how long the job would take, "having had no experience in shipbuilding. I must see how the work progresses before I can form any idea." They all labored from six in the morning until six at night. By the beginning of March Musgrave's hands were "so stiff and swollen with hard work that I can scarcely guide my pen." Within a week of writing this he had to stop working altogether, as his hands became so inflamed with boils that he had to wear a sling.

Worse still, Raynal, after many attempts to manufacture that critical auger, was forced to give up in despair. "We have got the keel, stem, and stern-post of the craft, and a number of timbers ready for bolting them together," wrote Musgrave; "but also here we are stuck fast, and find ourselves unable to go any farther. Mr. Raynal has made a saw, chisels, gouges, and sundry other tools. His ingenuity and dexterity at the forge have indeed surpassed my expectation, but making augers has proved a hopeless failure."

It almost broke Raynal's heart. He had done his absolute best, but turning the crucial spiral point at the end of the auger proved impossible with the tools and materials he had on hand—"For two whole days, I recommenced this operation again and yet again; each time I burned my iron, and, instead of finishing my work, destroyed it." Worse still, he had come to the conclusion that the task of building a ten-ton vessel was beyond their resources. He had been vastly overoptimistic; he hadn't realized that it would require such "an enormous amount of material, both of wood and iron," or that they "should be obliged to 'create' every piece with infinite trouble, the timbers of the old *Grafton* having no longer the necessary suppleness." It was no good going to the forest for the vast amount of planking that would be needed, the trees being so twisted.

In addition, he "had wholly failed to realise the immense number of nails, bolts, pegs, and the like, it would be requisite to manufacture." The problem "was the time so great a work would demand; I could not, all things considered, estimate it at less than a year and a half, or perhaps two years!"

Raynal had to brace himself to make this awful pronouncement, and, once he had spoken, the four others stood and stared at him in blank, disbelieving silence. For Musgrave the news "went like a shot to my heart." Already they had faced the hard reality that they were never likely to be rescued, and now this last hope was dashed. It was no wonder, as Musgrave grimly noted, that every face betrayed utter despair.

SEVENTEEN

Boats

In the far north of Auckland Island, the three last survivors of the wreck of the *Invercauld* successfully crossed the channel to Rabbit Island in their second, much more strongly built boat—which, at first seemed to be an excellent move. While January had been a stormy, gale-racked month, February had been blessed with unusually constant fine weather, and the cheerful sun shining on meadows that had been closely cropped by multitudes of tasty rabbits, and shingle beaches where sea lions and their newborn pups were bound to be in abundance, raised their spirits dramatically.

Finding good shelter on the side facing the bay, Dalgarno, Smith, and Holding chose a site about thirty yards up from the beach to build a hut under a sheltering tree. Then, however, Holding found to his disgust that he had forgotten the spade, which, with a few other implements, he had carried from Hardwicke to the camp on the promontory. As evidence of how his relationship with the captain and mate had altered, he promptly ordered them to take the boat across the channel to the old camp and bring him the tools, instead of rowing over to fetch them himself.

Apparently quite cowed by his constant demonstration of confident know-how, they obeyed, leading to a comic fiasco that could have resulted in still more tragedy. Even though the weather was warm, both men insisted on taking their overcoats, which almost drowned them when they capsized the boat just ten yards out from shore. Holding threw them a line, with the sardonic instruction to make sure they brought the boat and oars with them when they came ashore, but instead they floundered about, hampered by their coats, crying out, "For God's sake, save me, I cannot swim," which he found very amusing. Finally, however, he waded into the water and sorted everything out, and off they rowed again, without incident this time.

After they brought him the spade, Holding sent them to the beach to collect stones for the chimney, and then set to work cutting rectangles of turf from earth that had been cropped bare by the rabbits. When he had enough of these, he built up sod walls on the cleared patch, enclosing an area about eight or ten feet square. Then he cut rafters out of rata branches, thatched the roof, and used the boards left over from the boatbuilding for the floor. The fireplace and doorway were built within the most sheltered wall, and the inside of the sod house was lined with seal skins.

"When finished, we found it very comfortable, I can assure you," wrote Smith. "The bottoms of our beds were of seal's skins stretched upon a stretcher, and then we covered them with some withered grass, and for blankets we used seal-skins." Holding was pleased with the result as well, remarking that it must be the only house in history built with only one nail, as all the others had been used for the boats. Not so Captain Dalgarno, who later testified, "Gradually we collected a sufficient number of seal skins to construct with them a little hut, like the cabins of the Eskimos; but it protected us very imperfectly against the continual rains and the severity of that frightful climate."

As solitary by nature as ever, Holding then took himself off on long exploratory expeditions, keeping an eye out for game all the time. Despite the rosy picture he had painted when he was persuading the others to move to Rabbit Island, all three men were constantly hungry, Smith lamenting that because of the rabbits no *Stilbocarpa* plants grew on the island, "and we missed them very much." The sea lions had disappeared with the end of the rutting season, and while there were thousands of rabbits, they were all very lean, hungry, wild, and almost impossible to catch.

Occasionally Holding managed to knock one down with a thrown stone; once, to his amazement, he felled one with the flung adze. "Did I not wish I had a gun!" he exclaimed. As they got desperate, the men cut wood to make two 250-foot hedges, angled to meet each other at one end. Then they drove the rabbits toward the corner, the aim being to trap them there. Instead, as Andrew Smith described, they "jumped over our heads, or over the top of the hedge, or ran through among our feet." He also wrote about a failed attempt to shoot them with bows and arrows. Finally, he tracked the flights of hunting falcons to scavenge the carcasses of rabbits that the hawks had killed.

Holding had better luck when he thrust a hand down what he thought was a rabbit burrow. After the first painful jab, he realized that there was a bird in there—a fluffy chick with a very sharp beak. Ignoring the savage pecking, he hauled it out, killed it, plucked it, and cooked it, and found it very good eating.

He used to walk along the rocks, too, carrying short, stout sticks to kill birds on the wing, though this was only occasionally successful.

However, he noticed while exploring the tops of the cliffs that the roosting seagulls were quite tame, being unused to men, and so he was able to catch quite a few of these with sealskin snares. Apparently uncaring whether he fell or not, he took huge risks, creeping down cracks in the sides of the precipices. Once in a position overlooking a nesting terrace, he would dangle a snare, which he had weighted with a stone, and then drag it along the shallow nests. In this way he could scrape up a dozen fat chickens at a time. After he had done this a few times, flocks of albatrosses would follow his movements, and if a chick happened to fall out of the noose as he was drawing it up, an albatross would instantly follow it down, snatch the bird before it hit the sea, and rapidly tear it to pieces.

Though this dangerous activity currently yielded meat for the pot, Holding was very aware that the birds' breeding season would soon be over, so he also dug a garden and fenced it with brushwood, then sowed it with seeds from the cabbage and turnips that grew wild about Port Ross. "We had very hard work sometimes to keep the life in at all: yet, thank God, we always got a little of something," wrote Andrew Smith, going on to say—though without crediting Holding, "It was about the month of March, I think, when we commenced to clear a small space of ground on which we intended to raise a few turnips and roots, the seeds of which we collected on the island that we had left."

• • •

"Sunday, March 26, 1865," wrote Musgrave. "The sea booms, and the wind howls. These are sounds which have been almost constantly ringing in my ears for the last fifteen months." There was something horribly dismal about the hollow thud as rolling waves crashed against the distant, unseen western cliffs; "sometimes it makes my flesh creep to hear them." Such a wild sound in such a wild place might please lovers of the wild romantic, he ironically commented, but "I could not wish my greatest enemy to be similarly situated."

Musgrave had been even more deeply depressed since Raynal had delivered the news that building a cutter out of the bones of the *Grafton* was impracticable. With indomitable spirit, however, the men embarked on another project, having made up their minds to get to the far south of New Zealand in the dinghy. As Musgrave described, the craft was just "12 feet on the keel, and, I am sorry to say, very old and shaky," but he went along with the scheme, because his "tacit project and unalterable resolution" was to attempt a passage to New Zealand, even if it killed him. The plain, unalterable truth of the situation was that "starvation is staring us in the face, which, it will be admitted, is enough to drive men to desperation."

The plan was to strengthen and lengthen the boat for the voyage. She would need a sturdier mast and stout rigging too. The sails they had been using were full of holes, but by detaching the double layer of canvas that covered the roof of Epigwaitt and replacing it with thatch, they would have the cloth to make better ones.

While Musgrave claimed that the idea of modifying the boat was his, according to Raynal's version of events, the Frenchman himself was the one who had voiced it, at the same time that his shipmates absorbed his message that they could not possibly build a cutter within a reasonable length of time. He had even devised a schedule of work, he said—"put it on the stocks, give it a false keel, which would permit of its being lengthened fully three feet in the stern," raise its gunwales by at least a foot, and finally deck it over.

It is more likely, however, that the idea came spontaneously during a group discussion, just like the evening school and a great deal else. The summer was almost over; within four or five weeks the half-grown cubs would be competent swimmers and start taking to the sea with their mothers, and none of the men felt at all sure that they could survive another winter. It was by now patently obvious that if they were to escape this place, it would be by their own efforts, and they now accepted that the dinghy was their only means of doing so.

The first job was to fell stout trees and roll the trunks to the shore, where they were arranged to make a kind of shipbuilding yard. Once the struts were in place the boat was set upon them, upside down. One of the stoutest planks from the wreck was shaped into a new keel—"a keel longer than the old one," described Raynal—which was attached to the bottom of the dinghy, "solidly riveted by four iron bolts driven into the interior." That done, the boat was turned right way up again, settled on the stocks with her bow facing the water, and then wedged into place so she did not wobble about as they worked on her gunwales.

Despite the clouds of sandflies and the increasingly foul weather, the boatyard was busy from dawn to dusk, the men leaving it only when it was too dark or stormy to continue work. Even then, there was plenty to be done. Raynal labored at the forge, while one of the seamen worked the bellows, because every nail and every bolt had to be made by hand. At the same time, Musgrave stitched at the canvas they had taken from the cabin roof to make sails—something Raynal liked to see him doing during daytime as well, because the captain, while he was a fine sailmaker, was no good at carpentry, and was more likely to ruin things than fix them.

"I remember that one day I was working alone in the shed," Raynal reminisced later. He was busy forging some bolts to fasten new timbers to the boat, and from the corner of his eye could see Captain Musgrave working with the gimlet at the stocks. Then all at once the distant figure stiffened. "Suddenly I saw him ascend the rising ground and walk in my direction. He moved slowly, and with a face as pale as that of a criminal who had just been caught in a guilty act; one hand he held behind him."

Straightening in alarm, Raynal demanded, "What's the matter?"

"All is lost!" Musgrave miserably informed him.

"Why, what have you done?"

Musgrave brought his hand around, and showed him what he had there—the gimlet, with its sharp end broken! It was so reminiscent of the awful failure to turn a spiral on the point of the auger that he was on the verge of tears.

Raynal took one look, then couldn't help a bark of laughter. Only the very tip of the point was snapped off. He sharpened it with the grindstone, and the gimlet was as good as ever.

"TOWARD THE END of March we had attached a new framework to the stern of our boat," wrote Raynal. A stout piece of wood served as the sternpost, with one end set on the extremity of the false keel and the other end extending two feet above the original gunwale. Four bolted strips of iron, two on each side of the keel, bound this new framework to the old one. The same had been done at the forward end. A plank was added above the stem and fixed with two long iron bands, with a ring soldered to them at the bows to hold the end of the bowsprit, and which extended down each side of the bow to the false keel, where they ran along for some distance.

"Our next task was to raise the gunwale or bulwarks of the boat," Raynal continued; "which we accomplished by means of twenty-four new timbers, attached, twelve on each side, to the keel and original hull, rising above the latter fully two feet." To these were fixed twelve joists. "We had now only to plank it," and the sides would be the desired height.

The resourceful Raynal made it sound easy. In reality, the conditions slowed them down and turned the job into a nightmare. Despite the shortening days, the sandflies were perhaps even more malign than they had been the previous year, Musgrave recording that they "alight on you in clouds, literally covering every part of your skin that happens to be exposed, and not only that, but they get inside our clothes and bite there."

Last autumn, he had been able to escape them by retreating to the house. However, if they wanted to get the boat fixed by April, which was the target he had set, "we must grin and bear it, and persevere to get the job done." Accordingly, his face and hands were grotesquely swollen—"I do not think that at the present moment I could place the point of a needle on any part of my hands or face clear of their bites."

Musgrave had chosen April because the equinoctial gales

would be over then, and they could expect reasonable conditions for the passage. However, as he admitted himself, the deadline was far too tight. The weather was against them, the latter part of March bringing terrific gales. They were very hungry all the time too. With the boat out of commission, they were forced to hunt the woods about Epigwaitt, but the sea lions were scarcer than ever before.

Consequently, the day in early April that Musgrave had chosen to launch the boat was devoted instead to hunting for game. Right after breakfast all five men set off in different directions, some coming back with a handful of fish, others with nothing. As Musgrave put it, "we were all looking very blue at each other," when in came Alick in triumph, with a haunch over his shoulder, and the news that he had killed two large cows.

A meal was swiftly cooked and eaten, to give them strength, and then they set out to retrieve the rest of the meat, hastening because dusk was near and the tide was on the flood, meaning that parts of the beach would soon be under six feet of water. They collected the carcasses and killed two more cows, along with a calf. They got home soaking wet, as it had been raining heavily all the time, but, as Musgrave concluded gratefully, "we have been kindly dealt with, for Providence has always at the last push provided us with something."

There were more difficulties ahead, however. As April stretched toward May winter set in, with incessant gales, snow, and hail. One of their few solaces was the acquisition of another pet. For some time they had noticed a burrowing animal living in the nearby scrub, and when they set a trap in the forge they caught a young domestic cat who had come in for warmth. They gave her a box for a bed, and kept her tied up with a collar round her neck. She liked living at Epigwaitt so much that even after the collar was broken she still hung around, particularly at night. She was good company, enjoyed being petted and played with, and as Musgrave observed, "she soon cleared the house of mice, with which we were dreadfully infested."

Always, however, the overriding concern was the modification of the dinghy. Musgrave had vastly underestimated the amount of work to be done. "Small as she is, there has been a great deal of work about her," he wrote on April 16. "There are about 180 clinch bolts in her, and there will, when finished be about 700 nails and spikes in her. Raynal has had to make all these out of short bolts of all sorts and sizes, belaying pins, &c., welded together and drawn out."

According to Raynal's own description, these were no common nails, being three inches long, square at the head, and very sharp at the point, designed that way to avoid splintering their hard-won wood. The goal was to make fifty nails each day, and no one went to bed until that number had been made, so that it might be after midnight before they shut down the forge.

Despite their dedication, the work progressed with painful slowness. It was not until the start of May, marking the end of their sixteenth month on the Auckland Islands, that they had manufactured enough bolts and nails to start raising the sides of the boat. Whether they could turn the shaky dinghy into a craft substantial enough to cross the tempestuous 285-mile stretch of ocean between Auckland Island and New Zealand, was debatable, but they were all utterly convinced that it was the only hope they had.

Twenty miles to the north, events were proving them wrong —though not to their advantage.

AT RABBIT ISLAND, off Port Ross at the northernmost extremity of Auckland Island, the hunt for food had become very difficult indeed. The nesting seabirds had left the cliff terraces, the sea lions had vanished, and the rabbits were more wild than ever. To get anything to eat, Holding and his companions had to take out the makeshift boat to hunt for shellfish.

Despite the treacherous weather, Holding enjoyed the trips, because little Rabbit Island had come to feel like a prison. As always, he got great pleasure from watching the wildlife. On one such quest he spied sea lions on one of the nearby islets, their presence betrayed by the seagulls flocking and screaming around them. Paddling closer, Holding realized with fascination that the birds were deliberately teasing the sea lions by beating them with their wings and pecking at their heads, because the harassed animals retaliated by vomiting up the contents of their stomachs, which provided their tormentors with a feast.

As well as an interesting lesson in bird behavior, it was a chance to replenish the larder. After clubbing two seals and loading the boat to the gunwales with meat and skins, Holding thought it would be a good idea to shift their camp to this much more promising island. After the three men had conferred and agreed, he went into the scrub that clothed part of Rabbit Island, cutting suitable timber for building a hut. If they were to have any kind of dwelling on the islet, it was necessary to carry freight for a framework there, because it was quite bare of trees.

For a time his work went smoothly, despite an unpleasant fracas after Smith accidentally set fire to the sod house. Then

Holding's timber felling and any plans to move to the other side were suddenly and permanently interrupted.

THE DATE WAS MAY 22, 1865, twelve months and ten days after the wrecking of the *Invercauld*. Holding had broken the handle of his adze, and was heading back to the sod house to fix it. On the way, he heard such screaming that he started running frantically, thinking that the house was on fire again.

Instead, however, it was the captain, jumping up and down on the beach, calling and waving like a madman, and shouting over and over, *"A SHIP—A SHIP—A SHIP—A SHIP!"*

At the same time Holding arrived on the beach, Andrew Smith hurried up from another direction, asking, "What is it?"

"What have you been doing?" the captain wildly demanded. "Where have you been? I've been calling out for half an hour!"

It took some moments to calm Dalgarno down, but then at last they learned that he had glimpsed a full-rigged ship pass to the southeastward; she had been under reefed topsails and had been crossing the end of the channel they had negotiated to get to the islet with the seals.

But where was she now? The captain promised they would soon see her again, when she came around the point. As Holding remembered, it seemed to take forever, but then she reappeared, just as Dalgarno had prophesied. The three men frantically ran a blue shirt up a tall stick for a flag and built a fire, throwing green branches on top of it to send up clouds of smoke.

Then they waited, shivering with suspense. Was the ship going to pass by with the signals unseen? Horrifyingly, it seemed likely—but all at once Smith exclaimed that he'd heard the report of a gun, and then they all saw the ship lower a boat before passing on toward Port Ross. Silently, they watched it draw near.

Just as the boat arrived in the surf, Captain Dalgarno swung round to Holding and ordered him to keep his mouth shut. "Don't *you* speak to them," he said. "*I* will be the one who speaks."

Holding didn't object; as he commented later, he was too full of emotion for words. When the boat arrived they found that the crew did not know much English, anyway. As the halting conversation progressed, they learned that the vessel was the Spanish ship *Julian*—though Dalgarno called her a brig (a two-masted vessel) when he described the incident later, and Holding said she was sailing under Portuguese colors. She was from China, and was bound for Callao with Chinese coolies. "There was a plague raging on board, of which a great number of the Chinamen died," wrote Smith, but the three castaways were too elated at the prospect of rescue to feel any qualms.

Dalgarno, in his report, did not mention the *Julian*'s boat, saying instead that he and his men pursued the ship to Port Ross—"we launched the periagua, which we had hauled up on the shore, and seizing our paddles, rowed vigorously towards her. They perceived us from the ship," he went on. "The peculiarity of our equipment had attracted the attention of the crew, whom we could see grouped in the forecastle, attentively examining us. The officers in the stern-quarters were also observing us, with the assistance of a telescope."

Within moments, according to his version of what happened, the three castaways were standing "on the vessel's deck, where we were received by the captain, and questioned upon the circumstances which had plunged us in so lamentable a situation.

We told him our story," he continued, going on to relate that the tragic tale was received with much commiseration (by those who could understand it), "and from that moment we were welcomed by all with marks of the warmest sympathy."

This tale was nothing but fantasy and delusion. The actual events, as both Smith and Holding described them, were somewhat less elevated. Smith confirmed Holding's story that a boat was lowered while the ship went on to seek her anchorage—she "came close to the island, and sent a boat on shore," he wrote. It was dusk, so the boat's oarsmen were stranded, and the castaways had to put them up for the night in the cramped sod house.

"We made them as comfortable as we could," wrote Smith. For supper, he and Holding fried up some seal meat, "which some of them liked very well." The night, however, was restless. The castaways reeked of rancid oil and sea lion blood, and the men from the *Julian* were literally hopping with fleas.

At dawn Holding borrowed the boatswain's musket and had a fine time bagging three rabbits, using pebbles for shot, as the boatswain had forgotten to bring bullets. Then they all debated what should be carried to the ship. They had nine sea lion hides on hand, and the boatswain, when he saw them, said he could use them for chafing gear in the rigging. Holding helped the boat's crew load them in the boat, and then he, Dalgarno, and Smith "took our places in the boat and left at seven o'clock by the Boatswain's watch." After a lot of trouble and a day of searching, they found the ship in Laurie Bay, Port Ross.

"We were very kindly received; we got a suit of clothes each, and were made extremely comfortable," wrote Smith, referring to himself and Dalgarno. Officers got one kind of treatment, common seamen another. As Captain Dalgarno remembered with patent satisfaction, while he and Smith were entertained by the ship's captain and officers in the after quarters, the stubbornly insubordinate Holding was relegated to his proper station — "Our companion, the seaman, found a place among his forecastle equals."

That settled, the *Julian* lingered long enough in Port Ross to replenish her stocks of fresh water. Then she sailed for South America without troubling to make a search for any other survivors.

It is now more than two months since I wrote," began Musgrave in his journal entry dated June 23, and then gave an explanation for the long gap—"Since that time, we have had the greatest trials and difficulties to contend with." All five men had been struggling to keep meat on hand as well as adapt the dinghy for the long passage, the weather had been against them, with a great deal of snow, and Musgrave had been far too busy to keep any kind of written record.

"Rising at six in the morning, we immediately set to work, and with the exception of the brief intervals necessary for taking our meals, we did not leave off until eleven at night," wrote Raynal later. During the day, if the weather allowed it, they worked on the boat—"in the evening, the forge invariably occupied our attention, as we had to prepare the necessary materials for the morrow—nails, pegs, bolts, and so on. Sometimes Harry or George took Musgrave's place at the bellows, and assisted me to weld and forge the iron; meantime, Musgrave stitched away at the new sails we were making out of the old canvas of the *Grafton* or got ready the rigging for the boat."

All of it was unbelievably difficult. As Raynal described,

where they had anticipated using planking from the *Grafton* to raise the gunwales of the boat, "we found it would not stand bending, although well steamed." This meant that they had had to cut their own timber out of the bush, which, considering the twisted nature of the trees, was a formidable proposition—"Straight trunks, at least six feet in length, and six inches in diameter, the dimensions we required, were rare." Musgrave became their lumberjack, wading through thigh-deep snow to locate suitable trees, fell them, and heave them along to the shore, where the men built a saw pit fitted with a saw that Raynal laboriously fashioned from a piece of sheet iron.

"Each trunk was first squared, and then, according to its dimensions, sawn into three or four planks, about an inch thick, and five inches wide," Raynal wrote—"an exceedingly tedious operation," as Musgrave commented, because their primitive saw needed sharpening every half hour. The shortening of the days also meant that they couldn't work on the boat more than seven or eight hours at a time, and then only if the weather allowed it.

"On the other hand," as Raynal went on in buoyant fashion, "the evenings were long," which gave them more time to spend in the forge, making nails. "Mr. Raynal is still making his hammer ring in the forge," wrote Musgrave in that June 23 entry in his journal, noting that it was one o'clock in the morning. "There has been an amazing quantity of blacksmith work required for that small boat, which he has executed in a surprisingly skilful manner, and he has worked very hard."

As for himself, Musgrave reckoned that in all his life he had never labored as much as he had in the past six months: "We have had sails, masts, and everything to make." Then came yet another setback—"we were all seized with a violent attack of dysentery." They recovered, but Musgrave was "left with rheumatic pains and cramps, which will in all probability cling to me through life."

Food was shorter than ever, the men mostly keeping body and soul together with water and *Stilbocarpa* rhizomes, though occasionally a seagull was shot, and once a dreadfully savaged sea lion was discovered. "One of its fore flippers was entirely torn away from its body," Musgrave wrote, and went on to describe other ghastly wounds. She was a female in calf, and he blamed her condition on a fight with another seal, without thinking of predatory dogs, leopard seals, or sharks. Put out of her misery, she formed a most welcome addition to the larder.

"But, thank God!" Musgrave went on in the late June entry, "we are now in reality on the point of surmounting or ending our wretchedness and misery. The boat is finished, rigged, sails bent, and ready for launching."

The mainyard of the *Grafton* had been turned into an excellent mast, and they had also fashioned a bowsprit. The sides had been planked with steamed boards; the boat had been decked; and all of the seams had been caulked. "Furnished with a mallet and a very thin chisel," Raynal described, "I filled them with tow, made the evening before by Harry and George out of old ropes." They had no tar, so he had concocted a sticky mixture out of lime and seal oil.

The rudder had given him a lot of trouble, especially the design and manufacture of suitable hinges. However, it was now fixed solidly to the stern post and moved obediently at the slightest touch. Another challenge had been the provision of a pump. It would have been suicidal to venture to sea without one, so Raynal, remembering having seen one of the schooner's pumps lying derelict on the beach, went out in search.

"I was not mistaken," he wrote. "I found the pump in the same place. It was much damaged, but as it was ten feet long, I cut off a portion about four feet in length, of which it was possible to make use." With his hatchet, he chipped away at it to get it to the fit he needed—"at its base I fixed a valve; I placed another at the extremity of a piston terminated by an iron tringle, to which I attached a cross-shaped handle; and the result was a capital pump, which we fitted up in the boat, just behind the mast."

Then he followed up yet another idea, one that most probably saved all their lives. He cut three little hatchways in the decking, each about one foot square, and, after making five-foot sheaths out of canvas, he attached them to the edges of the hatches. The plan was for the three men who were sailing the boat to insert their legs in these and draw up the rest of the canvas about their torsos, fixing them in place with bands that hooked over their shoulders. "By this arrangement we hoped to gain a double end: to prevent ourselves from being washed overboard by the waves, and to prevent the water from pouring into the hold of our little bark.

"Moreover," Raynal continued, "as we should have to change places from time to time, to relieve the steersman," they needed good handholds. Accordingly, the men fixed eight stanchions around the deck, each about one foot high and pierced at the top to take a running cord. A half-hogshead of fresh water was set up in the hold, fitted with a tight lid that had a bunghole, and held in place with four planks. Finally, the *Grafton*'s compass was placed on the deck, between two of the hatchways and near the rudder, and similarly secured.

"Our work being completed, it presented to the gaze—at all events, to that of its authors—a very imposing appearance," wrote Raynal. "It was a decked boat, seventeen feet long, six feet wide, and three feet deep. Its capacity was two tons and a half. It was provided with a couple of jibs and a mainsail, in which we could take as many as three reefs." All that remained was to launch her, which meant they had to wait for more moderate weather. Despite this, as Musgrave wrote, "We are all in first-rate spirits, considering the misery with which we are surrounded."

There was one more relatively small task to be completed. To make sure that their hard work was not ruined, the men built a slipway out of planks, forming a smooth gutter that ran down to the low-water mark on the beach. Then at last the great day arrived.

"ON THE 27TH JUNE," recorded Musgrave, "we launched the boat, and took with us such things as we might require whilst lying at Camp Cove"—that being the bay where they would give her the finishing touches. "The flood lapped and bathed the extremity of our 'building-slip'," wrote Raynal.

With Musgrave and Harry on one side, and George and Alick on the other, and Raynal wielding a long lever at the stern, the boat was raised so that the props could be gradually knocked out. "And thus, slowly and tranquilly, step by step, as it were, it entered the liquid element, which soon uplifted it and bore it on its surface," Raynal described. This was the moment to christen her, and so, with marvelous optimism, they named her *Rescue*.

Once in the water, the boat jinked about in an undisciplined fashion, being so light—"There was not a moment to lose; we must quickly place some ballast on board." This was done by Raynal, who lowered himself through one of the hatchways into the hold. A pile of old iron from the *Grafton*'s ballast was lying ready on the beach, and the other men handed it along to him, piece by piece.

Once Raynal had dispersed it along the keel from stem to stern, the boat floated much more steadily. "When the boat was sufficiently loaded—the quantity required was nearly a ton—we covered the ballast with planks, which we nailed to the new framework." This, as on the old *Grafton*, would hold the ballast in place, and prevent the boat from tipping over. Then a load of salted sealskins was added. "Thus ballasted, our bark sank about two feet and a half in the water," so that all that could be seen was the new part of the boat, the old hull being under the water.

Because Musgrave was determined that everyone should go to New Zealand, all five were on board when she was sailed from the slipway to the cove—which was when he felt his first doubts. It was fortunate that the weather was perfectly calm, he admitted—"for on getting the boat into the water we found her so tender, the least movement put her almost on her beam ends; indeed some of the men were quite frightened, and would have gone on shore again." He calmed them with the assurance that they were safe because of the weight of the ballast but neverthe-less, he was disappointed in her himself.

The distance to Camp Cove was just seven miles, but they

didn't get there until dark, and had to camp on shore under a couple of spare sails. The weather trapped them there for two weeks, until July 11, during which time Musgrave changed the ballast around, and also altered the rig "from that of a cutter to a lug sail and jib, which latter rig I find the most suitable."

At the same time, he came to the full realization that it was madness to go to sea with so many on board, so he finally "proposed that two should remain on the island, whilst I and two others tried to reach New Zealand, when, if I arrived safe (of which I had very grave doubts), I would immediately find some means of sending for those who remained."

The others didn't like it, saying, "Well, if any of us are to be drowned, let us all drown together," though Harry did admit that he was not at all happy about going to sea in that "nutshell," and that he would probably agree to stay behind if someone else would stay with him. While the argument dragged on, they used the boat to get to seal rookeries for game, "and the oftener I went out the more I felt convinced that the boat was unfit to carry all of us," Musgrave mused.

The men still put up a fuss: "I now found that I was going to have some trouble with them; they were afraid to go, yet they objected to being left behind." Finally, on July 13, Musgrave decided that two of the men must stay at Epigwaitt, and chose George Harris and Henry Forgès. Harry was selected because he had said all along that he was afraid to go all that way in such a frail small boat, and George because he and Harry had always gotten along very well—"therefore I considered these the proper men to leave behind, giving them everything that we could spare."

They all returned to Epigwaitt, to await favorable weather. "On the 19th of July, a south-west wind began to blow," Raynal recorded; "the weather was clear, though cold (it was midwinter). The hour of departure had arrived." The moment that he, Musgrave, and Alick would be parted from Harry and George was nigh.

The good-byes were heartfelt. The five men had been comrades for the past twenty months. Since November 12, 1863, the day they had departed from Sydney, they had shared the same sufferings and struggles; they had worked in close brotherhood for the good of them all. Because of conscientious leadership, resourceful technology, unstinting hard work, and an outstanding spirit of camaraderie, they had survived unimaginable privations. Now, one way or another, the strange adventure was over.

"We were all of us profoundly agitated," wrote Raynal. Assembling in Epigwaitt for the very last time, they "joined in prayer to God, imploring his assistance for those who, in a frail bark, were about the confront a stormy sea, and those who remained on the rocky isle, to wrestle alone against want and despondency."

Then, with a final embrace by the slipway, they parted, and Musgrave, Raynal, and Alick set sail. The last glimpse they had of Epigwaitt was a plume of smoke from the chimney, beyond the scattered wreckage of the schooner. It was the morning of July 19, 1865. The *Grafton* castaways had been stranded in the Auckland Islands for one year, six months, and sixteen days.

NINETEEN

Deliverance

By eleven in the morning the little *Rescue* was sailing between the two big bluffs that stood on either side of the entrance to Carnley Harbour, and the open sea was before them. At once an icy blast of air filled their sails, sending them scudding over the waves.

Musgrave mistrusted the gale, knowing from experience that the wind would shift erratically about the western side of the compass, and was exceedingly anxious to get well away from the treacherous, reef-ridden northeastern shore of Auckland Island before the first strong gusts hit. "We did not, however, get more than 20 miles from the island before we felt the full fury of a south-west gale," he wrote—but twenty miles was enough.

"We found ourselves about three in the afternoon to the north of the Auckland group," Raynal recorded; "and we passed without accident the line of reefs which forms, in that quarter, a barrier of more than ordinary danger." After that, because of the eastward currents, all they had to do was keep steering north-northwest on the breast of that favorable wind, hoping to reach New Zealand before the worst of the weather began.

"We were making six knots an hour," Raynal went on. His mood at that moment was sanguine. Their destination was "about a hundred leagues" (three hundred nautical miles) away, and with a good breeze they should sail that distance in fifty or sixty hours. The *Rescue* was performing gallantly, though she took in rather a lot of water, forcing them to have a man working constantly at the pump while the other two steered and handled the sails, but "in all other respects she showed herself so seaworthy as to fill us with confidence." All that was necessary was to hang on and hope that the gale did not strengthen.

But as the first dusk fell "the wind increased, and very soon gathered into a hurricane. The surface of the sea was covered with enormous billows; they raised us upon their huge backs to sink under us immediately, and plunge us into the depths of their shifting abysses." Up and down the boat jerked and lurched, many feet at a time, until all three men were dizzy and sick. "It was impossible to think of food; we could do no more than swallow a few mouthfuls of water.

"Night came on," Raynal continued; "the hurricane, stronger and ever stronger, brought with it showers of biting hail and snow, to increase the horrors of our situation." They had already taken in two reefs of the big sail, and now they reduced their canvas still further. "The following day was no better," he went on. The horizon was black and bruised with cloud, and the sea was growing savage. When the *Rescue* sank in a trough, all they could see was gray waves that rose high above their mast, and all they could do was brace themselves for the lift and surge to the top. Even when they felt as if they could have eaten a little of the roast seal they had brought with them, it had become so rancid that they threw it overboard, utterly revolted.

By six in the evening the conditions were too dangerous to keep the little craft before the wind. "The monstrous waves broke around us with a terrible din, and besprinkled us with their phosphorescent foam," he wrote later. Captain Musgrave was forced to give orders to bring the little craft to, and meet the sea head-on, for fear that they would be swamped by an overtaking wave. Within half an hour, however, a huge wave rose high above them, reared its crest, and crashed down on the boat, sending her spinning round and round. According to Raynal, all three men screamed aloud in terror and panic. "We thought our last moment had come. And, in truth, we must have perished," he meditated, "had we not been fastened in our sail-cloth cases."

Luckily, the iron ballast they had secured in the bottom of the boat held firm, and when the huge wave passed on, the *Rescue* was floating upright again. The men gagged and retched to get rid of the water they had swallowed, and sailed doggedly on.

"July 21st," wrote Raynal. "Bad weather; the storm continued." However, they had managed to make sail in the intervals between squalls, and were back on their course. The third night was even more terrible than the previous ones—twice, within a half-hour period, they were seized and spun about dizzily by huge waves. When the fourth day dawned the three men were in a very bad way. Their clothes were completely drenched with the constant torrential rain; they were frozen with cold and faint with hunger; their hands and faces were burned with wind and salt. They stared feverishly north, "in the hope, always and always, of sighting land," but there was nothing but gray, heaving ocean and whipped foam to be seen.

Then, on the fifth morning, they glimpsed a distant bulge on the horizon. They had raised Stewart Island, the southernmost and smallest of the three islands of New Zealand, and were in reach of their destination, as Musgrave put it, "after a miserable passage of five days and nights." He himself had been on his feet the whole time, "holding onto a rope with one hand and pumping with the other," while the other two worked the sails and relieved each other at the tiller. "The wind, although fair, was so strong that we were obliged to lay-to nearly half the time, and the sea was constantly breaking over the little craft; and how she lived through it I scarcely know."

The men's physical state was precarious. "I had not eaten an ounce of food from the time of leaving until we arrived," Musgrave wrote; "and only drank about half a pint of water." Oddly, up until the day they sighted land he had felt no fatigue, but as they came close to the island he suddenly collapsed on the deck with exhaustion. He stayed there for a half hour, gaining just enough strength to get them to land—"but had we been out any longer I feel convinced that I should never have put foot on shore again."

Raynal himself felt so drained that the sight of land triggered just a fleeting sense of joy before he lapsed back into a state of dull endurance. The wind had fallen, though the sea was still turbulent, and they were making very little headway. They had oars, but not the strength to wield them, and so the *Rescue* dipped and rolled, getting nowhere, until they began to wonder if they would perish within sight of their goal. Toward evening a light breeze sprang up, pushing them toward the coast, but because dusk was upon them they were forced to lay to again and undergo another night at sea.

That night seemed endless, but day at last broke, and, said Raynal, "we united all our efforts to loosen sail anew, and at eleven in the morning we entered *Port Adventure*. It was the 24th of July 1865."

AT FIRST THE ARRIVAL was a terrible anticlimax. The hills of Stewart Island surrounded them, covered with primeval forest, apparently quite uninhabited. The waves broke hard on the beaches and the ebb tide was so strong they were compelled to beat to windward to keep out of the current. Raynal described how hard it was to work the ropes, their hands being grossly swollen with cold and salt water, and their arms very heavy and tired. "A few hours more, and nothing would remain for us but to lie down on the deck of the boat and await the coming of death."

Then, doubling a headland, they came across a Maori fishing village, where they saw their first sign of life—a large Newfoundland dog. Holding the dog's lead was a European man. Beyond him, some Maori women were spreading fishing nets on a fence to dry. As the *Rescue* glided in, the dog suddenly caught sight of the boat and began to bark. All those on shore turned and stared in astonishment. "A few moments, and our boat touched the shore," wrote Raynal. "The crowd surrounded it."

The three men were utterly overcome by the sudden attention. Alick passed out with the sudden easing of the strain they had been under, and Raynal and Musgrave had trouble summoning words to answer the flood of questions. Understand-

ing that they had endured an extraordinary ordeal, the crowd
helped them out of the boat, and tenderly assisted them to the
European man's house. Raynal, too overwhelmed by emotion to
talk, walked in silence, but "an immense joy, a profound gratitude, filled my heart." The European's house seemed a haven
indeed, with a garden, an orchard, and a vegetable patch. "The
simple sight of so much comfort was enough to console and
reinvigorate us."

The owner was Captain Tom Cross, who had married "a
young native woman, gentle and affectionate, who had already
borne him several children." Originally a seaman, he had settled here, and made a living out of growing fruit and vegetables
to supply visiting ships, and acting as a middleman for Maori
who wanted to exchange potatoes, fish, and flax for tobacco,
arms, and gunpowder. He was also the owner of a fifteen-ton
oyster-cutter named *Flying Scud*, which he used for fishing, collecting shellfish, and for carrying goods from Stewart Island to
Invercargill, the closest port on the mainland.

Tom Cross's wife immediately made the three men a warm
bath, in which they luxuriated while their clothes were dried.
Washed and dressed, Musgrave, Raynal, and Alick sat down in
front of a huge repast of fried pork, fish, "a pyramid of smoking potatoes," and bread—"bread all warm and fresh from the
oven!" As Raynal went on to comment, they were so hungry
they thought they could eat it all, but their stomachs had shrunk
so much that they could only manage a few mouthfuls—"And
these we had scarcely eaten, before a profound and irresistible
sleep fell upon us."

They slept soundly for twenty-four hours. When they awoke,
to their amazement they found they were at sea again. Blinking

confusedly, Raynal saw that he was in the between decks part of a ship, with his comrades, still asleep, on a mattress beside him. When he stood, they woke too, and the three men stumbled out on deck, to find they were on board the *Flying Scud*. The *Rescue* was with them, drawn behind the oyster-cutter on a tow rope. "A young Maori was at the helm," Raynal wrote, "and Mr. Cross was pacing the deck of his little vessel."

As soon as he saw them he strode up, asking how they were, and they all confessed that they were very hungry again. "Come below," he said, and when they were back in the cabin he hauled out a great quantity of food that his wife had prepared. "After our meal, to which *this* time we did full honour," they returned to deck, where Captain Cross answered their questions by telling them that they were crossing Foveaux Street to the port of Invercargill, where he would get a doctor to check them out, and also make arrangements for a vessel to be sent to Auckland Island to retrieve their two fellow castaways. And how had he spirited them on board his craft without their being aware of it? Some Maori helpers had carried them from the house to the cutter without disturbing "the jolly sleep" they were enjoying.

Getting over the bar and through the breakers into the port proved rather exciting, because it was well past high tide, but under Cross's sure, experienced hand, the *Flying Scud* made it safely. "But such was not the case with the unfortunate *Rescue*," as Raynal wryly described. The tow rope snapped, and the men watched the little boat driven onto the rocks, "where the breakers dashed her into fragments. Thus, in a few seconds, was destroyed, under our eyes, the work which had cost so much labour, and to which we owed our deliverance." Unsurprisingly, the sight brought tears to their eyes.

✦ TWENTY ✦

A Sentiment of Humanity

In the frontier town of Invercargill, it was a fine midwinter morning. Low sun reflected brightly on ice-crusted puddles in the wide, rutted street, and the air was clear, crisp, and very frosty. Horse-drawn drays rattled by, splashing up mud and water. The shadows of shopkeepers passed back and forth across the front windows of their clapboard stores, and housewives hurried along planked sidewalks, the wooden clogs called "pattens" that they wore over their slippers echoing loudly in the morning quiet. At the top of the street a dairymaid sang out for customers as she jingled her milk cans, while a placid cow ambled along at her heels. Beyond the shops, the *Flying Scud* glided into view, breasting to a mooring at the town quay, but the busy citizens took little notice. She was a familiar sight at the dock, just as her owner, Captain Tom Cross, was a familiar sight in town.

Then, however, the passersby saw the three men Captain Cross assisted onto the quay—scarecrow men with haggard faces and eyes set deep in hollowed sockets, their teeth glistening as white as bone amidst the dark tangle of their beards. The trio hobbled stiffly, supporting each other while Tom Cross gently urged them along. People gathered curiously, calling out unanswered questions as the three scarecrow men tottered up the board sidewalk of Clyde Street. At the first store the strangers reached, they stopped, evidently too weak to move any farther. The proprietor came out, spoke to Tom Cross, and then solicitously ushered them inside. After that, the street was quiet, save for the low babble of whispered speculation. After waiting a little while the onlookers dispersed about the township, taking their strange news with them.

That day, the local paper printed a notice:

INVERCARGILL, Thursday, 4:50 P.M.

Captain Musgrave, the mate, and Alick, a seaman, of the schooner *Grafton,* of Sydney, wrecked at the Auckland Islands twenty months since, have arrived. Two of the crew are left on the island.

"On the morning of the 27th July, 1865, I landed in Invercargill, and, in company with Captain Cross, walked up the jetty and entered, I think, the first store we came to—that of Mr. J. Ross," recorded Musgrave. "I had not been there more than five minutes when Mr. John Macpherson, of the firm of Macpherson and Co., came in." After hearing the tale, the merchant instantly offered all the help he could. "He took me at once to Mr. Ellis, Collector of Customs, who was the first person that I should see," Musgrave went on.

After giving Ellis the ship's papers, Musgrave asked for a vessel to be sent to the island to rescue Harry and George, but the government official said he could do nothing. "Mr. Macpherson then waited on the Deputy-Superintendent," but with the same disappointing result. Undeterred by these setbacks, Macpherson took the men to his house, and gave them lunch. Then he walked about town, going from store to store and house to house, soliciting money, blankets, and clothes for the poor destitute men, and telling the story of their astonishing escape from the Auckland Islands.

The response was generous, not just because openhandedness was typical of pioneer society, but also because the locals had a very good idea of the shocking ordeal the *Grafton* men had endured, many Invercargill men being mariners and fisherfolk who plied their trade in subantarctic seas. "For five days and nights did these brave men unremittingly battle with the winds and waves, sustained by the hope of life and the prospect of deliverance," related the *Southland News* on July 29. A benevolent publican, "Mr. Colyer, of the Princess's Hotel," immediately offered accommodation for the three men, free of charge, and the small community took the castaways to their hearts. Over the next two days a hundred pounds was contributed, besides clothing and blankets, which Musgrave proudly—and also to wreak a little revenge on Uncle Musgrave, no doubt—refused to accept without payment. According to his own account, he wrote out and handed to Macpherson "a bill for the amount on Sarpy and Musgrave," the total of which also covered the advance of a sum of money.

François Raynal, safely ensconced in the Princess Hotel, related that "a large number of the inhabitants came to see us, and express their sympathy." Mr. Colyer set apart three rooms for their use, and "Doctor Innes came to see us, and refusing to accept any other remuneration than our thanks, lavished upon us the most assiduous care." The illness that had nearly cost Raynal his life on Campbell Island had returned: "I could hardly move a step without supporting myself on a stout staff."

Raynal, like Musgrave and Alick, was appalled that the government, for unknown political reasons, was unable to do anything about saving Harry and George. Instead, the local officials promised in vague terms "that they would take the matter into consideration at a later date—in fact, as soon as they could. At a later date!" Raynal exclaimed in disgust. While they were waiting for the wheels of government to turn, Harry and George could be starving to death. Even if matters were going reasonably well with them, they were most certainly counting the hours until they learned whether their shipmates had reached New Zealand. There was no doubt about it: "Later meant—too late!"

By now, the indefatigable Mr. Macpherson had raised enough money to cover the cost of sending a ship to Carnley Harbour. Unfortunately, though, the only vessel available was Tom Cross's little oyster-cutter. "Several schooners were expected, but when they arrived they would occupy a certain time in unloading before they could undertake a voyage," Raynal went on—and how could anyone reconcile himself to such a delay?

A public meeting was held, and after due deliberation it was decided that though the *Flying Scud* was really too small, she was so well built, and possessed such excellent sailing qualities, that with a fine, practical seaman like Tom Cross in command, she could carry out the mission—as long as Captain Musgrave went with her as pilot.

As Musgrave himself phrased it, it was considered "incumbent on me to accompany Captain Cross, so as, from my knowledge of the place, to be in some measure a guarantee for the safety of the vessel, as she is not insured." After some heart searching, because he was overwhelmingly anxious to get to Sydney and find out how his family was faring, he agreed to go, even though he was still exhausted from the arduous voyage in the *Rescue,* and had an abscess in his armpit. As Raynal meditated, "Obeying a sentiment of humanity, this noble heart kept down his ardent desire to revisit his beloved family, and though just escaped from the clutches of Death, was willing to confront it anew, in accomplishing what he conceived to be a sacred duty!"

Provisions and gear for the voyage were collected, much of it donated, and the cutter was loaded. Musgrave, who had written a long letter to his wife, entrusted it to Mr. Macpherson to send to Sydney on the first available ship. Then, about four in the afternoon on Saturday, July 29, accompanied by Raynal, Alick, and just about the whole population of Invercargill, he walked down to the docks. "I grasped my friend's hand," wrote Raynal, "and penetrated by an emotion I could hardly restrain, I saw him set out again for the Aucklands, on board the *Flying Scud.*"

THE *FLYING SCUD* SAILED at 5 P.M., "followed by ardent prayers and warmest wishes of this community for a speedy and successful issue to her voyage of benevolence and mercy," according to the *Southland Times.* As it happened, the *Flying Scud* did not get very far that night. By the time the cutter arrived at the bar the tide was too low to cross it, so, as Musgrave noted, "we brought up for the night in a snug anchorage, at a place on the west side of the river called Sandy Point, about six miles from town."

Early the following morning they got through the break-ers with the use of long oars called sweeps (one of which they lost) because the northerly wind was so light. After a daylong struggle with the uncooperative breezes, they wafted into Stew-art Island at dark. Then the wind shifted to the northwest and increased, giving them a quick run into Port Adventure, the same fishing village where the castaways had landed just a week previously, and the place where Tom Cross had his home.

The wind promptly shifted again, this time blowing contrarily from the south, so that they were detained there for a week. Musgrave was still suffering from the aftereffects of the dread-ful passage to New Zealand, writing, "I fear that I am going to be attacked with some serious illness." However, it passed away. One of Cross's sailors rowed him about the port, so Musgrave could study the various anchorages. He stopped to converse with a Maori party who were gathering oysters: "They presented me with four or five dozen, which I must pronounce the finest I have met with in the Southern Hemisphere." The timber that grew on the surrounding slopes was interesting, too, in that it was very similar to the ironwood that had given the castaways such dif-ficulties at Carnley Harbour, but grew straight and tall.

Back at the cutter, the men were busily setting things to rights for "a sea voyage, which I believe the vessel had not yet been called upon to perform. She is nearly new," Musgrave added, "and has been wholly employed in the coasting trade." When the wind at last became favorable, on August sixth, he was exceedingly glad to proceed. They made their start at two in the afternoon, and by eight the following morning were four-teen miles south of Stewart Island.

After that they sailed merrily along—"the little vessel is

dancing about like a cork," he described, going on to say that it was exceedingly difficult to write up his journal, "as it is impossible to sit, or stand, or even lie, without holding on, or being well chocked off." However, the voyage that was starting out so blithely proved to be doomed. When they were within ten miles of the Snares Islands the wind veered to the southwest, which was dead ahead, and then it blew up hard, with a rugged sea. It was too dangerous to lay to in the gale, and so they turned back.

Then they got lost. "It is now 3 A.M.," Musgrave wrote nervously. "We have just hove the cutter to, and will wait for daylight, as we have not yet made the land, although we have run 20 miles farther than where we should have *found* it." There was only one compass on board, and Musgrave had every reason to believe it was faulty. Worse still, there was a strong possibility they were "in the vicinity of those ugly dangers, the Traps Reefs; and if the sea is running high and breaking all over, it will be impossible to see them before we should be on the top of them."

When day broke, there was nothing in sight. At nine in the morning Musgrave took a sight of the sun, but with indifferent results, because "the vessel is tossing about and throwing so much water over, and the sea is so rough." Accordingly, they stayed where they were until he could get better sights at noon — "We are all very miserable, everything wet, and we can get nothing cooked, for the man whom Captain Cross engaged, who was to have done the cooking, is a seasick, lazy good-for-nothing fellow, and can't, or won't do it, and Cross and the other man have to be almost constantly on deck. She is very wet and uneasy, and all this is bad enough, and we all wish the cruise well ended." However, as Musgrave then commented, it was a pleasure compared to his last experience in these seas.

At noon, he succeeded in finding that they were about sixty miles sou'sou'east of the East Cape of Stewart Island—meaning that he was right about the faulty compass—and he and Cross debated what to do next. Musgrave thought of going into a large New Zealand port, like Port Chalmers in Otago, but Cross had a hankering to go back to Port Adventure, because he thought he might be able to get a decent compass there.

So they steered for Stewart Island, arriving just in time to avoid the worst of a very heavy sou'sou'west gale, but only to find that there was no compass available. Someone told them there might be one twelve miles away, at a place called Paterson's Inlet, so Cross thought he would try to get there in the cutter's boat. "This trip is becoming so protracted that I am thoroughly sick of it, and am getting quite downhearted about it," Musgrave despaired; "indeed the question arises in my mind, am I doing an injustice to my family by prosecuting it?"

However, the storm continued, and it would have been madness to leave the harbor. After three days, the gale having somewhat abated, they set sail in the cutter for Paterson's Inlet, "where by good fortune a Mr. Lowrie furnished us with a compass," and the chief of Ruapuke, Tione Topi "Toby" Patuki, offered to lend them yet another. Musgrave was glad to accept, as it appeared to be in a better state than either of the others, and after getting back to Port Adventure—which they had to do with sweeps, as the wind fell away completely—he spent a lot of time and trouble comparing all three compasses, to try to ascertain which one was right.

While he was engaged in this, another gale blew up, this

time from the west-sou'west. "The bay was one continual sheet of foam all the afternoon, and since nightfall it has been thundering and lightning, with frequent showers. The New Zealand coast pilot says that thunder and lightning during a gale is indicative of its long continuance," Musgrave glumly continued. "We have had a great deal of it lately; so what may we expect now?"

The local Maori people prophesied that the bad weather would continue until the moon was past its last quarter, and it looked very much as if they were right. "All night the thunder and lightning were incessant, peal rolling upon peal, and keeping the earth in a continual tremor, accompanied by pouring rain," Musgrave went on. It was the heaviest thunderstorm he had ever known, and, true to the local superstition, even though the wind died away for a spell, it then blew up again from the south, with constant sleet and snow. It was bad enough here at Port Adventure, so what was it like for the two poor fellows on Auckland Island?

It was not until Tuesday, August 22 — thirty-five days after leaving George and Harry in Carnley Harbour — that Musgrave was finally able to record, "I am once more tossing about on Old Ocean. The little vessel is dashing the laughing spray from about her bows and galloping away, with a fair wind from the N.W.," he went on; "and I think we have a fair prospect of a speedy, and in some measure comfortable, run down to the Aucklands."

He was right, because the morning after that they raised land, which proved to be an island to the north end of the Auckland Island group. It was the twenty-second day since their departure from Invercargill.

TWENTY-ONE

Rescue

Musgrave glimpsed a line of breakers to leeward, stretching as far as he could see. Realizing that these were the reefs that broke out from the northeastern coast of Auckland Island, he advised Cross to haul off and stand about ten miles from land until they were well clear of them: "These reefs are very ugly dangers, and cannot too carefully be avoided until surveyed."

This hazard circumvented, they hauled in again, and sailed southward closer to the shore. Then all at once they saw smoke. It was on the side of one of the mountains, about eight miles north of Epigwaitt. Had Harry and George climbed up there, and set fire to the grass? Or was it a trick of the mist? There was nothing they could do about investigating the strange sight, and so they kept south.

The entry into Carnley Harbour was a desperate struggle against the westerly wind, which "drew down the sound with great fury," loaded with sleet and hail. For a while they felt doubtful that the *Flying Scud* could stand it, but they "hauled her up to it, standing by the halyards, and lowering away everything in some of the squalls, which would otherwise have capsized her, or blown away the canvas. We thrashed her up," Musgrave went on, "and nobly did the little craft do her work."

Cross was at the helm, while at every moment the gusts threatened to carry away the single mast, which was bending back and forth like a reed, or capsize the cutter, which was "frequently down, hatches in the water, while the spray flew in clouds over the masthead, smothering and nearly blinding us all." However, despite everything the weather could throw at them, at eight in the evening the *Flying Scud* made the haven of Camp Cove, and Musgrave was back at the place from where he'd set sail precisely five weeks before—"How very different are my feelings to then!"

"THURSDAY, AUGUST 24," he wrote next day. "We were up and on shore as soon as it was daylight." To his surprise, the tent that he and his men had lived in while they prepared the *Rescue* for her last-hope voyage was gone, along with all the tools and other gear. Evidently Harry and George had collected them—but how, without a boat? Perhaps they had made a raft, Musgrave thought, a notion that was reinforced when he found half a seal hanging in a tree, and "a rudely constructed oar and mast." The harbor was still white with foam, so they couldn't set out to investigate. Instead, they went on a hunt, Musgrave killing a cow and a calf.

This led to what he considered an amusing incident. Musgrave shot the calf, and after he had fired, "Cross saw the old cow running towards him, and at once bolted down the cliff and made for the boat." The female seal headed off in another direction, with Musgrave following her, so Tom Cross "took courage," and came back. Seeing the calf lying there, he thought it was asleep, set upon it with his club, and then cried out in triumph, "Where are you, boys? I've killed a seal!"

Musgrave returned, and thoughtfully studied the corpse. "Are you sure you've killed him?" he inquired.

"Killed him? Yes—his brains are coming out of his mouth."

On closer inspection, Musgrave saw that the pup had vomited milk in its death throes. He pointed out the bullet hole in the animal's head, and Cross was quite crestfallen. "Well," he said. "I thought I'd killed a seal."

IT WAS STILL very showery, but in the afternoon the rain eased and the wind moderated, and so they got under way and beat up to Epigwaitt, which was so enveloped in mist "the boys" didn't see the *Flying Scud*. Musgrave and Cross landed in the boat, "leaving the cutter underweigh, as there was too much wind and sea to anchor her," and hurried up to the cabin.

Harry, on seeing them, "turned as pale as a ghost," and staggered up to a post, against which he leaned for support, for he was evidently on the point of fainting; while the other, George, seized my hand in both of his and gave my arm a severe shaking, crying, 'Captain Musgrave, how are ye? How are ye?' apparently unable to say anything else."

After a struggle the Englishman managed to get control of himself, but still his "eyes were filled with tears" of utter joy. Crouching down by Harry, who was now insensible, George and Musgrave shook him and sprinkled his face with cold water that Captain Cross "brought in his oil-skin cap from the neighbouring brook," but it was a long time before the poor fellow opened his eyes.

As dark was falling, Musgrave and Cross rushed the two

castaways off to the cutter without pausing to ask or answer questions. Off before the wind they flew, and were at Camp Cove in good time for supper, which "consisted of fish and potatoes, tea, and bread and butter, and the two poor fellows set about with such a zest as I have seldom seen exhibited over a meal." Little wonder—one of their first revelations, as Musgrave related, was that at one time their food had become so short that they had been reduced to killing and eating mice. Worse still, they had had a falling-out—"were on the point of separating and living apart!" That nothing like this had happened before Musgrave had left the island was clearly a testament not only to his leadership but to the spirit of camaraderie that had bound them all together.

However, Musgrave's thoughts were focused on the smoke they had sighted as the cutter had come down the coast. Henry and George knew nothing about it, telling him that they had been nowhere near the mountains since the day the *Rescue* had sailed, so perhaps, he meditated, there was a possibility that there were other unfortunates living on the island. In that case, it was imperative to run back along the shore as soon as wind and weather allowed it. The thought of abandoning men who were suffering the same trials and tribulations he and his little company had endured for nineteen long months was utterly unacceptable.

THE NEXT MORNING dawned without any wind, so it was impossible to leave Carnley Harbour. However, the weather was otherwise relatively moderate, so Cross's crew put out the sweeps and rowed the *Flying Scud* to Epigwaitt, which gave Musgrave, Harry, and George an opportunity to retrieve what mementos of their long ordeal they might want. With thoughts of Raynal, waiting back in Invercargill, Musgrave detached the bellows from the forge, and carried it back to the cutter.

At the same time, Musgrave learned from Harry and George how they had retrieved the tent from Camp Cove. After having been reduced to catching and eating mice, they had made a raft with four empty casks, which had made a huge difference to them, because it meant that they had been able to get about the harbor to hunt, and also to retrieve the gear that had been left behind at Camp Cove. The badly made oar and mast had been abandoned after they had manufactured better ones. The half-carcass was the result of one of their hunting expeditions, they said; they had left it behind because a whole grown seal was more than two men could consume.

This talk of seal-hunting gave Captain Cross the urge to have another go, and so they set off with his dog—a large noble beast, as Musgrave described, "such as would have been of the greatest service to us while down here." When they flushed an old cow out of the bush the dog flew after it, and only let go after one of Cross's men, mad with excitement, hit the dog on the head instead of the seal.

However, the cutter's men gained both skill and courage over the next few stormbound days, collecting a few skins and rendering down a lot of oil, despite the constant heavy rain. For Musgrave, still exceedingly anxious about his family, the time dragged—"It is one month today since we left Invercargill," he wrote on August 30, "and a long dreary month it has been to me."

On the night of August 31 the wind increased with great violence, but after midnight it moderated considerably, and by daylight had fallen to a strong breeze. The sky was blue, the scudding clouds broken, and at ten in the morning they weighed anchor and headed out to sea, Musgrave feeling very glad indeed to depart from the place "in whose folds I have experienced the greatest misery of my life."

With due care to avoid reefs, they sailed up the eastern coast, while Musgrave took sightings and made notes. Everyone looked for signs of smoke, but saw nothing. About four-thirty in the afternoon they passed the northeast point of Auckland Island, and then cautiously ventured amongst the host of islets that hid the passage into Port Ross, still on the search for men who might have set the fire—though they were becoming less and less sure that what they had seen was smoke.

THE ONLY PILOT Musgrave had to help find an anchorage in this northern extremity of Auckland Island was a short chapter in a slender volume called *The History of Gold*, which had been published in 1853, and which he had acquired in Invercargill. After describing the island group as situated "in 51° South latitude and 166° east longitude," and "about 180 miles south of New Zealand, and 900 southeast from Van Diemen's Land" (Tasmania), this book went on to describe Bristow's discovery, the release of pigs into the territory, and the Enderby settlement in Port Ross. Then it launched into physical, biological, and meteorological descriptions—all from hearsay. The author, James Ward, had not even visited the island group, but had compiled his observations from letters sent to him by a friend, the surgeon of the Sydney whaler *Lord Hardwicke*.

Reading this book, Musgrave learned much about the early history of the islands, something he naturally found intriguing.

Of more immediate interest to him, however, was the set of instructions for entering Port Ross. "Port Ross is at the extreme north of the island, and contains secure anchorage for vessels," the book assured him. If they entered the bay from the north, and kept Enderby Island on the right while passing about a small wooded peninsula, they would be able to anchor "in perfect safety in any part." The inlet beyond the headland was "perfectly landlocked," the writer went on, "and the steep beach on the southern shore affords the greatest facility for clearing and reloading vessels."

As Musgrave and Cross swiftly found out, this advice was absolute humbug. It took them hours to get about the peninsula, because when Musgrave went down in a boat to test the soundings, he found that the bottom shallowed dangerously to less than a fathom. Finally they put out the sweeps and got the cutter to an anchorage just as the rain came pouring down—but surely this wasn't the right place? Around them, low hills clad in tussock and stag-headed bush rolled all the way to the water; the wind whistled freely in all directions; and there was no sign of a shelving beach. The scene was such a mismatch to the written description that Musgrave couldn't believe they had actually arrived—but, as it proved, they were there. "What a disappointment!" he wrote.

After an uncomfortable night rolling and pitching in a nasty swell that curled about the headland, Musgrave, with Tom Cross, went on shore to look around. Obviously, people had come before them, because a great deal of timber had been cut down—but where was the village of Hardwicke that Ward's book described? Like the *Invercauld* castaways who had stumbled on this place fifteen months earlier, Musgrave and Cross stared around in utter bewilderment.

"All gone," wrote Musgrave; "scarcely a vestige of a house remains; bare leveled places point out where many of them stood, as remaining traces of rude fences also point out where innumerable small gardens have been; but the ground everywhere, except where some of the houses have apparently stood, is choked up with a vigorous growth of thick long grass, and there is not the slightest sign of any edible vegetable." He was vastly relieved that he hadn't known anything about Hardwicke when he had been wrecked at Carnley Harbour, because if he had been aware of its existence he would have made a great effort to get here, and in the process most probably condemned all five *Grafton* castaways to death, because there were no sea lions to be seen at this place, "and there are very few of the roots here which we used to eat."

It began to rain heavily, with a hard gale from the northwest, so Cross and Musgrave returned to the cutter to drop a second anchor. After another nasty night, they went on shore again, this time with George Harris. Again the rain poured, so Musgrave took shelter under a flax bush while George and Captain Cross trekked on. Soon they were out of sight. Tiring of crouching in the downpour, Musgrave went back on board the *Flying Scud*. No sooner had he settled down than they came rushing back in a state of excitement.

Tom Cross and George Harris had found a dead man — "who had apparently died of starvation, and had evidently not been long dead, as flesh remained on his hands." A roof slate had been discovered alongside the corpse, and they had brought this

234 ISLAND OF THE LOST

with them, thinking it was interesting because it had squiggles scratched on its face — "which had no doubt been written by the deceased man, probably when dying," Musgrave guessed, having no idea that it might have been a memoriam inscribed by a fellow castaway, because the writing had been scoured off by the weather — "we found [it] impossible to decipher any further than the Christian name, James."

After a pause to eat their midday dinner, Cross and George led Musgrave to the place where the corpse was lying. Musgrave studied it with extremely mixed feelings, taking copious notes. "The body lay on a bed of grass, with some boards underneath raising it a few inches from the ground," he wrote; "and was close up against the west end of the house, which end and the sides had fallen outwards, while the roof, being pressed by the wind towards the other end, had just fallen clear of the body."

Later, he told Raynal that the arms were "stretched by the side of the body, and the fingers of the hands straight and untwisted," which he interpreted as "indications of a peaceful and apparently resigned departure. One leg hung a little out of the bed, the other was extended full length upon it," he went on. "A shoe was upon the left foot; the right leg, probably wounded, was wrapped up in a bandage. The dress was that of a sailor; moreover, several garments, one of which was an oil-cloth overcoat, were thrown upon the body to serve as coverlets."

In his written notes, Musgrave estimated that the body belonged to a man who had been about five feet seven inches tall, with light brown hair, a low forehead, high, prominent cheekbones, a protruding upper jaw, which was missing one front tooth, and a pointed chin. The skeleton was clothed in a sou'wester hat, three mufflers, a dark brown cloth coat with matching trousers, a blue serge vest, three shirts, "cotton draw-ers next to the skin, trowsers and woollen drawers over all, and three or four pairs of woollen socks and stockings." What Musgrave thought might be a Roman Catholic locket was strung about his neck; he removed this, along with "a lock of the unfortunate man's hair," as possible aids to identification. Beside the bed was a small pile of limpet shells, and a couple of glass bottles, one holding drinking water. "He has no doubt died from starvation," he somberly concluded.

The news of the loss of the *Invercauld* and the rescue of three survivors not having reached New Zealand yet, Musgrave, George, and Captain Cross could only make up theories about the dead man's fate. Perhaps, Musgrave speculated, a ship had foundered and this man had been the only survivor, though he had evidently managed to salvage a number of garments from his unfortunate shipmates before their bodies were car-ried away by the surf. Maybe a number had survived, and the rest had wandered off, leaving their wounded comrade behind. Or, worse still, the dead sailor could have been a man who was marooned by some brute of a captain.

Oddly, though it seemed as if the house had once sheltered this man, it looked as if it had fallen apart since his death. "When he died he was, no doubt, under the shelter of an old frame-house, *then* partly in ruins; and since his death, and very recently, it has fallen down entirely, but without touching the body, and leaving it exposed to the weather," Musgrave guessed, without suspecting that the boards might have been deliberately removed.

Inevitably, he meditated how this could so easily have been the fate of the *Grafton* castaways. "This lamentable spectacle would undoubtedly give rise to serious thoughts in anyone, but how infinitely more in me, whose bones might at the present moment have been lying about the ground under similar circumstances, had not the hand of Providence showered such great mercies upon me, perhaps the least deserving. What a field for serious reflection!"

The inspection of the corpse finished, the men dug a grave, and buried the skeleton after saying a few brief prayers. Later, Musgrave told Raynal that they placed a wooden cross at the head of the mound, and also lit a fire of green branches, raising great clouds of smoke to attract the attention of any others who might be in the vicinity. There was no response from the silent hills surrounding the ruined settlement, and searching the area on foot was too difficult to pursue for very long, partly because of the violent, snowy weather, and partly because the scrub was so extremely dense.

For Musgrave, this was most unsatisfactory. As he related after getting back to Invercargill, they had been unable to establish beyond doubt that there were no castaways left alive on the island—"and I confess the doubt torments me. The thought that some poor wretch should be left upon it to suffer what *we* suffered pursues me incessantly."

However, there was nothing more they could do. Captain Cross and Musgrave were very anxious to get to New Zealand—"for we are all heartily sick of the protractions of the voyage." Not only was Musgrave aware that Raynal and Alick, back in Invercargill, were tensely awaiting his return with Harry and George but his thoughts were constantly with his wife and family in Sydney, who should have received his letter by now.

At nine in the morning of September 13, the anchor was raised and the cutter was rowed out of Port Ross on the breast of the ebbing tide. Outside the heads there was a tremendous sea rolling in from the east, with torrential rain, but a favorable easterly gale blew up, driving them so swiftly to New Zealand that they dropped anchor at Port Pegasus, on the southeastern tip of Stewart Island, at eight that same night.

TWENTY-TWO

Reunion

In Invercargill, just as Musgrave guessed, Raynal and Alick had been counting the weeks. "Supported on one side by Alick, who gave me his arm, and on the other steadying myself with my cane," Raynal wrote, "I spent the greater part of every day upon the quay." There they handed a telescope back and forth, and "examined every white speck upon the horizon, in the hope of recognising the *Flying Scud,* and every evening we returned sadder of heart to our generous host, Mr. Collyer."

Time was plodding by. "A month passed, then another fortnight, then the seventh week. This extraordinary delay filled us with the greatest anxiety." The weather had been awful—had the little oyster-cutter foundered? The inhabitants of Invercargill, who shared their fears, were talking of mounting a second expedition when one morning the semaphore at the mouth of the New River estuary signaled that a cutter was in sight.

Was it Captain Musgrave? Raynal and Alick hurried to the dock at the back of the town. "It drew near; it was the *Flying Scud*!" Hearing the news, the entire population crowded to the shore as the little cutter glided up to the quay. Raynal's eyes were blurred with tears of excitement, but then he recognized the familiar shapes among the men standing on the deck. "Here he is! He lands! George and Harry are with him!"

It was September 15, 1865, the forty-ninth day since the departure of the *Flying Scud* from Invercargill, but at last they had arrived.

MUSGRAVE'S PUBLISHED MEMOIR concludes here, with the words, "the Journal of Thomas Musgrave, master mariner, recording the wreck of the *Grafton* and the adventures of its castaways on the Auckland Islands, may fittingly be brought to a close, with deep thankfulness to a gracious Providence for saving my companions and myself from a miserable fate."

The adventure was certainly not over, however. The next day Musgrave made his official report to the New Zealand government, which, as Raynal remarked, "this time thought fit to send a ship to explore the Aucklands," telegraphing instructions to the port authorities in Dunedin, in the province of Otago, to fit out the steamship *Southland* for the search. The ghoulish tale that Musgrave, George, and Tom Cross related about the discovery of a body at the ruined settlement of Hardwicke undoubtedly had a great deal to do with this change of stance.

Macpherson's schooner *Swordfish* was lying at Invercargill discharging her cargo, and Raynal, Alick, George, and Harry were offered passage in her to Melbourne. George Harris turned down the chance, as he had heard enlivening tales of the Otago gold rush, and had decided to stay on in New Zealand. However, Raynal, Alick, and Harry were glad to accept. Musgrave could have gone with them, but instead he opted to sail to Melbourne on a steamer that was also in port, and was commanded by one of his old friends—a coincidence that led to yet another voyage to the Auckland Islands.

After landing in Melbourne just one week later, Musgrave took passage to Sydney, where his wife and children were waiting impatiently. When she saw him, Mrs. Musgrave's feelings were compounded of irritation as well as vast relief. In her letter to Macpherson, thanking him for sending on Musgrave's message, she had expressed disappointment that her husband had returned to the Auckland Islands instead of coming straight to her side: "His protracted voyage back to the Islands is very distressing to me but I must try to bear up with it the best way I can." However, as she had also promised in that letter, Musgrave found her well, and his little ones in good health, too, so his joy should have been unsullied.

Instead of relaxing in the arms of his family, however, he hurried to the New South Wales government offices to make his report, being still tormented with thoughts that other castaways might be suffering terrible hardships in the Aucklands. At the same time, he offered to head an expedition to the islands, if the government would fund it, and because of his story of the discovery of the corpse, he got an attentive hearing. While they declined his offer of leading an expedition himself, the governments of New South Wales, Queensland, and Victoria immediately requisitioned the colonial steamer *Victoria*, with Captain Norman of the Royal Navy in command, his orders being "to convey relief to any such persons as may be discovered on the islands."

In a letter dated October 3, 1865, the three administrations begged Musgrave to accompany the search party, "as a cabin passenger," so that he could "advise and assist Commander Norman on all matters relating to the expedition, and specially to assist as pilot," as they considered that his "recent and intimate knowledge" of the place would prove invaluable. Then, most gratifyingly, they went on to state that while they fully appreciated his handsome offer to head an expedition free of charge, they could not allow it. Not only would they pay for a suitable outfit of clothes and gear, to the amount of £20, but they would provide a sum of £25, "to serve as a remittance to your family," and maintain them until he got back, when they would pay him "a further sum of £25." This was an extremely generous allowance—at that time a shepherd earned just five pounds a year—but all they asked in exchange, apart from his invaluable knowledge, was that he should keep a journal.

The steamer sailed the very next day, Wednesday, October 4, 1865, heavily laden with 189 tons of coal and provisions for two months, and, as Captain Norman noted in his report, "having on board as passengers, Captain Musgrave and Lieut.-Colonel Smith, R.A., as passengers." They arrived off the narrow western entrance to Carnley Harbour on October 10, "steam on, and all plain sail set," and after chugging along the tall cliffs of the southern coast of Adams Island, turned north, entered the harbor through the two big headlands, fired a gun, and steamed up to the wreck of the *Grafton*. Captain Norman landed a boat, to find that everything at Epigwaitt was just as the *Flying Scud* had left it—"we fired another gun, and proceeded down the harbor," and then anchored at Camp Cove, "but found that no one had been there since I left," Musgrave wrote.

All night guns were fired and rockets sent up into the silent darkness, with the same lack of response from the land. At dawn they got up steam again, left the harbor, and slowly sailed northward up the eastern coast of Auckland Island, exploring all the inlets by boat, and numbering them as they went. In the first, "Inlet No. 1," they found the remains of two huts, which had been abandoned many years before, and had undoubtedly been erected by sealers.

In the second inlet, they found old ax marks on the trees and attributed that to sealers too. There were also some turnips growing close to the water, where the soil was sandy. Because this bay was directly below the mountain where the cutter's men had seen smoke, the bush in the vicinity was thoroughly scouted, but the party saw no signs of life save for a few birds and a young sea lion, which they shot. Over the next two days they explored the rest of the eastern inlets, finding some beautiful streams, and trails through the bush that had been made by large pigs. In the ninth inlet they found an old whaleboat and the remains of a wigwam, but again they credited it to sealers, so kept on steaming north, firing guns as they went.

On the thirteenth they entered Port Ross, where the surrounding hills were white with a blanket of snow, which sent out echoes with every report. "Captain Musgrave and Colonel Smith proceeded with me to the head of Lawrie's Harbor, examining the old whaling settlement of Messrs. Enderbys' on our way," noted Captain Norman in his logbook. They found a brief inscription that had been carved on a rock by Musgrave when he had been here with the *Flying Scud,* but no sign "that afforded any probability of its having been inhabited for a very long time."

"We visited the grave of the unfortunate unknown whom I buried here," Musgrave wrote. After that, they took the boat to the head of the harbor and searched the shores in every direction, but saw no signs of human life. This led to one of his dark moods. "I feel the disappointment most severely," he went on, as he had held great hopes that he would find and rescue other castaways—"for having suffered myself, I would gladly have gone to the pole to have succoured others under similar circumstances." It was rather galling, too, that the expedition had proved pointless, though he was sure no one would regret the spirit of humanity that had prompted it.

The next day, October 14, after coming back from a long trek through the forest, he learned that Captain Norman had ordered that the corpse should be dug up and examined by the ship's surgeon. "In my presence, the body of the man found, and afterwards interred by Captain Musgrave, was exhumed," wrote Captain Norman in his official report; "and the skull examined by Dr. Chambres, who stated that the head was uninjured, and that the presence of a portion of skin and hair still remaining, led him to believe that the poor fellow had been dead about six months." The medic told Musgrave that all the teeth had now fallen out of the upper jaw. "Dr. Chambres is of [the] opinion that the man had been dead at least six months, and it is possible that he may have been dead much longer," Musgrave noted. Then, for the second time, the body was buried.

The following day was Sunday, and so the crew had liberty —an afternoon's vacation—and some of them found signs of a camp in Terror Cove, to the north of where the *Victoria* was anchored. Two of the men stumbled over "an old long-boat turned bottom up, as if it had been used for shelter; others found a sort of hut made of branches of trees, in which there had been a fire not very long ago, and close by were a heap of limpet shells, and a soup-and-bouillie tin."

Meantime, Musgrave and Smith took a boat to Shoe Island, an islet in the middle of the bay, but found no signs of human habitation—the jail, Rodd's Castle, that had been built by the Enderby settlers, was long gone. On the sixteenth, though it was snowing hard, Musgrave and Smith went out again, this time to climb the mountain that overlooked the bay, which they named Smith's Peak. To their astonishment, they found that a flag had been erected there. It was lying on the ground, along with its pole, so they set it up again, but the mystery of how it had gotten there remained unsolved.

Despite all these signs of past visitors, Musgrave had given up all hope of finding anyone alive—"for had anyone been alive on *any* part of it, they would have heard our guns and made signals, which we would have seen, for everyone on board feels deeply interested; every man is constantly on the look out, as well as a regular look-out being kept from the mast-head." Over the next few days, Captain Norman, a keen gardener, planted useful trees and sowed vegetable seeds. Goats and rabbits were released, and a signboard carved and set up. Though no one expected to see any shipwrecked sailors now, the strong possibility that more men would be cast away here in the future was on everyone's mind.

On the eighteenth, the *Victoria* got up steam, proceeded out of the harbor, and steered south along the other side of the island, finding that "the whole of the western coast of the island is one continued perpendicular wall, from 200 to 800 feet high," as Musgrave described. It was a forbidding vista—"If a ship should strike on this side of the island there would be but little chance of any life being saved; altogether this west coast, with its black dismal looking precipices sternly setting old ocean at defiance, and the now snow-clad mountains, towering above in majestic relief, is a scene never to be forgotten, and strikes one with a feeling of awe." So deeply did the sight affect him that he confessed that his chest felt too tight to breathe easily until those forbidding cliffs were left behind.

Having the advantage of steam, they were able to enter Carnley Harbour by the narrow western passage, though with the exercise of great care. Once inside the precipitous gorge, they "steamed slowly along, firing guns, and blowing the steam-whistle, and so proceeded to the north arm, and at 6 o'clock in the evening, anchored in 4½ fathoms of water above Figure-of-Eight Island. We had now made a complete circuit of the group," Musgrave concluded.

The steamer lay at anchor in Carnley Harbour for some days, partly because the weather turned foul, and partly to take on firewood to augment their coal. Epigwaitt was inspected again and proved to be a warm shelter still; they lit a fire in the hearth during a snowstorm and heated up a kettle of very acceptable cocoa. That indefatigable gardener, Captain Norman, took a lot of trouble to plant an avenue of trees from the door of the house to the steps where the *Grafton* men had drawn water from the creek, mixing the dirt with ashes and fencing off the saplings.

At last, on October 28, the *Victoria* left the Auckland Islands, making a call at Campbell Island on the way, just to make certain there were no castaways there. They dropped anchor at Perseverance Harbour that same afternoon, to find the landscape as empty of human life as the day Musgrave had left the island, on December 29, 1863. After planting some trees and liberating a boar and two sows, some guinea-fowl, and three geese, they erected a signboard, securing a bottle to it, which contained a letter that listed the animals and requested visitors not to shoot them, as it was hoped that they would breed, providing food stock.

Then they set sail for New Zealand, with Musgrave satisfied that no stone had been left unturned in the hunt for castaways. However, as he remarked wistfully, "I should like much to unravel the mystery as to how the man came here, whom we found dead."

It was a puzzle that was going to be solved much more quickly than he expected, and by none other than François Raynal.

⇥ TWENTY-THREE ⇤

Answers

Raynal, Alick, and Harry, meanwhile, had been deeply regretting their decision to sail to Melbourne on the *Swordfish*—the passage, which should have taken a couple of weeks, eventually lasted three months! First, a westerly gale forced the schooner to take shelter in a bay in the north of Stewart Island. It was a week before it was safe to depart from there, and then a second storm sent the captain scurrying for refuge again. "The sailors," Raynal pronounced, "thought the schooner enchanted," and were muttering about a Jonah on board.

Their grumbles turned to growls after the third attempt to leave Foveaux Strait—"A heavy wave crushed in two of our hatchways, deluged the cabin, and flung the schooner on her beam ends. She would have heeled over had I not cut, at the moment, the main sheet," Raynal bragged. Because there was so much damage, they were forced to put into Port Chalmers, the deep-sea anchorage for Dunedin, to carry out repairs—repairs that took up most of the following month. Accordingly, they were still there on November 8, when to Raynal's vast surprise Captain Musgrave arrived on the *Victoria,* replenishing her coal on the way to Sydney.

Amazed, Raynal learned that Musgrave had been to the Aucklands yet again. As it happened, though, he had some startling news of his own. When the English mail steamer had arrived in Port Chalmers the previous evening, he had bought a newspaper, and a headline on an inside page had leapt up at him—"Narrative of the Wreck of the *Invercauld* on the Auckland Islands, by Captain Dalgarno." It was the first clue that any of the *Grafton* men had that there had been another shipwreck while they were on the island, and that other castaways had suffered the same ordeal.

The story that followed the headline gave Captain Dalgarno's version of the awful story, along with some of the circumstances surrounding the deaths and disappearances of sixteen of the nineteen wreck survivors. Much, however, was left undescribed. Not once did he mention either Holding or Smith by name, instead using the all-inclusive word "we" when describing accomplishments such as coracle making or sea lion killing—"We thought ourselves very fortunate when we fell in with a sea lion, which we killed with cudgels cut from the trees with our pocket-knives," he wrote. Nor did he offer any kind of explanation for his strange failure to persuade the captain of the *Julian* to search the island before departing for the far side of the Pacific.

At the conclusion of this unrevealing narrative, Dalgarno also made the odd mistake of claiming that the ship *Julian*, after rescuing himself and his two companions, "steered for Valparaiso, where we landed a few weeks later." The ship, in fact, arrived at Callao, Peru, on June 28, 1865. There, Smith was sent to the hospital, while Dalgarno and Holding reported to the British consul. Dalgarno was given his fare to return to

England and left on the mail boat the very same evening, leaving Holding and Smith behind.

A week later he arrived in Panama, and after crossing the isthmus to Aspinwall he caught the steamship *Shannon* to the English port of Southampton, where he paused to write to the owners of the *Invercauld,* informing them of the loss of their ship. "In about twenty minutes after striking, she was in atoms," he wrote in this gloomy communication, which the *Aberdeen Journal* printed on August 2, 1865:

> The boys Middleton and Wilson, and four seamen were drowned; the remainder nineteen of us, getting washed ashore through the wreck, all more or less hurt—the night being dark and cold. We saved nothing but what we had on our persons; and before being washed from the wreck, I hove off my sea boots, so as to enable me to reach the shore.
>
> We all crept close together as we could to keep ourselves warm. The spray from the sea reaching us made it one of the most dismal nights ever anyone suffered, and we were all glad when day broke. We went and collected a few of the most suitable pieces of the wreck to make a hut to cover us from the weather, where we made a fire, the steward having saved a box of matches.
>
> We remain[ed] four days at the wreck, [then] we proceeded to go on the top of the island to see if we could find food or any inhabitants. It was no easy matter to reach the top, it being 2000 feet high, and almost perpendicular. On the following morning we made towards the bay that was on the east side, which occupied some days, the scrub

being so heavy to walk amongst. The cook and three sea-men died during this time. All of us were getting weak for want of food and from cold. We reached the bay and found some limpets on the rocks. We caught two seals and found them good food.

After living three months on limpets, they got done, all we had again was roots and water, seeing no more seals. By the end of August the only survivors were myself, the mate and Robert Holding; the carpenter, the boys Liddle and Lancefield, being among the last that died.

Because of legal necessity, Robert Holding was named in this (though with no mention of his resourcefulness), but Andrew Smith was not, the assumption being made that the owners would know whom he meant by "the mate." In the longer "Narrative" that Dalgarno wrote for a local newspaper after getting home—the same one Raynal, Musgrave, Alick, and Harry read in Invercargill—Dalgarno did not mention Holding by name at all, simply calling him "the seaman," and again, Smith was referred to only as "the mate."

Having posted this notification to the ship's owners, Captain Dalgarno was free at last to go to Aberdeen, pausing only to pen his longer "Narrative" for newspaper publication. That done, he returned to the house in the hamlet of Buxburn, four miles northwest of the port, where his young son and daughter had lived ever since their mother, Helen McMillan Dalgarno, had died. "His health is still delicate," noted the local paper. This was confirmed by Dalgarno himself, who had ended the "Narrative" with the words, "I took my passage on board the mail-packet to return to England, where, thank God, I arrived some days ago;

ANSWERS   251

but with my health so completely broken up, that I fear I shall be compelled to abandon for ever my profession." Prophetic words, because he was never given another command.

Andrew Smith—the man who wasn't named in either of Dalgarno's accounts—arrived in Aberdeen sometime in August, the *Aberdeen Journal* recording on September 6 that "Mr. Smith, late mate of the *Invercauld*," was in good health when the writer visited him, "with the exception of a feeling of pain and numbness in the legs and feet." The journalist was there to press him to write his own version of the castaway ordeal, but Smith resisted all such appeals until the following year, when he wrote a short account for the Glasgow publishing firm of Brown & Son and Ferguson, with the title *The Castaways: A Narrative of the Wreck and sufferings of the Officers and Crew of the Ship Invercauld of Aberdeen, on the Auckland Islands.*

It begins, "Having been requested to give a narrative of the wreck and sufferings of the officers and crew of the *Invercauld* of Aberdeen, I have to state, as some excuse for the delay in its appearance, that I understood Captain Dalgarno was to give an account of them, and in this expectation I deferred drawing up this narrative." However, it is unlikely that he was unaware that Dalgarno had produced his own version, which indicates that the relationship between the two men had soured. Having produced this document, Andrew Smith, like Dalgarno, dropped out of sight. The newspaper stories stopped that same month of September 1865, and neither he nor Dalgarno appeared in the records again.

At least, they had had their little moment of fame. No newspaper writer was ever interested in Robert Holding. Back in Callao, the British consul had sent him to a common seamen's boardinghouse instead of giving him a ticket home — "such is the difference in the treatment of officers and men that poor Jack has to take his chance." He was penniless, but three of the seamen from the *Julian* gave him five dollars each, which tided him over for a while. The crew of a visiting British warship saw his plight too, and "made a whip around and presented me with $35.00. I don't forget the Navy," he commented.

After waiting around in the Peruvian port for three weeks, occasionally visiting Smith in the hospital, Holding managed to get a seaman's job on a small Welsh vessel, *Mathewan*, which was bound for Europe. "Having been round Cape Horn I cannot say that I relished the idea," he wrote, but, being a beggar, he had no choice. And so, in this humble fashion, he left the Pacific Ocean and its terrible memories behind.

Robert Holding took his discharge from the *Mathewan* at Rotterdam on October 21, 1865, and then, after visiting his family in England, he resumed his seafaring career. In 1888 he gave up the sea, migrated to Canada, and then after working as a machinist in Toronto and Kingston, Ontario, he headed for the goldfields of West Shining Tree. Having had some luck in the prospecting way, he bought a hotel with the proceeds and became a publican. This colorful and varied career ended when he died on January 12, 1933, his legacy to his family being the remarkable memoir of his experiences as a castaway, which he commenced in 1926, at the age of eighty-six.

BACK IN NOVEMBER 1865, despite the implications of the report of the loss of the *Invercauld*, Captain Norman came to the firm conclusion that there was no one left alive either on

Campbell Island or in the Auckland Islands group. Accordingly, he ordered the anchor weighed, and the *Victoria* departed from Port Chalmers for Melbourne, Australia. As a measure of their respect, the pilots who accompanied him out to the heads did not charge for the service.

A few days later, Raynal, Alick, and Harry sailed out of the same port in the schooner *Swordfish*. This time, as Raynal described with patent relief, "our voyage was fair and favourable," so they arrived in Melbourne just a few days behind the *Victoria*. Meanwhile, the three comrades had lost track of George Harris: "I do not know whether he still resides in New Zealand, and if he has succeeded in his new trade of gold-digger," Raynal wrote later.

A month after arriving in Melbourne, Alick Maclaren returned to sea, joining the crew of a Liverpool clipper. Harry Forgès, who reckoned that he had experienced more than enough of the ocean and its hazards, went to work for an uncle who kept a large sheep station two hundred miles inland, which for him was a good safe distance from the sea. This left François Raynal alone in the port, where he had to remain under medical care because his health was still very poor. Soon, however, Musgrave joined him, having come to Melbourne to settle with his family. In his report of the voyage of the *Victoria*, Captain Norman had strongly commended Musgrave for his assistance, which he had found invaluable, and this reference, accompanied with warm backing from the Invercargill merchant John Macpherson (who was also a personal friend of the Minister of Trade, James G. Francis), landed Thomas Musgrave a job with the Department of Trade & Customs in that port.

This triumph was soon followed by the launch of Musgrave's book, which was published by the local firm Henry T. Dwight late that same year, 1865, with the title *Castaway on the Auckland Isles: a narrative of the wreck of the 'Grafton': from the private journals of Capt. Thos. Musgrave, with a map and some account of the Aucklands.* Whether Musgrave consulted with Raynal as he compiled the book is unknown. What is certain is that Musgrave's editor, a local luminary by the name of John Joseph Shillinglaw, had a great deal to do with its final form.

Shillinglaw was a noted raconteur and prized dinner guest— and a talented editor. Not only did he persuade Musgrave to pad out the bare bones of the intermittent journal he had written to turn it into a book, but, understanding that Musgrave's style rang with a natural sincerity, he allowed him to tell it in his own voice. The book, dedicated to John Macpherson and the Minister of Trade, James G. Francis, "as a tribute of gratitude," was very successful locally, leading to another edition, published in London by Lockwood in 1866, as, *Castaway on the Auckland Isles: a narrative of the wreck of the Grafton and of the escape of the crew after twenty months suffering: from the private journals of Captain Thomas Musgrave, together with some account of the Aucklands,* and which, despite the slight difference in title and the order in which the appendices (which describe sea lions and the Auckland Islands) appear, was identical to the first.

In 1867, Thomas Musgrave was given the job of "harbour boat captain"—or pilot—for the Gippsland Entrance of the harbor, with a salary of £200 per annum and a staff of six. Subsequently, he was put in charge of a number of lighthouses, and eventually died at one of these, Point Lonsdale lighthouse, Victoria, on November 7, 1891, at the age of just fifty-nine.

Now, he lies under a marble headstone in picturesque Queens-cliff Cemetery, close to the wife who predeceased him by just a few months. Aptly, he is surrounded by the graves of many men who drowned at sea, and the lighthouse keepers and lifeboat men who saved many more from shipwreck.

"As for myself," wrote Raynal, "when I recruited my strength I quitted Melbourne, carrying with me the most agreeable recollection of the generous attentions lavished upon me, during my stay there, by its inhabitants." What he had done in the meantime to keep body and soul together is unknown, though there was an unlikely report printed later in *The Australian* that he "practised mesmerism." The writer of this report also claimed inside knowledge of the mysterious lode on Campbell Island—which, he says, was copper, not argentiferous tin. Charles Sarpy, according to this piece of unfounded speculation, was married to a granddaughter of the firm of Underwood & Co., which had a vague mercantile connection with the Enderby-inspired colony, and had heard about a copper mine from one or other of the people who had lived at Hardwicke. Though Raynal came from a good family, and was an excellent scholar, as the writer averred, he claimed that the Frenchman joined the expedition just to get his hands on the copper.

According to Raynal's own account, after leaving Melbourne his sole ambition was to get to France. He went to Sydney first, however, and "waited upon our partners. With respect to *them*, I had not only a personal resentment to satisfy, but an act of justice to accomplish," he said, and went on to relate that he "reproached them in severe terms" for their callous indifference and "their guilty forgetfulness of their solemn engagements."

Charles Sarpy and Uncle Musgrave had plenty of excuses, including their lack of funds to finance a rescue mission. They also emphatically assured him that they had reported the missing ship to the authorities. When he checked, however, it was to find that they had waited *thirteen months* before doing so, well outside the administrative deadline.

Finally, "on the 6th of April 1867," as he went on, "I sailed from Sydney on board the *John Masterman*, bound for London." He arrived there on August 22 and just a few days later, "with a heart overflowing with joy, I landed in France; I trod my native soil." He had been away from home a total of twenty years.

François Raynal found his parents living in an apartment in the 17th arrondissement of Paris. For some time afterward he lived with them while he worked on his book and found a publishing firm — one that had an even greater influence on the form of his book than John Shillinglaw had had on Musgrave's publication. This was Librairie de L. Hachette, which has a very interesting history.

Its founder, Louis Hachette, came from a poor family, but had been allowed to attend a prestigious school in Paris because his mother was a linen maid there. No sooner had he passed his final examinations as a teacher, in 1822, than the school was closed down by the authorities, being considered too left-wing, and so he was unable to claim his certificate. In 1826, Hachette somehow raised enough money to buy up a tiny bookselling business on the Rue St. Germain. The following year, in a curious echo of Raynal's early career, he assumed the responsibility of his whole family, taking care of his mother and sisters as well as his wife and two small children. At the same time he launched into publishing, becoming the first publisher in history to specialize in textbooks for elementary schoolchildren. When rail travel became available to the common crowd, Hachette pioneered the practice of putting stalls in railroad stations that sold cheap, light, readable books, later supplemented with travel guides. By the time he died, in 1864, he was one of the richest men in France.

Though Louis Hachette was no longer around at the time Raynal submitted his manuscript, his liberal traditions had been carried on by his successors, which meant that Librairie L. Hachette was the perfect publisher for his book. Raynal's description of the egalitarian domestic arrangements of Epigwaitt had particular appeal to the democratically minded editorial board, and this part of the story was given due prominence. Everything that was inspiring—Raynal's technical resourcefulness, Alick's gallantry, Musgrave's conscientious leadership—was emphasized, as an eloquent testament to the triumph of the human spirit in the face of tremendous difficulties.

Editorial policy also influenced the selection of an illustrator. The man commissioned was Alphonse de Neuville, a very popular artist who also illustrated books by Jules Verne and Alexandre Dumas *fils*. As was typical with Hachette, de Neuville worked closely with the editor, who chose the subjects of the pictures for their inspirational and educational value. Even the placement of the illustrations was carefully thought out, each one preceding the relevant text by two or three pages, with the idea of keeping the reader's curiosity and interest alive. As usual, too, it was claimed that the scenes were taken from sketches made by the author—who, unlike the illustrator, was unnamed, being kept mysteriously anonymous. It is, in fact, only possible to be sure that François Raynal is the author by comparing his book with Musgrave's.

The marketing of the book was carried out with equally deliberate care. Extracts were published in three installments in the very popular Hachette-owned magazine *Le Tour du Monde,* starting July 1869, to whet public interest. Then, the following year, the entire story was published under the title *Les naufrages; ou, Vingt mois sur un recif des îles Auckland: recit authentique, illustré de 40 gravures sur bois dessinées par A. de Neuville.*

It was an immediate best-seller, translated into Italian and German in 1871, into English in 1874, and Norwegian in 1879. Printing followed printing, while reviewers breathlessly compared it to the classic *Robinson Crusoe.* There were obvious reasons for this. Like Defoe's book, *Les naufrages* involved as well as enthralled the reader; like *Robinson Crusoe,* it celebrated the value of hard work and the importance of human labor. At a time when technological advances were booming, it brought renewed awareness of the blessings of tools and engineering. It even affected the leisure time of its readers—a fashion arose for such activities as gardening, camping, pottery, sewing, leatherwork, and the keeping of pets. In the past, these basic skills had been dismissed as the kind of thing our lowly peasant ancestors did to keep body and soul together, but now they became therapeutic recreational activities for educated city-dwellers. Because of its inspirational appeal, Hachette put it out in special editions, some intended for family collections and others, particularly handsomely produced, for end-of-year school prizes. Both English and French editions are in print today—still without Raynal's name on either the cover or the title page.

HELPED BY A RECOMMENDATION from a director of the publishing company, Raynal secured a good job with the Paris Municipal Council, and from then on moved up steadily through the ranks of public servants. He was recognized by the literati, too: In 1868 he was nominated a member of the Geographic Society of Paris, and in 1873 he was invited to talk at the Académie des Sciences during a meeting of the Commission of the Transit of Venus, giving them the advice (which they followed) to site their observatory on Campbell Island rather than in the Aucklands. In 1874 *Les naufrages* was awarded a Montyon prize by the Académie Française, which involved a fat purse of 1,500 francs in addition to a flattering citation; in 1875 Raynal was a delegate to the International Congress of Geographical Sciences; in 1881 he was admitted to the Order of Palmes Académiques.

However, Raynal's health was as precarious as ever. In 1888 he was forced to take sick leave, and was never well enough to work again. On August 18, 1889, he was granted early retirement on medical grounds. Less than a decade later, on April 28, 1898, he passed away at the age of sixty-eight, his remarkable life finally over.

Unknown to any of the *Invercauld* survivors, the discovery of the corpse of their erstwhile shipmate, James Mahoney, had led to a great deal of interest in the Auckland Islands, which resulted in the ultimate provision of castaway depots for the survivors of future shipwrecks. Because of the death of the second mate of the *Invercauld,* their awful ordeal was eventually to be the inspiration that saved the lives of many others.

Back on October 14, 1865, while Captain Norman and the surgeon of the *Victoria* were busily disinterring the remains of James Mahoney, the paddle wheels of the steam tug *Southland* churned up mud and water as she turned around and then chugged out of Invercargill. Her captain was James Greig, a flamboyant Scotsman who had arrived in Southland in 1862 after several years on the Australian goldfields, and who currently held the position of harbormaster. A remarkably energetic man, he not only completed his allotted task, but also produced a long and chatty statement that was published in the New Zealand papers—much of it highly irritating, as Captain Musgrave confided to Macpherson in a letter.

In this gossipy account, after reporting that he had seen

nothing but "the ordinary accompaniment of sea fowls and porpoises" on the passage south, Greig announced that he had arrived at Port Ross at four in the morning on October 21—to find a notice carved on a tree informing him that the *Victoria* had beaten them to it, along with a message in a bottle, signed by Captain Norman, giving all the particulars of their search. Well, as he candidly confessed, this surely did have the effect of "considerably dampening the enthusiasm" of everyone on board the *Southland*. However, he and his men searched on, undaunted, and in the process turned up traces of past occupation that the *Flying Scud* and *Victoria* parties had missed.

The first was the "frame of a boat, made of small sticks woven together, and lashed together with strips of seal skins." Without realizing it, Greig's men had discovered the coracle that Holding, Smith, and Dalgarno had constructed in November 1864, almost exactly twelve months earlier, and abandoned after they had built a wooden boat. The second was the hut Holding had lived in by himself while ostracized by Smith and Dalgarno—"A thatched hut about nine feet square," which, Greig deduced, had been built by someone "who had no axe, and who subsisted on limpets, to which fact a large pile of shells bore testimony." A track led from this to a promontory, where they found a tall pole with a bunch of white grass attached to the top, which had fallen down in the meantime.

Having noted all this, Greig then turned to another piece of business—to dig up Mahoney's body yet again. Dr. Monkton, the Invercargill surgeon who was with him, inspected what was left of it and came to some conclusions that were truly remarkable, as Thomas Musgrave tartly remarked. Indeed, as he ironically commented in a letter to Macpherson after reading the newspaper account, he wondered if they had dug up the same body.

Dr. Monkton declared that the deceased had been no ordinary seaman—that, judging by his clothes, he had never been accustomed to hard labor. The dead man's hair was "medium" brown, not light, the way Musgrave had described it, "cheekbones not high, nor chin pointed." He was similarly derisory about Musgrave's conclusion that the deceased had been Catholic, saying that a small heart-shaped locket with some kind of token hidden inside was poor evidence of any such thing.

Having dug Mahoney up for the second time, the *Southland* crew then buried him for the third time—in a coffin, which they had carried for that purpose. As well as this, they had prepared a board, which read: ERECTED BY THE CREW OF THE P.S. 'SOUTHLAND,' OVER THE REMAINS OF A MAN WHO HAD APPARENTLY HAD DIED OF STARVATION, AND WAS BURIED BY THE CREW OF THE 'FLYING SCUD,' SEPTEMBER 3, 1865. Having set this up at the head of the grave, they left their own message in a bottle, and then made steam and chugged down the east coast of Auckland Island.

On October 28, having stopped to shoot pigs and sea lions every now and then, they dropped anchor in Carnley Harbour. In the course of the following survey, they slept two nights in Epigwaitt—"a very comfortable sort of place about 12 feet by 18 feet, with a large stone chimney," Greig decided. "The only objectionable feature," he went on, "was the slightness of the rafters, which bent so much to a gale we experienced the second night, that some of the nervous ones of the party, before turning in formed a complete network of rope between the wall-plates to catch the roof if it fell"—which, as he went on to comment, created a strangely mysterious effect in the firelight.

"We found a quantity of smoked shags and pieces of seal inside the house," he went on; "and a variety of little articles, evincing the expenditure of a considerable amount of patience and ingenuity in their construction." The bush had been cleared all about the house, and there was "an old forge, charcoal pits, tannery, &c.," too—an important confirmation of the achievements Musgrave and Raynal described.

Greig himself was not particularly admiring—"Musgrave's party appear to have had no garden whatever, and to have cut very few tracks in the bush," he criticized. He had heard that Musgrave considered the forest about Carnley Harbour "*impenetrable*." Well, he reckoned, if Musgrave ever lived in New Zealand, he would learn what "*impenetrable*" forest was really like.

Finally, on November 7, after some exciting days of hunting sea lions—and being chased by more than a few infuriated sea lion bulls—the crew of the *Southland* raised the anchor and set course for New Zealand, Greig having come to the firm conclusion that there was no one left alive in the islands. "Having now seen all that is to be seen of this group, it is obvious that no one at present exists thereon, or, with the exception of Musgrave's party, have existed on any of these islands for some time past," he wrote. Obviously, it was a big surprise to him when he arrived back in New Zealand and learned about the *Invercauld* castaways.

IN JANUARY 1868, public interest in the Auckland Islands was electrified again when the papers broke the story of the American-built 1,200-ton *General Grant*, which on May 13,

1866, crashed into the cliffs of the western side of Auckland Island and became a total loss.

"Wreck of the ship 'General Grant'—sixty-eight dead—ten survivors confined for eighteen months upon a desert island," ran the heading in the *Sydney Morning Herald*. "On the morning of the 10th of January, a telegram announced the arrival at Bluff of the whaling ship *Amherst*, Captain Gilroy, having on board ten persons (one of them a woman), the sole survivors of the crew and passengers of the ship *General Grant*, which sailed from Melbourne for London in May 1866, with a valuable cargo of wool, skins, and gold."

According to the riveting report that followed, the ship sailed into "a deep crevasse of volcanic origin, against whose sides the hull was shattered before foundering," and only fourteen men and one woman (the stewardess) survived, the captain going down with his ship. They rowed in the two unscathed ship's boats to Port Ross, where they lived in the ruined house at Hardwicke—the same house where the corpse of James Mahoney had been discovered a few months earlier—after closing in the sides to render it more weatherproof.

The goats and pigs Captain Norman had liberated were still running around, and they managed to kill one or two of these. However, their main food supply was sea lion. In the pupping season of January 1867, having collected a good store of meat, the first officer, Bart Brown, set off for New Zealand with three other men in one of the ship's boats, which had been decked over and loaded with skins of fresh water as well as the provisions. Unlike Musgrave's *Rescue*, this boat was never seen or heard from again.

The remaining ten men and one woman struggled on. On

September 3, 1867, one of the men, sixty-two-year-old David McLellan, died. On October 6, a sail was sighted, but though fires were lit and the day was clear, there was no response. Like Robert Holding earlier, the castaways decided that they should move to an island that was closer to the open sea, and the whole party was ferried to Enderby Island in the remaining boat, only to see another ship pass without seeing their signals. Just two days after that, however, on November 21, 1867, the colonial whaling brig *Amherst* called by, and Captain Paddy Gilroy carried them to New Zealand, to relate their dreadful tale.

The resulting public uproar led to a government decision to establish castaway depots on both Campbell Island and Auckland Island, and the *Amherst* was sent out with building materials, livestock, and provisions. Paddy Gilroy was again in command and a justice of the peace, Henry Armstrong, was on board to keep an official record. The first depot they established was at Port Ross, where they strengthened the house at Hardwicke and left a strongbox with supplies. On the lid of this Armstrong wrote, THE CURSE OF THE WIDOW AND FATHERLESS LIGHT UPON THE MAN WHO BREAKS OPEN THIS BOX WHILST HE HAS A SHIP AT HIS BACK.

Then they steered for Perseverance Harbour on the same mission, with a large spar in tow, Captain Gilroy being determined to hoist a flagstaff on treeless Campbell Island so that those in need could fly a signal of distress. They arrived at the mouth of Perseverance Harbour on February 14, 1868, but for some days the wind blew so hard from the interior that it was impossible to enter, and so it was not until the twenty-fourth that they were able to drop anchor. There were no traces at all of the animals the *Victoria* had landed, so they released some more. Then they erected the spar a hundred yards from the notice board that had been set up by the *Victoria*, and put a strongbox and a spade at its foot.

At the same time, they stumbled across the grim sight of six graves and, alongside them, the skeleton of a man, evidently the remains of the crew of some ship that had been wrecked since the *Victoria* had left. Further impelled by this ghoulish discovery, they fixed up a hut that had been built by these unknown castaways. It was about ten feet long and eight feet wide, with overlapping deal boards and a pitched roof, with thatch that they repaired. Then, after placing a chest of provisions inside, Gilroy and Armstrong sailed away, their mission in the dangerous subantarctic seas accomplished.

THESE DEPOTS, OCCASIONALLY checked and restocked by navy ships and government craft, were to save the lives of many shipwrecked sailors. Eight of these were survivors of the *Derry Castle*, which foundered off the north coast of Enderby Island in 1887. The men knew there was a castaway hut at Port Ross, which gave them the courage to live in rough shelters made out of tussock while they constructed a boat from the timbers of the wreck. Having crossed the channel, they lived on the stores and what sea lions they could catch until rescued by the *Awarua*, which was sealing illegally, as by that time the trade had been banned by the New Zealand government.

In March 1891, the ship *Compadre* caught fire to the north of the islands, and after finding the situation was hopeless, her captain deliberately steered for the rocks of a cape off Port Ross. All fifteen crew climbed onto the jibboom, and when she hit they jumped for it, landing battered and bruised, but alive, on the shore. One man died during the first night, but the rest survived on the stores they found, until saved by the schooner *Janet Ramsey* on June 30, in what the newspapers called a remarkable state of good health, considering the privations they had endured.

Particularly eloquent is the story of the survivors from the *Dundonald,* which piled up on Disappointment Island in the middle of the night of March 7, 1907. According to the reminiscences of one of the survivors, Charles Eyre, when dawn broke eleven men were clinging to the rigging, while five more were hanging onto precipitous cliffs, having jumped there from the sternmost mast. Like the *Invercauld* men, many of them had discarded their boots and heavy clothing. The first officer, who was the most badly hurt, was in command, as the captain and the second mate had gone down with the ship.

For a while, they thought they were on the main island, Auckland Island, and that a simple walk would take them to the castaway hut. Struggling over rock and plateau, they finally realized with horror that they were on Disappointment Island, and Auckland Island was on the other side of a turbulent five-mile-wide channel. Worse still, the rocky islet had no running streams of fresh water. On the twelfth day, the mate died, but the men kept together as a reasonably democratic group, catching rainwater and sharing out the meat from mollymawk albatrosses and the occasional seal. For shelter they dug seven or eight little burrows, roofed them with tussock, and lived in them in pairs, like rabbits, while they debated how to get across the channel to Auckland Island.

Finally, they built a coracle out of long twigs and seal skins, and three of the men crossed over in it. Days later, they returned to say that the big island wasn't worth the trouble—the terrain was impossible, and they had not been able to find the depot. The other castaways, however, determined to make another attempt, which they finally accomplished in October. This second party was successful in locating the depot, which, to their joy, was by this time furnished with a boatshed and boat. The rest of the castaways were fetched from Disappointment Island, and on November 15 the New Zealand government steamer *Hinemoa* arrived—not to inspect the castaway depot, but on another mission altogether, having a party of scientists on board. The castaways, though furnished with more provisions, were forced to keep on living in the depot hut until the scientific survey was completed, when they were carried to New Zealand.

THIS WAS BY NO means the first scientific expedition to call at the islands, one of the most important being the German one that in 1874 set up a base at Terror Cove in Port Ross to observe the transit of Venus. They, unlike the French expedition, which had gone to Campbell Island on Raynal's advice, were lucky in that the weather cleared at the critical time of the planet's passing. The three brick pillars erected as bases for their instruments are still there.

The Enderby experiment was to be imitated too. In 1894 the island group was divided into three pastoral runs, and offered for lease by the New Zealand government. The following year nine longhorn cattle and twenty sheep were landed on Enderby Island, but, like their predecessors, they did not thrive. In 1900 another leaseholder landed two thousand sheep at Carnley Harbour and farmed Adams Island, but the climate worked its evil spell again. Within ten years most of the sheep had perished, and the lease was forfeited.

With the end of the windjammer era, the route along the fifties latitude in the southern ocean was abandoned, and the Auckland Islands group, being out of the shipping paths, was no longer infamous as a graveyard for ships. A different future beckoned. As scientists explained the unique character of the flora and fauna, ideas of conservation began to take hold. In 1934 the group was declared a nature preserve, and the fur seals, sea lions, birds, and native plants were protected. Once again, the hills and beaches were shrouded in silence, distant from the touch of man.

Abruptly, war intruded. In August 1939 the German steamer *Erlangen* was at anchor in Dunedin Harbour when her master, Captain Grams, was warned by the German consul that hostilities were imminent. He immediately made a quiet departure, but, having only five days' fuel on board, headed first for Carnley Harbour, where his men cut down tracts of rata forest for firewood. When the New Zealand government heard about this, it was decided to set up coastal watching stations. These, established in 1941, were manned by scientists, partly so that the islands could be properly studied and surveyed, and partly so that men with valuable qualifications would not be lost in the theater of war. Despite the constant rain and mist, the men rowed about the entire coast, surveying as they went. All the heights were surmounted, named, and measured, too, and so the first complete, accurate map of the Auckland Islands was drawn up.

Thomas Musgrave, without a doubt, would have thoroughly approved.

At every heave of the swell she is dragging the anchor home, and getting nearer the shore. From 10 P.M. till midnight the gale blew with the most terrific violence, and precisely at midnight the ship struck.

—logbook of the *Grafton*,
Saturday, January 2, 1864

Remains of the wreck of the *Grafton*, at Epigwaitt, Auckland Islands. Alexander Turnbull Library, National Library of New Zealand, Wellington, reference number 1/2-098 181-F.

✄ AUTHOR'S NOTE ✄

In the Macpherson collection (MSX-4936), which is held at the Alexander Turnbull Library, National Library of New Zealand, there is a clipping of an undated review from the *Saturday Review*, which compares Musgrave's *Castaway* with Raynal's *Les naufrages*. The writer concludes by saying, "The relation between the two books has been rather a puzzle to us; and though we have given to the comparison as much trouble as the question seemed to be worth, we do not feel confident that we have obtained a satisfactory explanation."

He was right in saying that there are puzzling inconsistencies. While both men told the same basic story, there are constant contrasts in timing and emphasis. This reflects not just the influence of the men's editors but also the writers' differing memories, because *both* men padded their diaries with remembered anecdotes when preparing them for publication. The only difference is that Raynal openly admits he did this, while Musgrave does not. Deciding which version of each little event was closer to the truth was an interesting challenge.

Musgrave wrote his journal only intermittently, initially

about every Sunday but with increasingly longer gaps as he became involved in projects or wandered off on long treks. On October 30, 1864, he complained he "must now forego about the last bit of comfort that was left to me, which is writing a little on Sundays; for if I continue to do so, my only remaining book of blank paper will be filled up. I may yet have something of moment to insert, for which purpose I must reserve the few remaining pages," he added. Ten thousand words follow this entry, far too many to fit into a "few remaining pages," so the conclusion that he added a lot of material when preparing for publication is inescapable.

This is confirmed by the occasional little mistake. For instance, on January 10, 1864, just seven days after the wreck, he says that Raynal "is our blacksmith, and makes nails for us"—which was impossible, because Raynal had no means of making nails then, not having a forge, tools, or materials, let alone the physical strength. Evidently Musgrave intended to add that tidbit to an entry for January the following year, a time when Raynal really was busy with his hammer and anvil, but somehow turned to the wrong page.

Raynal kept a daily record, Musgrave also writing on January 10, 1864, that "my time has been so much occupied in hard work as to leave me no time to make even daily notes, but Mr. Raynal, who is improving fast, keeps the diary." Raynal himself noted that he updated the logbook every evening, usually with mundane details of weather, but occasionally adding "a brief narrative of our doings and adventures; sometimes I allowed myself to jot down my individual impressions." These were easily elaborated from memory, and—perhaps after an editorial decision, or maybe because of Raynal's natural flair for narrative—repositioned for dramatic impact.

Because of this more romantic approach, there are times when Raynal is less reliable than Musgrave. For instance, Musgrave noted that the earthquake occurred on May 15, 1864, while Raynal placed it at a more portentous time, in June, when provisions were getting very low. Where Musgrave admitted that he went off on long solitary treks, Raynal glossed over this, once (January 24, 1864) saying that George and Harry had gone with him when it had not been so. It seemed more probable, in view of his mental state, that Musgrave's version was the right one.

Raynal reckoned the first sea lion the group killed and ate was a one-year-old female, yet his vivid word picture of the black, oily, disgusting meat makes it plain that this was a bull. Either the original identification was wrong, or his memory was faulty. Working from the translation has hazards too. Though very competent, the English version is at times more effusive than the French original. For instance, while describing the storm that almost sank the schooner on the way to Campbell Island, Raynal said simply, "*Le ciel est noir,*" but the translation reads, "The sky is literally black." For some unknown reason, too, the translator played fast and loose with Raynal's dates, his simple notation "*1er mai*" becoming "*Wednesday, May 1,*" when May 1, 1864, was actually a Sunday.

A puzzling difference is the sad wrecking of the little *Rescue*, which Raynal places at the time the *Flying Scud* first crossed the bar of the New River estuary, providing an emotional moment in his story. Musgrave, while he also describes the little boat breaking its towline at the bar, says it happened when the *Flying*

Scud arrived at Invercargill the second time, after the rescue of Harry and George from the Auckland Islands. It seems logical that if the boat had survived the first crossing, the curious populace would have flocked to inspect it, and the newspapers would have printed a firsthand description, and so I opted for Raynal's version.

The ownership of the gun posed a problem, as both men claimed that it was his. It seemed more plausible to me that someone who had spent a decade on the goldfields would be armed, and so I decided in favor of Raynal. A curious discrepancy is that Raynal did not mention heaving over the wreck of the schooner. For those interested in the technicalities, the process of heaving down a ship to expose her bottom is described in detail in Albert Cook Church, *Whale Ships and Whaling* (New York: W. W. Norton, 1938), pp. 24–25. In a shipyard, the ship would be moored close to the wharf, so that the cable rove between the two heaving blocks (one on the mast, one on the heaving post) was short and steep, helping the process along. Considering the circumstances the *Grafton* sailors faced, tipping over the wreck was an extremely ambitious project, involving a huge amount of physical work, so it is very surprising that Raynal failed to describe it.

At times a good guide for deciding the true order in which things happened was to see what the sea lions were doing at the particular times described. Their breeding pattern is described in *Preliminary Results of the Auckland Islands Expedition 1972–1973*, compiled and edited by J. C. Yaldwyn, and printed by the New Zealand Department of Lands and Survey in 1975. The papers relevant to sea lion breeding cycles were "Report on the Natural History and Behaviour of Hooker's Sea lion at Enderby Island, Auckland Island, 1972-73," by H. A. Best (pp. 159–70); "Observations on the Breeding Cycle of Hooker's Sea lion on Enderby Island, 1972–73," by B. J. Marlow (pp. 171–75); and "Report on the Collection of Anatomical and Osteological Material of Hooker's Sea lion during the Auckland Islands Expedition 1972–73," by Judith E. Marlow (pp. 176–82), this last being a charming dissertation, which I briefly quoted in the discussion of sea lions in Chapter 6.

I am indebted to Creative New Zealand for a grant I received in the year 2000 to research the history of sealing in the subantarctic islands, and to the J. D. Stout Fellowship for a year's tenure (2001) at the Stout Centre for New Zealand Studies, an institute that still provides a great deal of intellectual support. The job of comparing the various editions of the two books was carried out in the reading room of the J. C. Beaglehole Library, at Victoria University, Wellington, New Zealand, where I was greatly assisted by the librarian, Nicola Frean, and her assistant, Tracey Williamson. They were not only helpful but enthusiastic, even organizing a most valuable panel discussion of the two publications.

Their volume of *Les naufrages* is an 1870 edition, and is a large, splendid book with a handsome crimson cover and gilt-edged pages. The English translation I used is an enlarged facsimile of an 1880 reprint by T. Nelson and Sons, printed in 2003 by Roger Steele, of the Wellington publishing firm Steele Roberts. This edition is augmented with commentaries on the Auckland Islands; François Edouard Raynal and his book; Alphonse de Neuville, illustrator; Captain Thomas Musgrave; and the influence of Raynal's *Wrecked on a Reef* on Jules Verne's novels, all researched and written by Verne scholar Christiane Mortelier.

There is a third edition of Musgrave's book. In 1943 the New Zealand publishing firm A. H. & A. W. Reed produced a version with almost the same title, *Castaway on the Aucklands: the wreck of the Grafton, from the private journals of Thomas Musgrave, Master mariner, edited by A. H. and A. W. Reed.* However, though the reader is not warned by the foreword, it is by no means a true reproduction. Instead, in an inappropriate effort to make Musgrave's plain, workmanlike writing more accessible to the ordinary reader, the editors paraphrased his account— replacing his "I went to bed" with "I turned in," for instance. As I could not comfortably quote from this, it was set aside.

The Macpherson collection (MSX-4936) at the Alexander Turnbull Library, National Library of New Zealand, includes three letters, one fragmentary, written by Musgrave to Macpherson; a letter of thanks from Mrs. Musgrave to Macpherson; an unsourced newspaper clipping, dated October 20, 1865, reprinting Andrew Smith's account from the *Glasgow Mail;* a statement of accounts from the *Grafton* Relief Fund; a receipt for Mahoney's gravestone (£3); and the review of Raynal's book, mentioned earlier. Additionally, a notebook kept by Musgrave on the island is held by the Queensland Maritime Museum. However, if it were not for Captain Greig's detailed description of what he found at Epigwaitt, which was printed on page 5 of the *Daily Southern Cross* on November 27, 1865, after the return of the *Southland,* it would be easy to believe that both *Les naufrages* and *Castaway* are largely works of fiction. Questions were certainly asked—the Macpherson collection includes a copy of a letter from the Geneva branch of Librairie Hachette, dated February 11, 1870, and signed by Nancy Coulin, which asks John Macpherson for authentication of the wreck, saying that while

Hachette publishers have no doubt of Raynal's veracity, during a lecture tour doubts were expressed by some who heard him.

The ordeal of the *Invercauld* survivors, which runs in such terrible parallel to that of the *Grafton* castaways, is described in detail in a book called *Wake of the Invercauld*, which was published in Auckland in 1997 by Exisle Press. The author, Madelene Ferguson Allen, was Robert Holding's great-granddaughter. An adopted child, she discovered her birth family in 1984, and at the same time learned about her remarkable ancestor. Upon reading the memoir Holding had begun in 1926, a handful of years before his death in January 1933, she was inspired to embark on a mission that included two trips to the Auckland Islands, and ended in the publication of her book, which encompasses a complete transcription of Holding's journal, with a running commentary of her journeys and researches.

Painstakingly researched, *Wake of the Invercauld* authenticates everything he wrote—as long as allowance is given for the fact that Holding started his chronicle on an old Remington typewriter at the age of eighty-six, sixty years after the actual events. Natural lapses in recollection are particularly apparent where nautical details are confused; for instance, Andrew Smith, the mate, said the *Invercauld* had single topsails, while Holding described a ship with the new (at the time) double topsails. In the text, I have glossed over these inconsistencies, and am grateful for the technical advice given by Captain Nick Burningham. The credit is his; the mistakes are mine.

Holding's descriptions of both Smith and Captain Dalgarno are derogatory, but seem to be justifiably so. The inescapable conclusion is that if Holding had held rank, and had been allowed to take control, more of the *Invercauld* group would have

survived. Though he did not know about the part that Holding played, Thomas Musgrave confirmed this, writing to Macpherson on November 9, 1865, that Dalgarno's account "proves that there has been no unity amongst them, neither has the Captain attempted (or he has not been able) to hold any authority or influence over them; to which cause I atribute [sic] a great number of their deaths." It must be added, however, that while Musgrave's moral strength and Raynal's ingenuity played a large part in the survival of the *Grafton* group, they were fortunate in that they were stranded in the early summer when the sea lions were gathering to pup, and that they were able to cannibalize the wreck to make a sturdy house. Though they were just novice sealers, they were mentally prepared to kill the animals, which the survivors from the *Invercauld* were not. (The *Grafton*'s real mission was almost certainly to scout out sealing grounds; as Bob Braithwaite, a Wellington geologist, confirmed to me in a helpful discussion, the fabled silver-tin mine can be dismissed as just that, a fable.)

Captain Dalgarno's *Narrative of the Wreck of the "Invercauld" among the Auckland Islands* is an appendix in Raynal's book. Evidently, Raynal kept the newspaper that carried the story, and it was translated into French to be added to *Les naufrages*. Then, when *Wrecked on a Reef* came out, Dalgarno's narrative was translated from the French back into English. Consequently, the phrasing is unlikely to be exactly the same as the original. Unfortunately, Raynal neglected to tell his readers the name of the newspaper, and it has been impossible to track it down since.

There are just a few other published sources. In 1866 the official journals kept by Musgrave and Captain Norman on board the *Victoria* were printed in Melbourne by F. F. Baillière, with

the title *Journals of the voyage and proceedings of H.M.C.S. Victoria: in search of shipwrecked people at the Auckland and other islands, with an outline sketch of the islands.* This was bound into the copy of the Melbourne edition of *Castaway* that was presented to John Macpherson, but I read it as a separate volume at the National Library, Wellington.

The strange little book that Musgrave used to navigate the *Flying Scud* into Port Ross was *A history of gold as a commodity and as a measure of value: its fluctuations both in ancient and modern times, with an estimate of the probable supplies from California and Australia.* Written by James Ward, and published in 1853 by the London firm of William S. Orr, it devotes chapter five (pp. 81–90) to the Auckland Islands. As mentioned in the text, Ward himself had never been there, but instead related what he had been told by the surgeon of the *Earl of Hardwicke.*

This unnamed fellow could well have been one of the three doctors whose drunken frolics were noted with such despair in the daybooks of two of the unfortunate officials who administered the settlement, William Mackworth and William Munce. These can be read in *Enderby Settlement Diaries: Records of a British Colony at the Auckland Islands 1849–1852,* edited by P. R. Dingwall, C. Fraser, J. G. Gregory, and C. J. R. Robertson, and published by Wild Press and Wordsell Press (Auckland and Wellington) in 1999.

Because of the lack of documentation, the seven-year effort by the Ngati Matunga chief Matioro and his people to colonize Auckland Island has never been described, though it was significantly more successful than any other attempt, leading to the successful introduction and acclimatization of the New Zealand flax, *Phormium tenax.* I thank Wilford Davis for sending me a short account of one of those colonists, his great-grandmother Kurapa, which was originally published as "Captives on the Auckland Islands," *NZ Genealogist,* November/December 1999: 375. *Coastmaster: the story of Captain James B. Greig,* by John McCraw, was published by Silverdale Press (Hamilton, NZ) in 1999. The story of the *General Grant* castaways, begun by Madelene Ferguson Allen, and completed after her death by Ken Scadden, was published by Exisle Press (Auckland) with the title *General Grant's Gold,* in 2007. The enthralling story of the *Dundonald* castaways is documented in the book *The Castaways of Disappointment Island* by H. Escott Inman, published by Partridge & Co. of London in 1911. It was here that I learned that eating *Stilbocarpa* bleaches the teeth. Plant information is from the *Plants for a Future* species database, a Web search engine by Rich Morris that is linked to www.ibiblio.org. Many other dietary details come from J. C. Drummond, with Anne Wilbraham, *The Englishman's Food: a history of five centuries of English diet* (London: Jonathan Cape, 1957), and Donald S. McLaren, *Nutrition and its Disorders* (Edinburgh: Churchill Livingstone, 1976). The *Grafton* castaways were suffering from an abnormally elevated concentration of ketones in the body tissues and fluids, the result of their fat and protein-high diet, plus carbohydrate deprivation and deficiencies in essential vitamins and minerals.

There are remarkably few books about the history of the Auckland Islands, most of them outdated and out of print. Roger Carrick's *New Zealand's Lone Lands: being brief Notes of a Visit to the Outlying Islands of the Colony,* was published in Wellington by Didsbury in 1892. More balanced and reliable is Fergus McLaren's *The Eventful Story of the Auckland Islands,* published in Wellington by A. H. & A. W. Reed in 1948. Two comprehensive accounts of the subantarctic islands that include the

Auckland Islands are Allan W. Eden, *Islands of Despair* (London: Andrew Melrose, 1955) and Rosaline Redwood, *Forgotten Islands of the South Pacific: the Story of New Zealand's Southern Islands* (Wellington: Reed, 1950).

The story of the scientific coastwatchers during World War II was written up from their journals by Graham Turbott and published as a monograph by the Department of Conservation in September 2002, under the title *Year Away: Wartime Coastwatching on the Auckland Islands, 1944*. Though out of print, it has been partially digitalized, and can be read on the Department of Conservation Web site, www.doc.govt.nz. Also of great interest is I. S. Kerr, *Campbell Island: A History* (Wellington: A. H. & A. W. Reed, 1976). A particularly beautiful book is Conan Fraser's *Beyond the Roaring Forties: New Zealand's Subantarctic Islands* (Wellington: Govt. Printing Office, 1986). Extremely useful is a revised and updated edition of *New Zealand's Subantarctic Islands* (originally edited by Tim Higham and published in 1991), edited by Tom O'Connor and published with the same title by Reed in 1999, under the auspices of the Department of Conservation.

A useful summary of shipwrecks on the Auckland Islands and the establishment and provisioning of castaway depots was provided by Rachael Egerton, officer with the Southland Conservancy of the Department of Conservation. For those interested in seals and sea lions, the department posts information on its Web site, as does the New Zealand Forest and Bird Society. The birds mentioned are all described on www.nzbirds.com.

Apart from those people already acknowledged in these notes, thanks are due to my husband, Ron, who listened patiently to endless repetitions of the technical parts of the book and gave valuable advice; Roger Steele; Christiane Mortelier;

Paul Dingwall; Brett Fotheringham; Ken Scadden; Dr. Simon Nathan; the publishers at Algonquin; my editor, Antonia Fusco; my loyal agent, Laura Langlie; and the fellow historian to whom this book is dedicated—Roberta McIntyre, whose early encouragement could not have been more well timed.

Today, the Auckland Islands is a World Heritage Area, UNESCO having assigned the group the highest possible conservation status. The island group supports the world's largest populations of wandering albatross and mollymawk and protects the breeding ground of the New Zealand, or Hooker's, sea lion, now one of the world's rarest seals.

It is possible to visit there, but only under the most rigorous conditions. Tourist entry permits are issued, but only if a representative of the New Zealand Department of Conservation accompanies the party. Landings are allowed only at designated sites on Auckland Island and Enderby Island, the other islands being absolutely off limits. Footwear, clothing, and gear are thoroughly checked; strict measures are taken against the accidental release of mice or rats; no plants or rocks are allowed to be disturbed or removed; no animals may be closely approached; the collection of specimens or souvenirs is absolutely forbidden; no rubbish or refuse may be left behind, and smoking is not permitted.

Further information is available from:

Department of Conservation
Southland Conservancy
PO Box 743
Invercargill, New Zealand

JOAN DRUETT is a maritime historian and the award-winning author of several books, including *Petticoat Whalers*, *She Was a Sister Sailor*, *Hen Frigates*, *Tupaia*, and *The Discovery of Tahiti*. Her interest in maritime history began in 1984, when she discovered the grave of a young American whaling wife while exploring the tropical island of Rarotonga; she subsequently received a Fulbright fellowship to study whaling wives in New England and California. Her groundbreaking work in the field of seafaring women was also recognized with an L. Byrne Waterman Award. She is married to Ron Druett, a maritime artist. Visit Joan Druett's blog at joan-druett.blogspot.com.